DRAGONS, DONKEYS, AND DUST

DRAGONS, DONKEYS, AND DUST
Memoirs from a decade in China

Rudy Kong

BLB
BING LONG BOOKS
Vancouver

ISBN: 978-0-9813003-2-0

Library and Archives Canada Cataloguing in Publication

Kong, Rudy, 1971-
Dragons, donkeys and dust: memoirs from a
decade in China / Rudy Kong.

Includes index.
ISBN 978-0-9813003-2-0

1. Kong, Rudy, 1971-.   2. China--Biography.
I. Title.
DS712.K66 2009   951.06092   C2009-906745-5

Printed in the USA
10 9 8 7 6 5 4 3 2 1

For Hanna and Cosmo,
lest you forget the life we lived in China.

Acknowledgements

As will become clear while reading this book, one does not just plonk themselves down in China and start living life without a tremendous amount of help from others. There are several Chinese friends that I owe so much to for their help at various key times in my stay in China: (Alice) Zhou Shu Bo, for translating at our daughter's birth, and then showing us our first home-cooked Chinese meal (including Coca-Cola chicken); (Alice) Ma Xiao Ya, for helping with my motorcycle registration so many years ago and helping us countless times, in countless ways; Sun Ming Cai, for years of help in many circumstances; (Sandy) Hu Shan Shan, for helping so much during our apartment purchase and renovations; Ella for help with the driver's licenses; (Eric/Wonger) Wang Jun, for introducing me to hockey in China; Yin Nan Chang, for all his lessons on Chinese culture and customs disguised as chitchat on hockey trips and at his parties; and (Paul Coffey) Zeng Zhe, for showing us how to play beautiful hockey, China-style. The greatest help has come from Ayi, Li Cun Hua, who has been grandmother, cleaner, cook, shopper, masseuse, friend, and more for a decade. Without her life in China simply wouldn't have been so good.

Canadians helped too. I am especially grateful to Suzanne Williams for coming to the rescue when our son was born and for being a best friend to my wife, keeping her grounded and sane all those years in China. When other foreigners appeared with families and children it did a world of good, convincing us we were not reckless fools for raising kids in China. They were, and still are, terrific friends: The Blights of Australia; the Primaveras, Olafsons, Naminis, Potters, and

Colorados of Canada; the Gustafsons and Mastrorillis of the USA; and the inspirational Ghalilis, the one family that was there when we arrived and still there today, solid rocks in the community's foundation.

Thanks to Anne, Tom, Steve, Charles, Paulette, and Jim at Bing Long Books for supportive words and critical editing, and especially to my editor Craig Stanley Engleson.

Above all else, thanks must go to my love Sara, for being so supportive of this endeavour, and all our adventures thus far.

Transliteration from Chinese

There are various ways to transliterate Chinese characters for readers of English. In this book all Chinese words are expressed in the Pinyin system. Readers will likely be somewhat familiar with the Wade-Giles system often used in the past that recorded the capital of China as Peking. Today it has largely been replaced by Pinyin, the system favoured by the government of the People's Republic of China. In the Pinyin system Peking becomes Beijing, Kung Fu becomes Gong Fu, and Mao Tse-tung becomes Mao Zedong. The Pinyin system also includes four symbols to indicate the four tones of spoken Mandarin Chinese. This book does not include the tone symbols because most readers (me included) will butcher the pronunciation anyway; no need to worry about tones.

A note on Chinese names: The Chinese give their family name first and their given names last. Typically, the Chinese have given names made of one or two words. Sometimes the given names may be written in Pinyin as one single word but at other times the two words are separated. For example, Li Xiaolong (Bruce Lee's Chinese name) could be written as Li Xiao Long. Likewise, Chinese place names that are made of two or more words are sometimes written as separate words. For example, Shanghai could be written as Shang Hai. In this book I have written Chinese place names as one word but people's names I have written in the manner that seemed best to me at the time.

Currency, Weights, and Measures

Renminbi (RMB) is 'the people's money'. While the exchange rate fluctuates significantly, on average over the past decade one Canadian dollar has been equivalent to six *yuan* of the people's money.

Some approximate conversions:

1 RMB=15 cents

10 RMB=$1.5

100 RMB=$15

Weight is normally measured in *jin*.

1 *jin*=500 grams

List of Maps

Contents

China and neighbouring countries.
* Taiwan remains a disputed territory.

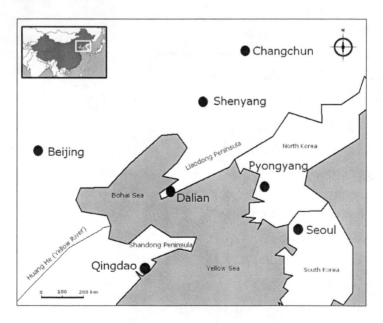

Dalian and environs.
Most of the events of this book took place in or around Dalian.

Preface

'I heard the markets are all closed today. It's Union Day,' said the young Italian woman, answering my wife's question. My jaw dropped and my brow furrowed, according to Sara.

'It's your last day in Myanmar. Are you going to do some shopping?' Sara had asked.

Three weeks earlier, while standing in the hot sun, feeling like Merseault in Camus' *L'Etranger*, ready to kill an Arab, I had convinced Sara not to buy some paintings she really wanted. It made absolutely no sense to me to lug paintings around Burma for a month. They would be heavy, too big, get ruined, I thought to myself.

'We'll be back, you can buy them then. I guarantee it!'

Spouses have a way of not forgetting these kinds of things and Sara reminded me of my guarantee almost immediately. Damn it! The Bogyoke Aung San Market, known as Scott Market in the old colonial days, surely couldn't be closed today. We were flying to Bangkok in the morning and let's face it, you don't get to Myanmar everyday. It had been 13 years since my last visit.

Sometimes it's little things that cause the universe to implode and today it was these paintings. I had an ominous feeling that if Sara didn't get these paintings I would be in the dog house for a long, long time. I kept up an optimistic exterior while we went to see for ourselves. Yep, the market was closed.

'Try Shwedagon pagoda' someone said. 'East gate...no, north gate...north, east, south, west...uh...yes, east gate of Shwedagon'.

We jump into a taxi, a Japanese relic circa 1980. Yesterday, I got stuck, literally, in one of these crap buckets. The driver had to fetch his pliers from the trunk to get me out. Shoes off, up we march through the East Gate. No paintings. Trudge over to the South Gate. Up and down. No paintings. Sara's silent rage is no longer silent. I mention the irony: we are at a holy Buddhist site and cursing each other because of material things. Hmmm, Buddha was right, our desire did bring suffering.

Shwedagon pagoda shines brilliantly, standing over 300 feet tall, covered completely in gold. 5000 diamonds and nearly as many rubies ensure that it sparkles day and night. Legend holds it to be over two thousand years old and it is truly a sight to behold, one of the most impressive monuments humans have built, not to mention a place of spiritual importance and serenity. But its awesome beauty, charm, and holiness did nothing to help solve the problem at hand— finding the paintings and restoring harmony in my family.

'Many paintings, many galleries' says a Buddha-head vendor who suggests we try Golden Valley.

Back into a Datsun, or perhaps it was a Mazda, as old as I am. Golden Valley has galleries and expensive paintings but we confess that we want the cheap stuff sold at the market. The tropical heat is stifling and by now the kids and Sara are wiped out, done. We return to the hotel, drenched in sweat. I feel dejected for being the chump who ruined the last day of an otherwise terrific trip to Myanmar.

With the family up in the room, I'm back in the Datsun, this time to Sule Pagoda in the centre of Yangon. There will be something there for sure. There is tons of stuff, but no paintings. I walk back up to Bogyoke Aung San market and am intercepted by Wilson.

2

Wilson is not Scottish, he's a 73 year old Indian with a moustache dyed jet black but showing ashy roots, wrapped in a green *longyi* with leathery feet sticking out underneath protected only partially by cheap synthetic flip-flop sandals.

'Market is closed,' he says with an accent decidedly not Burmese. As if his ethnicity needed confirmation he bobbled his head like only marionettes and Indians do.

'Yes, I know. I'm looking for the paintings that are sold at the front entrance'.

'I will help you. I am Catholic,' he added. I was desperate and I would have followed a Satanist to Hell if the paintings were down there.

Back to Shwedagon pagoda, East Gate. Wilson talks to every Buddha-head vendor and gets directions. Half an hour later I find myself apologizing to a famous Burmese artist who sells paintings at shows in Singapore for thousands of dollars and explaining why I want $10 market specials and not his real art. Wilson condemns him as a greedy artist as we walk away down a filthy street and he tells me a story of how monks were shot dead just here on the street one year earlier. Wilson stops to talk to some pedi-cab drivers. Next, we waltz into an artist's living room that is surprisingly bare and free of art or even colour, wake her sleeping baby and apologize again.

Back on the street we are vigilantly watched by a group of under-employed pedi-rickshaw drivers, scrawny and dark, holding up their patterned *longyis* so as not to dirty them on the bicycle chain. Wilson predicts a rebellion in the spring, sometime between April and June, but definitely after the Burmese New Year. Then he comes up with a brilliant idea. We return to the market to find the gatekeeper and get into his registry book that contains information on all of the

3

market's vendors. The book is full of writing that to me looks like circles, semi circles, quarter circles, and circles with squiggles attached. I have to take his word when he says that he has no address for the painting seller.

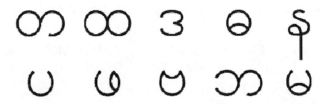

A sample of Burmese script.

At this point I have finally given up, my stomach is aching from hunger. I'm exhausted and I calculate that I have now spent three hours with Wilson, and now Sara will be worried as well as angry. I didn't tell her I was going out. Wilson stops and asks another man. He knows of a painter in the surrounding countryside. I tell Wilson not to worry and thank him for his help. I am giving up.

Two of the ubiquitous street urchins approach selling postcards. Don't they know that because of email nobody sends postcards anymore? I hear Wilson scolding them in Burmese. Or is it Tamil? No, he hasn't scolded them. He turns to me with his weathered hands clasped at his chest.

'I prayed to Jesus to show us the way to your paintings and he gave us this boy. The boy's auntie is the woman who sells the paintings!'

Well thank you Jesus! Mind you, I would have thanked the Great Satan if that's who led us to the paintings.

We follow the boys down a disgusting alley that hadn't changed, or apparently been cleaned, for a hundred years.

Three hundred flies erupt from an open sewer and there we ascend a dank stairwell. A brown wooden door opens to reveal a sweatshop, only it is postcard assembly, not textiles, being done by three generations of an extended family. No paintings in sight though. I sit with Wilson on a plastic chair. Fifteen minutes later the paintings arrive. They look awesome; brightly coloured monks on the dry Irrawaddy River bed and silhouettes on an ancient teak bridge. Sara will be pleased. I return to the hotel to find her on the street with the kids. I am gloating, thinking I'm the cat's ass. The sceptical look on her face gives way to a smile. She knew I would find them.

The life I live isn't that of my friends at home, I think to myself, trying to fall asleep in a drab room, the only colour coming from squashed mosquitoes on the walls. We have no windows or escape route. I should write today's events down and use them to illustrate a point in the preface to my book, I say to myself.

From my Little Green Notebook, February 13th, 2009.

I wrote this book in a little green notebook bought for my daughter to do her holiday homework. While sitting at the pool with our friends, the Colorados, in Bangkok's famed Atlanta hotel—famed for it's slightly dilapidated old time luxury at budget prices—I told a story and someone said 'You should write a book'. And that was it. Our holiday, which took us to Guangzhou and Macau, Bangkok, and finally to Myanmar, became my 'time off' to finally write something of our dozen years in China.

Why write a book about China? Here's a tongue in cheek answer: When people ask me the same questions over and over I can say 'Read my book'. Seriously, my wife and I have been fielding the same questions about our life in China for the past decade. When we go to parties in Canada, our life often becomes the focus of conversation. It became clear that people think our life and experience is interesting. Even people who really do live their own fascinating lives think our experience is yet even more interesting. This book is for those people.

This book has another purpose too. The anti-China bias in the Western media has become unbearable for me. I simply cringe every time I read the nonsense that is written because it is either so far from reality or horribly biased. I should be clear, however, that I'm not a China apologizer, and I am often very critical of the government and the way things are done. This book aims to present a picture of the real China, at least as I have seen it. I neither want to paint a picture of an idyllic traditional China, nor the booming economic power-house. I simply want to tell our tales from twelve years of living and traveling in China with two children. There are points in the book when I digress and offer opinions, some-times strong opinions. I would be a fool to attempt to keep my biases out of this book. As a writer, they are as inevitable as the biases of each reader. Further, I believe my opinions are rooted in my background and interest in the history and geo-politics of Asia; I hope, therefore, that while they may put off some readers, others will find them worthy.

It is my sincere hope that readers will be interested in, even amazed or horrified, or better yet, enthused and inspired by the stories herein. In short, my wish is that these true tales are entertaining and that readers may overlook my shortcomings as a writer. I did pick up a copy of *Style: 10 Lessons in Clarity and Grace* but unfortunately not until *after* I finished writing.

Part One:
OPENING CEREMONY

It's cold and you are standing in a line before a flag pole. Your ears are burning from the frigid wind and you long to be allowed to pull on a toque. A young Chinese man stands erect at the front wearing a suit a size too large, holding a microphone. He tests the mike with a tap of his fingers, attempts to keep a piece of paper in his other hand from blowing away, and begins:

'Ladies and gentlemen, honoured guests, and dear leaders, *da jia hao!*' *Da jia hao* literally means 'everybody good' and he yelps it with an enthusiasm not shared by anyone else present. You begin to shift uncomfortably in your line, wishing you weren't here, hoping it will be over in a few minutes. You tune out, but catch a few key words.

'...hard work...bright future...'

It seems to go on and on and now your toes have gone numb. You can't take it anymore but the speaker continues, he is relentless. You hear the word 'harmonious' for the third time.

'...cultural understanding...love the Motherland'.

Finally, the speaker barks out '*xianzai kaishi!*'—now begins! The Chinese clap. The translator continues, now in English...

There are almost as many ceremonies in China as there are bicycles, and to date I have stood through over four hundred flag raising ceremonies. Let this page stand as the opening ceremony for this book. Think this page is useless? Reread it four hundred times!

I now declare the book reading ceremony begins!

1

The Dream

'**G**et up, get on up!'
'Get up, get on up!'

James Brown screamed at me while Flight JL 797 bound for Dalian, China was taxiing down the runway at Narita airport outside of Tokyo, Japan. I was listening to JEN, Japan Airlines Entertainment Network, and I couldn't agree more with James Brown, I wanted to 'get on up' in the air and get home. Home is Dalian, China, or more precisely, a small town that was a village not long ago called Manjiatan— meaning Man family beach—located an hour north-east of Dalian proper, in China's north-east Liaoning province. Dalian is a modern prosperous city but Manjiatan remains a dusty Chinese backwater town, where goats are still slaughtered on the sidewalk each morning, rabbit skins hang on the main road outside barbeque restaurants, local residents cook communally outside over woks placed on barrels stocked with burning corn husks, and donkey carts compete on the roads with modern vehicles.

'Can we hit it and quit?' James Brown screams, the JEN play list now on its second rotation.

'Can we hit it and quit?'

At this point I think James Brown's lyrics are a bit inappropriate for a plane flying not far from North Korean air space. No, I don't want to hit it and quit, I want to go home. We've been away from home for six weeks and the kids are really excited about seeing their cats, their *Ayi*—nanny—, playing with their toys, and sleeping in their own rooms again. Somehow, James Brown knew there was inclement weather in Dalian and the pilot 'hit it and quit,' sort of. Actually he circled Dalian a couple of times and then turned around. We travelled all day but ended up back where we started, in Japan at the Hotel Nikko Narita. We would try again tomorrow to get home. It is at moments like this when we question why we live as we do, overseas in a very strange and foreign environment and we wonder if our life would be easier, better, if we had stayed in Canada. Whenever I have doubts I think back to the dream that started this whole adventure.

Like a scene out of a Spaghetti Western film, I am walking down a dusty road where old familiar faces hitch horses to posts and loiter around saloon doors. Ignoring them, I continue down the road, eventually coming to an intersection where I enter a huge building. I find myself in a hotel room with a beautiful young woman. She is friendly, to say the least, and I soon find myself pulling down her pants and biting her bottom on the right cheek—don't you just love dreams?! Just as things are getting interesting, I hear a commotion outside and go out onto a balcony that overlooks a large courtyard in the inner section of the hotel. In the courtyard is a magnificent classical Chinese garden, complete with carp-filled pond, fragrant chrysanthemum, and gnarled 'bonsai' trees. A huge bird, which I now interpret as a phoenix, swoops down, its talons just missing my head, and morphs into a hideous pterodactyl-like creature, then becomes an even more frightening beast. Terrified, I return to the room to alert or perhaps protect the gorgeous young woman who has now become very important to me. The room is empty but I notice another door, ajar, that opens onto a road behind the hotel. Panicked, I rush outside and down some steps to the road. The street is no longer the Old West. It is now chaotic and oblivious to my predicament. Red Volkswagen Santanas jerk past one another honking excessively. I step out in front of one and frantically wrench open the door. It's a taxi. Somehow the scene has become China!

'*Wo de tai tai zai na li?*'—Where is my wife?—I yell at the driver and jump in.

At this point I woke up, feeling a mixture of confusion, exhaustion, and yet somehow thrilled that I had just dreamt what I had. I immediately realized that my wife in the dream was in fact a girl in three of my classes in the B Ed program at the University of British Columbia. I had been living and travelling with a girlfriend for the previous two years but we had decided somewhat casually and amicably to go our separate ways, and she moved out. Because I was planning to move to Victoria on Vancouver Island in a couple of months, and being an impoverished student at the time, I temporarily moved in with my mother and step-father to save on rent. The dream occurred on the first night at my mother's house, the first night not with my then ex-girlfriend.

The girl, named Sara, had written her name and phone number in my notebook and casually mentioned that I might need to call her to 'study' some time. She was a stunning looking girl, just turned 25 and in good shape, who I noticed on the first day of classes. She wore her hair very short, accentuating her green eyes, with all the boldness of Sinead O'Connor but gentler, so that mum would approve instantly. When several gay classmates made a display that challenged our views on sexuality, I spotted her photo on their display and froze. It seemed that this beauty was a lesbian and this thought made me feel sick with angst. I realized then that I had feelings for her. Strangely enough I also noticed an unbearable body odour that I seemed to produce whenever I was around her. It repulsed me, but apparently attracted her.

I ate breakfast and drank a coffee, but I couldn't shake the feelings the dream had aroused. Normally, I would never act on a dream but for some reason I dug around in my notebook for her number, dug even deeper for courage, and called her.

'Hi Sara, it's me. I don't really know how to say this but... I had a really weird dream and you were in it'.

'Really? I'm just dying my hair. Why don't you come down to my place and tell me all about it?

I did, and her short hair looked great orange, like Annie Lennox but sexier. Sara ordered vegetarian Chinese takeaway and I stayed for supper.

That week an uncle passed through town and took the family out for Chinese food. My fortune cookie read: YOU WILL GO TO CHINA! I laughed because it seemed a bit unlikely and a bit late. I'd already been to China three times and had no plans to return. I was going to be a teacher on Vancouver Island, if all went as planned.

As fate would have it, the following Saturday, one week after the dream, I did pull down Sara's pants. Thinking it unwise to bite her bottom on our first intimate occasion I did notice that in the very spot I had taken a bite in the dream she had a tattoo; a yin-yang, the ancient Chinese symbol of harmonious opposites of male and female.

Within two months, on Valentine's Day, we inadvertently conceived a child. We were 25 years old and $40,000 in debt from student loans, with virtually no prospects of teaching jobs in British Columbia. Instincts kicked in and I became seriously anxious about how I might provide for a family. I began furiously playing the stock market, quickly losing the little money I had. I even contemplated growing dope. One day I saw an ad in the newspaper for British Columbia certified teachers needed in China. I knew the instant I saw the ad that the job was mine for the taking. Alas, what crazy woman would head off to China pregnant? It seemed absurd to even consider it but I reluctantly told Sara about the job as I was leaving town for a one-week stint planting trees in the forests of northern British Columbia.

While I was gone Sara wrote a cover letter and sent in my resume. When I returned she had already set up an interview. And that was it. Two 25 year old Canadians, who barely knew each other, broke, and expecting a child, set off for China in August 1998 to start a life together.

My dreams come true.

2

Map of Dalny, as published in Scribner's Magazine, April 1903.

Far Away

'Whereabouts in China do you live?'
'Dalian,' we say, and pre-empting the blank expressions add 'it's in the North-east, half way between Beijing and Seoul, Korea.

Very few people in the West know of Dalian and neither

did we before we arrived. But it wasn't always unknown. The older generation and history buffs are familiar with the naval base at Port Arthur, named by the British—perhaps for a Navy captain or perhaps for Queen Victoria's son—who were sniffing around the region by the mid 1800s. A day's march north of Port Arthur, the British settled briefly in a place known by the Manchu as Qing Niwakou. Another march farther north was the fortified, walled Chinese town Jinzhou, which remains today.

The name Dalian interested and perplexed me from the moment we arrived. With the help of a dictionary I surmised that it meant Big Link but locals laughed when I suggested as much. That was too literal a translation and they insisted that Dalian was just a name and that it had no meaning. I still like to think of Dalian as Big Link; it's a fitting name for a port city.

As it turned out the British, who returned Qing Niwakou to the Chinese in the 1880s, weren't the only foreigners interested in the area. The Japanese occupied the region following their defeat of the Chinese in 1895 only to be denied by the Tripartite Intervention of France, Germany, and Russia. The Russians then moved in following a lease from the Qing dynasty and began building a modern, planned city at Qing Niwakou in 1898. They named their model town Dalny, meaning Far Away, a reflection of the remoteness as viewed from St. Petersburg. With Dalny the Russians gained an ice-free port just a few hours by ship from the European concessions at Tianjin and Germany's settlement at Qingdao. With the extension of the Trans-Manchurian railway Dalny was not so far away, just a week or so to St. Petersburg by rail.

Of Dalny the New York Times wrote in 1903:

One sees by it that each section has been planned to serve a special purpose. Everything has been segregated. In the commercial city a building to be used as an auction hall and exchange is in the centre, and surrounding it are private banks, the Russo-Chinese Bank, a town club, a theatre, the Judges's office, a Post and telegraph office, the Police Office, and the offices of the Town Council. Slightly to the east are the Mayor's office, the quarters of the military employes, the Mayor's residence, and the boys' and girls's museums. Still further east are the private residences for Europeans.

I give full credit to the Russians for a job well done. The Dalian seen in the map above still exists as the heart of the city. In fact the features of Dalian that locals and anyone who has visited recall are all visible on that map. The 'square,' or roundabout, in the centre of the map is now *Zhong Shan* square and other key landmarks—Victory Square, Friendship Square, People's Square, and Gangwan Square — are all clearly seen. The park that carefully separated Foreign Town from China Town remains as Labour Park. These places give Dalian a very distinctive feel and make it much more charming than most other Chinese cities.

The remarkable accomplishment of the Russians was not admired by the Japanese however, still upset by the Europeans taking what Japan had won in the treaty of Shimonoseki in 1895. From the New York Times:

> Just what Japan is going to do in the matter seems at present to be 'one of those things that no feller can find out'. She wants to do something and feels that she can. But tackling Russia is a big job for her. It has been the private opinion of

17

those in Japan, publicly expressed on numerous occasions, that she can whip almost any nation that she tackles. Her difficulties by no means include want of pluck, and perhaps at the start she may have supplies and material enough. It is the financial problem that is the great difficulty.

As it turned out the Japanese had both the pluck and the finances to carry out an attack on Dalny. They launched an attack on the Russian forces and laid siege to Port Arthur in 1904. By September, 1905 the Manchurian Campaign—AKA the Russo-Japanese War—was over. The Russian Empire was humiliated and left in ruins, helping foment revolution and eventually leading to the takeover by Lenin's Communists.

Under Japanese rule Dalian was further developed. They built a network of electric streetcars, à la San Francisco, that still charm the streets today and added a large section of two-story European-style houses that are steadily and surely being torn down. It's a shame because the Japanese district is one of the most pleasant and quiet parts of urban Dalian. Its tree-lined streets hold hundreds of washed-out yellow fixer-uppers just waiting to become million dollar character homes. Let's hope the government has the sense to preserve at least some of this unique area of the city.

The Russians returned to push out the Japanese at the end of WWII and the Soviets continued the development of the shipyard they started prior to their defeat by the Japanese. Once the Soviets gave up control of Dalny to the Chinese in 1950 their shipbuilding efforts became the China Shipbuilding Company, which produced both China's first submarine and destroyer equipped with guided missiles. Shipbuilding, along with oil and gas refining and more recently IT manufacturing, continues to sustain Dalian's economy.

The rise of modern Dalian as an important and booming metropolis is very much attributed to the success of one individual in particular, a man named Bo Xilai. The son of a first generation Chinese revolutionary, he made his mark in Dalian through beautification projects—the city has been recognized nationally as 'National Sanitary City' and internationally as 'very liveable'—and a policy of openness to the world. Under his guidance Dalian became connected to the provincial capital by expressway and festivals sprang up all over town, notably the fashion festival that shuts the city down each September. The Chinese love monikers and Dalian, under Bo's leadership, gained plenty: Fashion City, Soccer City, Hong Kong of the North, Home of Track and Field, Apple Land, Rat-free City, and Pearl of the Bo Hai.

Southern Liaodong Peninsula.

Once I had determined that Dalny, or Far Away, was a legitimate and apt Russian name and not just a phonetic wannabe of the Chinese name Dalian, I wondered if Dalian was a phonetic rip off of Dalny. Did Dalian really have no meaning? Had the Chinese simply taken the Russian name? Apparently not. Eventually I discovered that the body of water near Dalian had long been known to the navigators of the world as *Talien wan*—and it appeared as such as early as

1860 in the Illustrated London News. In pinyin this is Dalian wan, or Dalian harbour.

Once, in 1998, when my mother came out to visit after our daughter was born, we were walking along the coast in Jinshitan, the seaside resort area north-east of Dalian where I worked. The Siberian winds were ripping down over the Liaodong peninsula and we found ourselves desperately seeking shelter from the wind and cold and needing a hot cup of tea. Struggling through the minus twenty degree wind-chill to get to the only restaurant in the near vicinity, we arrived to find the doors locked. Like desperate homeless refugees we rapped on the glass door only to be told to go away by the staff inside. Frozen and dejected, my mum turned to me and said 'this place is the end of the world!'

We were indeed far away.

3

Baby Hanna, 8 months, in the Potala, Lhasa.

Life Is Cheap

We lived in a suburb about thirty minutes north of Dalian called Kaifaqu. *Kai fa* means development and *qu* means region or zone. The Development Zone was a village of farmers and fishers until 1984 when the local government, following Deng Xiaoping's maxim 'to get rich is glorious,' created a zone with tax incentives for multi-national corporations to set up factories. Residential neighbourhoods of identical blocks of six story apartments are surrounded by electronics and pharmaceutical factories. For four years we lived kitty-corner from a Toshiba plant that ran 24-7, every eight hours spilling hundreds of young men and women into the streets who walked noisily under our window on their way to eat, shop, or hang out.

When we arrived in China, Sara was seven months pregnant and by that point her impending labour was very clear to everyone. On our first day in Dalian we were out for a stroll in Kaifaqu through a neighbourhood known as *wu cai cheng*—Five Colour City. *Wu cai cheng* had been designed with a grand vision. Set up as an entertainment district, it contained a myriad of small lanes and side streets made up of the most bizarre and gaudy buildings. Elves, dwarfs, giants, crabs, and a monstrous pencil, were some of the typically weird statues that adorned the shop fronts and streets. Seedy looking *KTV*—Karaoke—clubs with girls in traditional Chinese dresses called *qi pao* waiting behind windows in red-lit rooms, giving the vibe of an Amsterdam brothel, sat side by side with shops selling fruits and veggies, or ornate blue Dalian glass. The KTV girls, before things got busy inside, played badminton with one another on the street. They smashed and volleyed the birdies back and forth over an invisible net, all the while dressed in high heels and dazzling tight silk *qi pao*.

Walking through this area we were perplexed by the absurdity of the scene. In the middle of *wu cai cheng* was a large square that by 1998 had been left to dilapidate just long enough for nature to begin to take back what it once governed. The 'square' was mostly covered with knee-high wild grass, where there were several camels grazing and waiting for people to climb up and snap a photo, or go for a short camel ride for ten *yuan*. It was here that our daughter Hanna rode a camel before ever riding a pony, perhaps even before seeing a cat or dog.

Meanwhile, under the camel ride wasteland there was a subterranean roller skating rink, where teenagers, university students, and young factory workers strutted their stuff on old-school roller skates.

The author and his daughter on a camel in five colour city, 2000.

At night if a man walked through Five Colour City prostitutes emerged out of the darkness—were they lying in the grass?—and accompanied him to wherever he was going, which in 1998 was likely to a pub called The Watering Hole. It was here, between the camel square and The Watering Hole that we found ourselves walking past The Friendship Store, a government run, overpriced department store. Incidentally, if you find yourself living in China and want to propose to your girlfriend, don't buy the ring at the Friendship Store. The stones will fall out—more on this story in a later chapter.

23

To our surprise, just beyond the Friendship Store and across the street, we came upon two white men sitting in chairs outside underneath a sign that said 'Mike's Pizza'. The younger man, with long hair in a ponytail, was Mike. He had opened the pizza place with his wife Gao Jing. The older fellow, bald, with a belly almost as large as his Texas drawl, was Bob Smith. In those days the expat community in Kaifaqu was small, and you didn't pass another foreigner without at least a friendly 'hello'.

'Howdy' called Bob, and noticing Sara's figure added 'hope y'all be getting on a plane to have that baby'.

We introduced ourselves to Mike and Bob and explained that yes, we were indeed having the baby in Dalian. Mike and Bob were both pretty much in disbelief. That just wasn't done. Any foreigners who got pregnant in Dalian returned home or went to Hong Kong, or at least to Beijing for the birth. We got the impression they thought we were insane. Over the next few weeks we got to know Bob well. He was a great guy. He worked at the plant that produced cans for Coca-Cola and drove a SUV, one of the very few foreigners who drove in Dalian at that time. Most foreigners took taxis everywhere unless their companies provided a car and driver. Bob insisted that we should call him, day or night, when the time came for a ride to the hospital.

For the first pre-natal check up in China we went downtown to the Women's and Maternity hospital in Dalian. We were accompanied by three Canadian friends. The Maternity hospital was a decrepit building built by the Japanese during their occupation of Dalian, which they called *Dairen*, in the 1930s and 1940s.

As we entered we were greeted by human foetuses of various stages of development, displayed like grotesque pickles in jars. God only knows why the hospital staff thought that pregnant women would want to see these gruesome corpses. Somehow our friends and I were able to distract Sara and thankfully she never did see them. But after seeing the state of the toilets she decided not to give birth at the Maternity hospital, preferring the local Kaifaqu hospital, closer to home.

To better understand why the foetuses were on display, something that seems so offensive and inappropriate to many Westerners, we should consider the Chinese views on birth control and abortion. Just below our apartment was a small women's clinic. A Chinese-Canadian friend pointed out a plaque that hung on the clinic's wall. It read

> **Congratulations on 10,000**
>
> **successful abortions performed!**

Perhaps my memory fails me and the number was not quite so high but it was terribly shocking to us nonetheless. Clearly abortion is routine in China. Later when I was teaching population control in my class I introduced abortion as a controversial issue. The class of grade 11s, mostly 18 or 19 years old, was unanimous in believing that abortion was a non-issue. It was neither a woman's right nor an abhorrent murder; there was no moral or ethical question for them. The only exception came from the few Korean students who often were Christians.

I feel the reasons for this are twofold. First is the belief in science and the destruction by the Communists of religious institutions in China. Although there has been a renewal of intensive religion and spiritual movements (Falun Gong being an expression of this trend), generally speaking the modern Chinese are atheists who see abortion as a helpful and useful feature of modern science and medicine. Second is their overwhelming support for Deng Xiaoping's policies, including, or perhaps especially, the One Child Policy.

China's population is extremely large, at 1.3 billion and still growing, or approximately 20% of the world. Although China is massive, barely smaller than Canada and roughly the size of the USA, its population is stuffed into the eastern and south-western portions of the country. The largest provinces, Tibet, Qinghai, Xinjiang, and Inner Mongolia are sparsely populated for good reason—they are barren! The world should thank Deng Xiaoping, yet the Western media continue to point to the One Child Policy as an example of oppression by the Communists.

Arable versus barren land in China.

The Western media tell us stories of Chinese murdering infant girls and the prevalence of female abortions. It is true that the sex ratio statistics—as severe as 130 boys to 100 girls in some provinces such as poor agricultural Anhui, several hundred kilometres inland from Shanghai—do suggest a significant problem. A good friend of mine from Qiqihar, way up north near the Russian border, told me he saw abandoned dead babies under a bridge when he was a child on at least three occasions. Qiqihar is a poor region and that was nearly thirty years ago. Times have changed—that is not to suggest that it doesn't still happen—but the reporting on China hasn't.

The Western media stories leave the readers with a mistaken view of the whole Chinese nation as sexist, barbaric, and murderous savages. I, personally, have never met a Chinese who didn't absolutely treasure their one child, whether boy or girl. My best Chinese friend has two daughters from two marriages—allowed under the One Child Policy—and he loves them dearly. A female Chinese colleague of mine proudly told me how she and her husband had spent 8,000 RMB (nearly $1,500) on their daughter's first birthday party. Of course, many people would prefer to have more children and it is true that we've been told by numerous Chinese how lucky we are to have two children, especially one boy and one girl, but there is an overwhelming understanding and support for the policy. Then again, it is hard to distinguish support from acceptance in China, so pervasive is the propaganda.

The preference for boys does linger from previous times though, and now that my children are older I can see it whenever we are out together. Many of our Chinese neighbours absolutely adore my son and will lavish him with attention, telling him how handsome and smart he is, ignoring his sister who sits right beside him. Our daughter doesn't get upset, however, preferring to be left alone than to be constantly pestered by locals.

On Halloween we attended a party at the most prestigious of Kaifaqu's gated communities, the Beverly Gardens, where expats lived in brightly coloured ginger-bread houses. Sara, now absolutely bursting at the belly, danced all night and on the walk home scaled a five foot metal fence rather than walk another couple hundred metres in the cold.

We had agreed that if a girl was born she would be named Katie, but at 5 am on November 1st I was awoken by Sara who had got up excessively early to clean the apartment and was told that if a girl was born she should be named Hanna.

'Okay dear, whatever...' I said and went back to sleep. In my semi-conscious state I could hear Sara muttering 'Hanna, she will be Hanna'.

When I woke we decided to go for a breakfast buffet that we had heard so much about at the nearby Kerren Hotel. We were craving Western food by then, especially breakfasts, and making bacon and eggs at home meant an hour-long bumpy and dangerous bus ride to the city centre, where a new Japanese department store, Mykal, sold bacon. We made it about 200 metres from the apartment before Sara apologized and said she needed to return home—she had peed her pants! We realized within a short time that actually her water had broken and she was in labour. We packed our bags, called

Bob Smith, ordered a pizza from Mike and had it delivered to the Kaifaqu hospital.

The first thing you have to do in a Chinese hospital is pay. No money, no service. Canadians would sure appreciate Canadian Medicare after a visit to a Chinese hospital. Tommy Douglas *was* the greatest Canadian! I can't remember exactly how much I paid, but it was a deposit somewhere in the neighbourhood of 2,000 RMB. Sara wanted a natural birth but the option of changing her mind and having drugs soon evaporated because you have to order and pay for any 'extras' like medication in advance and I hadn't done so.

We were shown to a room with three other women in various stages of labour or nursing their newborn babies. Their families crowded around each bed and mould coated the walls.

'Could we have our own room?' we asked optimistically.

The staff at the hospital, on some level, wanted to please us since we were the first foreigners to trust this hospital with our child's birth. Remarkably, a number of Chinese actually thanked us for trusting their medical system. Eventually we settled on the only 'private' room available—a storage room full of boxes of medicine, equipment, and apples. A bed was wheeled in for Sara and we settled in to count contractions, accompanied by our friends Linda, Kathy, and Suzanne.

In China, the government controls if and when you will have heat. Back in the 1950s the government had to decide where to provide heat and where it was not necessary. They drew a line from the Huai River, about half way between the

Yellow and Yangtze Rivers, to the Qinling Mountains. This roughly followed the 0° isotherm in January. In other words, north of this line it is literally freezing but south of this line it isn't and is technically considered a subtropical climate. It doesn't feel very tropical to the locals who suffer through cold, damp winters though, with temperatures often hovering just above 0° Celsius inside and outside their houses. Periodically it does snow, such as happened in January/February of 2008 when not only were people freezing, but their pipes froze too.

North of the Huai-Qinling line there is heat provided via coal burning plants that pipe hot water through radiators into apartments. Even though this is a utility that the customer pays for (expensive enough that many Chinese go without heat) the government decides when it comes on and off. In Dalian, most years it is turned on November 15th, regardless of the temperature outside. In 1998 it was already freezing at night by Halloween.

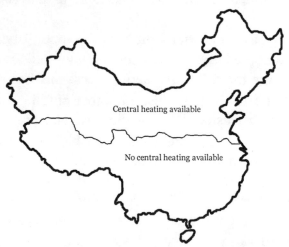

Availability of central heating in China.

Hospitals receive no special treatment and on November 1st, 1998 the Kaifaqu hospital was COLD! Somebody, I can't remember who, must have returned to our home and picked up an electric heater that we plugged into an outlet in our store room. There we sat, the five of us, in the glow of the electric heater, eating Mike's pizza, and counting contractions. Following each contraction Sara belched. It was the onions on the pizza, she said, adding a touch of humour to an otherwise intense situation.

I had hoped to be present for our baby's birth but the doctors were very clear: No one was allowed in the delivery room except for our translator, Alice Zhou, then working in our school's foreign affairs department. When Sara was led into the delivery room I didn't know what to do with myself. I aimlessly paced the halls and wrung my hands nervously. Eventually I spotted a stretcher in the hallway and decided to get horizontal, thinking that it might calm my nerves if I lay down. I contemplated what was happening. Sara was in the delivery room fighting a fierce battle with her body while I lay apparently in a state of meditation. In fact I was battling my own internal war with my nerves. When Sara came out of the delivery room to go to the washroom (a nasty experience in itself—the washroom was dark, cold, and filthy) I was busted for having a nap. The irritated look on her face said 'Get off your ass!' and I scrambled up off the stretcher. I guess I can see how from her perspective it might have looked like I was not taking the whole situation seriously.

At some point I noticed that there were windows above the doors and that by bringing out a chair and standing on it I could see everything happening in the delivery room. Although not physically in the room I was just a metre or two away from the birth scene. Two doctors and two nurses, all

31

female, attended to the birth. The head doctor spoke some English but instead of helping, her limited English hindered things considerably. She was giving the wrong instructions, perhaps nervous about delivering a foreign baby.

At about 11 pm I saw through the window an inexplicable scene. A nurse was heaving herself on Sara's stomach. I guess she was trying to help push out the baby. With the nurse's 'help' and a few blood curdling screams from Sara our daughter entered the world. Given Sara's words from the morning I knew she was Hanna. After cleaning her off, weighing her (4 kg), and rubbing her cheek against Sara's cheek, they brought her out to me. I quietly wept with my baby Hanna all to myself in my arms. I have never felt such joy and been so sure that the world was a wonderful place as at that moment. If a movie were made of this story this scene would be accompanied by violins playing so softly and sweetly that not an eye in the cinema would be dry. The violins and dream-sequence that I was experiencing with Hanna was interrupted by a barbaric and primal screaming coming from somewhere nearby in the hospital. It was Sara screaming in pain being stitched up without anaesthetic because her cheapskate husband hadn't pre-paid for any. Her screams dwindled to whimpers as my blue-eyed little girl looked up at me in the cold, dark hallway outside the delivery room.

We were told that we should stay a week, but considering the hospital condition we insisted on leaving as soon as possible. The next day Hanna was given a half-hearted bath— they didn't quite get all the amniotic fluid off her—and given a TB shot, from which she still has a scar, and we were ready to leave. Before we were officially checked out I took our paper work to the cashier to settle the bill. For the delivery, the 'private' room, boxes and boxes of maternity medicine, both traditional Chinese herbal teas and antibiotics (we threw it all out at home) we paid 1100 RMB. $200 Canadian for a beautiful girl; Life is cheap in China!

In 2000 we repeated the whole process when our son was born. This time we knew what to expect, hospital wise, but we didn't count on arriving at the hospital so early. Sara's labour started in the early morning and I took my time getting prepared, calling work, etc. The second child comes fast and before I knew what was happening Sara was grunting and groaning—this baby was on the way!

Outside we stumbled around in the dark trying to find a taxi. Ideally, a father will have arranged a ride to the hospital for his wife and child to be. Not this dad. I ran up the road and eventually found a cab and we got to the hospital within a few minutes. Because of the early hour the hospital wasn't open and we had to find our way to the emergency entrance. Once there, we were greeted rather pathetically by a sleeping attendant, slumped behind a glass window. I don't know what exactly I said to the woman, but I probably just said 'haizi lai!'—child coming!—and pointed to Sara who was buckled over in contraction pain in the dark foyer.

'San lou,' was all the attendant offered. I understood that to mean 'third floor'.

Up to the third floor we went, feeling our way in the dark. I hurried ahead and found nothing but locked doors. Sara panted behind me, crouching down with each worsening contraction. She badly needed to get to the maternity ward.

There was nobody there.

I rushed downstairs to the attendant and demanded some help.

'*San lou,*' she repeated.

'*Mei you!*'—there is nothing there!—I frantically spurted back.

Seeing Sara arrive back on the scene in the sad shape she was in, the attendant found it in her heart to actually get off her arse and point us in the right direction.

'*San hao lou,*' she said with a frustrated expression and pointed us out the door.

I had misheard her. *San lou* means third floor, while *san hao lou* means building three. Surely the tones are different but I can't hear the difference.

We made it to the maternity ward, much improved since Hanna was born, and the doctors got Sara right to the delivery room. I ran downstairs to get something and bumped into Suzanne, who had made the 30 minute trip from the city and arrived just minutes after we had. That's how long we had been lost and wandering around. Suzanne saved the day, because the woman who was going to translate had left her phone off the hook. Suzanne had been at Hanna's birth and knew what to expect. She guided and calmed Sara during the labour, while I watched through a door window. It was barely 30 minutes before our son Cosmo was born. Like at Hanna's birth, he was looked over, weighed, wrapped in a blanket, and after a cheek rub was brought directly out to me to hold.

I hadn't wanted a second child. I thought I couldn't love a child as much as our first. But I was overwhelmed and found immediately that love for your children is unlimited.

Cosmo was bathed and given an immunization at noon and we checked out, after signing a waiver and fighting off the doctors' protests that it was too soon to leave, by two pm. Cosmo was cheaper than Hanna: 900 RMB. By not staying overnight Sara had saved us thirty bucks!

Sara and Hanna in our apartment with baby Cosmo, the day he was born.

Later that week I returned to the hospital to fill out forms and apply for a birth certificate. Things got funny when they attempted to input Cosmo's name into their computer program. He didn't fit. Chinese names are generally two or three characters, unless they are from a minority group such as Mongolian or Uyghur, in which case they might be up to five or six characters. Cosmo has two middle names and his full name is 23 letters. There was a 15 minute discussion about how to solve this problem. Eventually I convinced them that hand writing the name would be fine. This document would be translated and notarized and sent to Sydney, Nova Scotia, for a Canadian citizenship card anyway. It wasn't a crucial problem for us.

Many people ask us if our kids are Chinese citizens. No, they are not. China does not give citizenship by birthright. Essentially, their policy is that one parent must be a Chinese citizen for the child to be a Chinese citizen. In mixed marriages it is usually the case that the parents opt for the foreign citizenship. In fact, I have never heard of any mixed couple choosing Chinese citizenship and China does not recognize dual citizenship.

The next step after translating and notarizing the birth certificate was to send the papers to Beijing for a passport. Normally a passport application requires proof of Canadian citizenship. Because it takes six months or longer for citizenship papers to be processed, the Canadian embassy in Beijing issues a temporary passport for the child that is good for just one year. Without this, we wouldn't be able to take our kids with us on holiday or home to Canada to meet their grandparents.

Shortly after Hanna was born, when we hadn't yet taken care of her paperwork, Sara got news that her father was dying. She got the news Friday and we flew to Beijing that night hoping that Sara and Hanna would be able to fly to Canada the following morning. You will hear plenty of stories of complaints about the service at Canadian embassies around the world, but on this occasion a particular embassy official went above and beyond the call of duty for us. I can't recall her name now but she came into work on a Saturday morning (unusual for a Canadian government worker, I know) and inserted Hanna into Sara's passport, despite the fact that we didn't even have her birth certificate yet. One hurdle remained: Hanna didn't have a Chinese visa. In other words, even though she was born in China, she wasn't legally entitled to be there, and therefore, paradoxically, wasn't legally able to leave either. The embassy official's Chinese secretary had *guanxi*, or connections, at the local *gong an* office —the public security bureau, or PSB—and a phone call was made.

'Go down there and give them this note. If they give you a visa your daughter can travel with you, if they don't she can't leave China'.

Sara was now all the more distraught with the prospect of her infant daughter not being allowed on the plane while her dad was on his death bed on the other side of the Pacific.

We were very fortunate that the *gong an*, not always known to be cooperative, gave us a visa on the spot. I still feel considerable gratitude to both the Canadian embassy staff and the PSB officer who helped us out that day. This would not be the last time that *guanxi* would come in handy in China. After buying a $200 ticket for Hanna—infants require tickets even though they don't eat food or get a seat—Sara and Hanna got on the plane; I returned to work and caught up with them a week later.

Canadian citizenship cards with baby photos.

Once the citizenship card arrives the passport's validity may be extended for another four years. One hilarious result of this system for Canadians born overseas is that their Canadian ID card, which they keep for life, has a photo taken when they are newborn infants. I chuckle to myself thinking of my kids handing over this ID to enter a nightclub when they are 19, their photo showing a six week old baby held up by their parent's hands.

There are a number of interesting traditions in China following child birth. The first we encountered was a special mother's meal. Our friend and translator for the birth, Alice Zhou, returned to the hospital with a bowl for Sara. Think hospital food is bad at home? Try a meal at a Chinese hospital. There you get slop so bad the locals won't even eat it. Most Chinese who are staying in a hospital will have meals delivered from home. So when Alice showed up she was doing two good deeds. First, she was making sure Sara didn't suffer through a Chinese hospital meal, and second, she made sure that Sara was getting the nourishment a mother needs after giving birth.

Sara looked sceptically at the bowl of mothers' *zhou*, a congee or porridge with egg and dates, as we heard all about how it was traditional mothers' food and quite important and necessary. Even the best *zhou* doesn't look too appetizing— think porridge with unknown Chinese elements added. She smiled politely, took a bite for diplomacy's sake and left the rest.

The Chinese mother and child are supposed to be shut up at home for a month with considerable restrictions on their lives.

The new mother isn't to bathe or even brush her teeth for thirty days. Thankfully, Sara didn't even wait a day for a shower. The baby is to be held horizontally and at all times is bundled in so much clothing and blankets that you wonder if the kids will bake to death in their cocoons.

So when we ventured outside with Hanna after five days we could hear everyone talking about the one month old foreign baby. If we dared to tell them her true age of less than a week the crowds would have freaked out. And yes, there were crowds everywhere we went. In those days just being a foreigner of Caucasian or African descent was enough to get a healthy dose of stares. A personal favourite memory from those days was a man so mesmerized by the sight of us that he drove his bicycle straight into a parked van, his basket of apples spilling all over the road as he scrambled to get his composure. When we walked with Hanna we couldn't stop, because if we did, a crowd of twenty or so gawkers would soon swarm us.

'Zhen bai ah!'—How white!—they shrieked, and everyone tried to touch her face.

The Chinese have a real sense of community that allows pretty much anyone to grab your baby right out of your arms and walk off for a while. We found ourselves battling the masses to keep our precious Hanna out of the clutches of all and everyone. On our first trip to the market, a meat seller, her hands oozing with chicken slime, tried to pinch Hanna's cheek. Yikes! The locals were also amazed by the way we carried Hanna in a baby carrier on our front. Despite the fact that many minority groups in Southern China sling their babies over their backs this was too shocking for the Northern Chinese and we were lectured that we were harming her back irreparably.

The Chinese are also obsessed with temperature.

'*Leng bu leng*?'—Are you cold?—they call out, almost as a greeting.

They were maddened that we dressed our baby so lightly. The same routine occurred whether outside or in a stiflingly hot mall or underground market. I recall visiting my friends Darren and Alice in the same Kaifaqu hospital a few years ago when their son was born. Alice, being Chinese, got no special treatment and was stuffed into one of the regular maternity rooms with several other families. There, Darren engaged in open warfare with the others. The battles were won whenever he managed to open the solitary window allowing some fresh air into the mouldy room crowded with sweaty bodies, his newborn son breaking out in a heat rash in the 30°C June day. But inevitably each victory was short lived and the others insisted on closing the window for fear their bundled red babies would catch a cold in the muggy summer air.

Our kids still get a lot of attention in China but it faded considerably as they got older. The Chinese sure do love children and this has benefits. If you want to go out for supper you don't need a baby sitter. Unlike in the West, babies are always welcome, even at the finest restaurants. Chinese restaurants are *re nao*—hot and noisy—so a screaming child doesn't disrupt the other patrons—they are all screaming too! You don't have to ask, a waitress will soon scoop up and entertain your child while you eat. This is terrific provided your kids like the attention. Our kids didn't always appreciate the attention but it was humorous to see Hanna in a restaurant in Canada when she was a toddler giving cute puppy eyes to the waitresses and being ignored. She couldn't figure out what was wrong. In China our kids are special, almost famous in our community; in Canada they are nobody.

In short, while the conditions of the hospitals are often truly appalling, the walls in the maternity wards covered with mould, child birth, it seems to me, is largely a solitary battle the mother wages herself. When the battle has been won, the spoils of war are your children, who are now your preoccupation. It wouldn't matter if you were lying on the hot stones of the Gobi desert.

4

Sara makes a friend at the furniture market in Jinzhou.

Zai Jia Li

When I was hired I was told that the school would arrange our accommodation but that we would have to pay rent, a very reasonable $300 a month for a large three bedroom apartment. We were also responsible for furnishing the apartment and I was told we could do that for about $2500 Canadian. The premise was that most of this investment we could get back when we left by selling our furniture to the incoming teachers who would replace us. Because I had taught ESL in Guangzhou previously, where I shared an apartment with two other Canadian teachers, I had an expectation of what the apartment would be like. When we arrived at the apartment the first day we were a little overwhelmed. The brand new apartment was indeed large, about 120 square metres, but it, like all new apartments in China, was simply a concrete shell. There was no flooring, no cupboards or wardrobes or closets, and no curtains. Nothing had been finished, except a tiled kitchen with sink and two tiled bathrooms, *sans* mirrors. The rest was bare concrete. The school had purchased, on our behalf, a small fridge, a stove with propane tank, a telephone, a simple ringer washing machine (no dryer), a hot water heater and a bed. These purchases were later to cause conflict with the school.

That first day we were advanced some pay and taken on a shopping spree. We were taken first to a market we would later know as *jin ma shang chang*—Golden Horse Market—to buy all the little things you need to run a household: plates, utensils, pots and pans, towels, bathmats, etc. It was a strange experience to feel so helpless and dependent, four of us being led by Alice Zhou, who had to translate and bargain for us. When you travel you don't need much but relocating and starting a new life and setting up a home requires major purchases and decisions. Things were unfamiliar and we really didn't know how long we were settling down for. What was necessary and what was available? We couldn't find an oven or a toaster. Did we need a wok? How about a rice cooker, the one indispensible appliance of every Chinese kitchen? The shopping decisions were made more difficult because at that point we couldn't say much more than counting to ten in Chinese. Shopkeepers aggressively demanded *'yao mai shenme'*—What do you want to buy? Even today after twelve years in this environment I sometimes don't have the patience to deal with shopping at Golden Horse Market—one always feels pressure to buy from the vendors, so much so that I often leave the market frustrated and empty-handed. If only they would shut up and give you a few minutes to think you might be able to buy something.

The next morning we were taken to the furniture market in the nearby town of Jinzhou. Jinzhou is an older more established centre than Kaifaqu and even had a McDonald's restaurant. I confess, we made a dozen or so trips just for the Mickey D's in our first couple of years in Kaifaqu. There was also an indoor playground for kids in the next building. Outdoor playgrounds with swings and teeter-totters for kids don't really exist in China as they do in the West, so going there was a real treat for all ages.

At the furniture market we waded through a sea of kitschy, cheap crap, but nevertheless settled on a sofa set, wardrobe, and table and chairs. Unlike some single teachers, who could afford to be more frugal, we needed to build a nest comfortable enough to start a family in. Despite spending more than our colleagues on furniture, most of it was junk. Our sofa, although comfortable enough to sit on, broke within weeks. When I opened it up I found that major wooden supports were inches too short and were barely held together by nails. I can't remember how many times that sofa crashed apart after someone sat down on it heavily and how many times I had to repair it.

We made do with what we had. To add colour to the house we filled old juice concentrate bottles with coloured water and set them on the window sill. I bought three Buddha image posters from a hawker under a bridge for 10 RMB each.

With Sara's talent for arrangement our cold, empty shell soon became a warm home.

Later we found that gorgeous Chinese 'antique' furniture was available in Beijing and some other large cities. The genuine antiques, which traders scoured the country for, were sent down to towns in the Pearl River delta and were refurbished. They then appeared in expensive shops in the touristy streets of Macau, just below the famous ruins, the facade of St. Paul's. Still more was sent to the expensive and trendy shops of Hollywood Street in Hong Kong's Mid-levels district.

The growing demand for antiques led to outfits that built authentic looking new furniture. Many of these shops opened near Beijing's awesome market at *Panjiayuan*, known as the Dirt Market in English. Aptly named, the Dirt Market is a collection of antique and trinket vendors from all over China who spread their wares on the ground, hence the market's name. Old coins, fragments of antique pottery, *Quotations from Chairman Mao* (the Little Red Book), and old clocks are standard stuff available for sale. More interesting were the hawkers from China's hinterlands: The Miao women (known as Hmong in S.E. Asia) with red betel nut-stained teeth and hands turned violet from the dyes they use to make their embroidered aprons and clothing; Tibetans with coral and turquoise jewellery and collections of their odd fur and felt hats; Muslims from Qinghai and Gansu selling furs from various wild cats and wolves; Turkic speaking Uyghurs with jade from Khotan, near China's frontier with Pakistan and Afghanistan.

These days the Dirt Market is no longer dirt—it is open-air but covered—and prices have risen, but I still enjoy a couple of hours strolling around and I never know what I'll come home with. The furniture shops around the Dirt Market furnished our whole apartment. One of our first purchases was a Chinese medicine chest. Each of the many small drawers has the name of a traditional Chinese medicine engraved on it in Chinese characters. Satisfying the demand of the foreign market, the medicine chests are now modified so that each drawer fits CD cases perfectly. Because DVDs cost only a dollar in China, the chests fill up pretty quickly. Another modified piece we've bought is a large *armoire* made to hold a TV, which can be shut up and covered by the two beautiful doors. When new teachers or Chinese friends, both groups of people with relatively barren living quarters, come to visit they always comment on our lovely Chinese furniture and the artwork we have picked up from a decade of travels around Asia.

Although Sara created such a warm home, our Chinese apartment certainly tested our nerves at times. The power often went out without warning. It went out once when Hanna was just a week old in early November. The government-provided heat wasn't yet on and without electricity our own portable heaters wouldn't work. Nor would our electric hot water tank, so we were left in the dark, cold and stinky. Luckily we could cook, because our stove ran on propane. After determining that power was not cut for the whole building and confirming that we had paid our bill we called the school but were told that the electrician was busy getting married that day.

'I don't care who, just get someone down here. We've got a six day old baby!' I barked into a phone, echoing what I had heard Sara say moments earlier.

That afternoon a motorcycle pulled up driven by the school's carpenter with the groom on the back. They were drunk for sure, as Chinese weddings involve a lot of drinking, especially for the groom who has to have a drink with each table of guests. The poor guy was dragged away from his own wedding. The drunken groom/electrician proceeded to fiddle around with some wires in the building's main switch box and nervously switched the power back on. This hilarious moment is the only time I have ever seen an electrician doubtful of his work. He was very clearly scared when he flicked the switch back on, jumping back, seemingly expecting an explosion of sparks or some other catastrophe. There was no explosion and off they went drunk on their motorcycle back to the wedding.

Propane had a habit of running out at the most inopportune times too, like when we were hosting a kid's birthday party. That was simple enough to remedy.

'*Yong mei qi*'—need propane—we stuttered in halting Chinese into the phone and it would arrive and be hooked up within the hour.

But nothing drove us mad like Chinese plumbing. Poor infrastructure combined with cheap materials and worse workmanship made for all around nasty conditions in the bathroom and under the kitchen sink. When we first turned on our taps they ran black for several minutes, and once our hot water tank exploded, covering the entire bathroom in black goo. Toilets perpetually ran and in one of our apartments the toilet's intake pipe burst every year for four years, flooding the apartment if we weren't home to catch it right away. We had no hot water in our kitchen our first year and went eight days without any hot water at all. That's fine if you are in a bungalow on a tropical beach, but in Manchuria during the winter with two babies at home it's not so popular. Here's a little tip: If you want to keep your wife and mother of your children happy then make sure you have hot water. In China this is easier said than done.

The most persistent plumbing issue, however, was Ivan. Ivan was the name given to the invisible ogre that left the stench that emanated day and night from all the drains in China. Try as you might to cover drains with plungers, caps, or waste paper baskets, you just couldn't keep Ivan out. The Chinese plumbers are strangers to the gooseneck pipes we use in the West to prevent Ivan from getting into our homes. When we leave China Ivan is one fellow I won't miss.

When we returned from our first Chinese New Year holiday we were informed we had to move apartments the next day. The new apartment was in the same building but in the next stairwell and on the 1st floor, which meant we would need to have bars on our windows for security. The apartment was identical to our first except the layout was opposite. We moved everything and put it all in the same places, the only problem being the wall-to-wall carpeting that had to be cut up because the floor pattern was opposite to the original. This gave the apartment a raggedy, patchwork appearance. We weren't too happy about the forced rush move but were reassured that we wouldn't have to move again.

Five months later, a meeting with our boss informed us that he had purchased a group of apartments in a nearby neighbourhood and that they would be provided completely furnished, with hardwood floors for the same rent. Other than not wanting to move again we had another concern. The apartments were going to be furnished, but we had previously spent $3500 furnishing the first apartment with the understanding that we could sell the furniture to the new teachers when we left.

'No problem' we were told, the school would move our furniture and buy it from us.

That sounded great, but when it was time to be reimbursed major problems appeared. First, the school's accountant, who seemed to be the most powerful person around, insisted on using a depreciation scale so we were to get only 70% of what we had paid for everything; it was now second hand. The next issue was what everything actually cost. We were being cheated but Sara had kept all the original receipts, especially from the items the school had bought for us. This way we proved that we had been overcharged by the school. For example, we were originally charged 1400 RMB for our washing machine but come reimbursement time they produced a receipt for only 700 RMB. After we showed our receipts they had no choice but to pay. A final battle, which we lost, was over transferring the phone line. When we arrived, a land line cost 1700 RMB (over $300) just to set up and when the cost of the actual telephone was added we were charged 2000 RMB. We protested that this was outrageously expensive and said we would live without a phone. Who were we going to call anyway? Our only friends lived in the same stairwell of the building.

'Sorry, it's already done' we were told and the money was deducted from my first month's pay without my agreeing to it. By this time the state-owned phone company had drastically reduced their fees to meet the growing challenge to their monopoly from cell phone providers. Why get a land line at all? We were out a couple hundred dollars on that deal. This is how things worked in our early days in Dalian. There was, and still is, a lot of mistrust between the company I worked for and the Canadian employees teaching there. But to be fair, much of distrust over money comes from the handling of money matters by the Chinese employees, not from the owner. Our boss has tended to be honest when it comes to legal and contractual arguments that arise and in the case of the telephone lines, after a year's fight we eventually got our money back.

Sara and friends have a 'pearl party' in our apartment.

Our third apartment lacked natural light due to its location and was so cold in winter we had to cover the windows with plastic. After four years of putting up with it we decided to break free from the control our employer held over our living conditions. This was a smart move because it reduced the connections between our life and our work. Any apartment hassles could no longer be blamed on the company and this reduced resentment towards my employers. I noticed that in subsequent years the Canadian teachers that were dependent on the school for housing had numerous complaints that led to unhappiness at work as well. It was too hard to separate the two.

We decided to move into a new upscale neighbourhood. Our new apartment cost us 40,000 RMB a year to rent (generally in China you are required to pay six or even 12 months rent in advance). Our rent nearly doubled but our quality of life more than doubled. Our living room view of a concrete corner wall became a mountain and sea view; one small bathroom became two; one story became two; and dark was replaced with bright sky lights. Four balconies enhanced our lifestyle and I even set up a portable hot tub on one of the balconies. The grounds at Song Hai Zhuang Yuan—Pine Sea Gardens—were also a radical improvement. In our old neighbourhood broken glass and human excrement littered the communal square where our children played. Songhai boasted tennis and basketball courts (although we had to paint the lines on the empty tennis courts ourselves and then all of a sudden tennis became popular), two playgrounds for children, and well manicured gardens. We were able to hop the fence and access trails in the adjacent Dong Shan—East Mountain—park which is home to a small population of local wildlife, notably pheasants, rabbits and snakes, some of which were poisonous and pretty big too.

Life in Songhai was great but we still had a few complaints, mostly about the plumbing, which perpetually leaked and Ivan made his visits there too. When a Chinese fellow, who I will call Pengyou—friend—in this book, who worked for a housing complex in a beach resort area close to our work, informed us they were building phase two, it was time to buy.

After eight and a half years in China we were going to be home owners... sort of. Although foreigners had legally been able to buy apartments (technically nobody owns land in China, instead owners hold 70 year leases) for a number of years in the more developed areas, this particular developer hadn't got a license to sell to foreigners. We turned to the person we trust most in China, Ayi. We had trusted Ayi with our children's well being for eight years, surely she was trustworthy. Our apartment was purchased with our money, but in Ayi's name. It's a little scary to have your home, your largest investment, owned technically by someone else but as Sara says 'if she really is the kind of person who would cheat us out of our home, what can we do?' The idea is that after a period of two years we can 'buy' back the house.

Hanna and Cosmo in our Song Hai apartment.

Buying the apartment involved some instances that seem humorous, but only in retrospect. First of all, we had to bribe someone just to be able to buy the apartment! It was a bit of an insider deal I guess, but Pengyou had got us a chance to pick out and pay a deposit on an apartment the day before they were available to the public and for a cheaper price per square metre. It turns out that this was phase two of the bribing because some apartments were already gone, and in fact, Pengyou had secured his for even cheaper.

Neither Sara nor I like the idea of bribery and we have tried to be principled about not contributing to the corrupt system in China. It's not always a case of black or white corruption though. The grey area is large, due to the importance of *guanxi*, a concept of paramount importance in China that refers to the connections that one needs in order to get anything done. Related to *guanxi* is *mianzi*, or face. Because of *guanxi* and *mianzi* one is called upon and calls upon others. We paid the bribe to buy the apartment. When in Rome...

I wasn't able to get a mortgage in China for a couple of reasons. First, the apartment wasn't in our name and second, we didn't have the minimum 30% to put down. I borrowed the money from a Canadian bank and had it wired to my Chinese bank account. This was simple enough and cost about $30. On the Chinese side it was not so simple. After we paid the deposit we had been told that they would inform us when we were to pay in full.

'Don't worry, not now' we heard every time we asked.

'*Shenme shihou?*' When?

'*Bu yiding. Qiu tian, ke neng*'. Not certain. Maybe in the fall.

As usually happens in China there was an urgent call one day. 'You've got to pay by the end of the week or you'll lose the apartment!'

No worries, the money is in the bank. Or is it? When I went to withdraw it, I was told that actually all the money in my account was Canadian dollars and I would have to exchange it to RMB before I could withdraw it.

'Ok, let's do that now'

'*Bu keyi*'. Not possible. 'Only US$10,000 can be exchanged per day and maximum $50,000 per month'.

So everyday for several days I trundled up to the little Bank of China branch on the main corner of the little town of Manjiatan and exchanged $10,000 into RMB until I had 465,000 RMB in my account, the total cost of the apartment. To pay for it I was to deposit the money into an account at the China Construction Bank, across the street from the Bank of China.

'Can I wire the money to the Construction Bank?'

'*Bu keyi*'.

I had no choice but to pack 465,000 RMB, all in red 100 RMB notes, into my bursting laptop bag. Many locals, those who are employed anyway, make less than 1000 RMB a month, so I was a tad nervous about walking around with all that cash. Imagine crossing main street in your home town with half a million dollars in a bag. I asked the bank's security guards if they would escort me to the other bank.

'*Bu keyi*'.

So I scurried across the road alone, rushing nervously past a line of moto-taxi drivers who won't make that much cash in their lifetimes.

Then all we had to do was wait for the building to be finished. It had gone up so quickly but once the building was up, it stalled. Electricity and water were perpetually coming 'maybe next week'. Chinese contractors are, generally speaking, not to be trusted, either for quality of their workmanship or for their habit of cheating the customer by using cheaper materials when you paid for better, or charging more but using less. Chinese homeowners will always have someone they trust watching over the construction 24 hours a day. Because we both were working we weren't able to do this, so we were pretty excited to hear that a British outfit called B&Q had just opened a superstore in Dalian city. B&Q is similar to North America's Home Depot, but in addition to the building supplies they also had interior designers and construction crews. Going with B&Q was to give us peace of mind. How wrong we were!

The whole B&Q experience was a gong show. They sent out the designer, a great guy whose card said Tony Xing, who wandered through the apartment saying *keyi*—it's possible—and *mei wenti*—it's no problem—to everything.

'Can we knock out this wall?'

'*Keyi*'.

'Can we enclose this balcony?'

'*Keyi*'.

'Push out this wall?'

'*Keyi*'.

'Move the front door down a flight of stairs?'

'*Mei wenti. Zai Zhongguo duo mei wenti*'. In China everything is possible. No problem.

This was going to be a lot of fun. Basically, there seemed to be no rules or regulations limiting our creativity and renovations. Two other friends had also purchased apartments in the same complex and together, the three families exchanged ideas on how we would design our homes. When one of us came up with a good idea, the other two would poach it, so in the end, while each of our three homes is distinctive, they share several common features. One great idea from Brad, who in turn had seen a Chinese neighbour do it, was to 'steal' some space at the top of the hallway.

We had all bought sixth floor apartments. Most apartment blocks in China are six stories because any higher and regulations require an elevator, which of course increases costs to the developer which are then passed on to the owners. Foreigners often choose to rent top floor apartments because they are more likely to have a balcony or even several balconies. Our apartment had a narrow balcony that extended the entire length of the apartment on the south side, stretching in front of the living room, Hanna's bedroom and the master bedroom. From this balcony we have an unobstructed view of all of Jinshitan beach resort and the Yellow Sea. There was also a three metre wide balcony stretching the width of the apartment on the east side. On the north-west corner was another balcony. The balconies, which you don't pay for in the square metre count, and the view, were the reasons Sara had picked that particular apartment. The drawback of course is the six flights of stairs that you have to walk up and down. Floors one to five have apartments on each side of the stairwell but our 'penthouse' is the only apartment on the top floor. The actual front door to our apartment is on the landing half way between the fifth and sixth floors. Here the ceiling in the stairwell is very high, extending to the top of the sixth floor. Brad's idea was to fill in this space above the stairwell. Nobody would care because it didn't affect anyone else's space. This way we were able to build in a loft attached to the smallest bedroom (in fact we had to build a wall to create the small room from a nook in the original layout). A local guy built a wooden staircase up to the loft with drawers built into the stairs (this was Blake's idea) and it became the perfect room for our son Cosmo. When the head of the *wu*

ye—the maintenance department—whom we named Crazy
Eyes Killer, saw our lofts, he freaked out.

'It's your place. Who cares what he says. Who is he? He
can't stop you once it is done' our Chinese friends all encouraged. They were right, this time.

Another really exciting experience was designing our
kitchen. Typically, Chinese kitchens are very small and are
shut off from the dining or living room by a sliding door. This
is because Chinese cuisine involves a lot of frying in woks and
the oil splashes all over the place. There is also a lot of smoke
and chilli dust that permeates the whole apartment. The
Chinese kitchen has very little counter space and the counters
are way too low. Every foreigner living in China complains
about back ache from preparing food or washing dishes in a
hunched over position. The Chinese don't bake so there are
no ovens, and the stove is generally only two burners. We
were set on creating a real Western-style kitchen and we
succeeded, with the single exception that our oven and stove
are on opposite sides of the room, because under the stove
there is a propane bottle. The bright colours, open plan—we
knocked out a window into the entrance way, another one of
Blake's ideas—, the 90 cm high, artificial marble counters,
and a large two door fridge and freezer (a rare luxury in
China) make our kitchen the envy of all our expat teacher
friends.

The original kitchen sub-contractor disappeared, delaying
our kitchen cabinets and counters installation, but B&Q
refunded the 5000 RMB we had paid as a deposit. I guess
that was one benefit we got from B&Q. We had to go through
the difficult task of picking out colours and patterns again.

In Canada when you buy a condo, you likely choose one of
several colour schemes; there are few options, making it a

relatively simple procedure. In China the new apartment owner has an infinite number of potential decisions to make. How many electrical outlets do you need? Where should they go? If you don't make these decisions they will be made for you by the workers who really don't give a damn, and seem to lack common sense when it comes to these kinds of concerns. This may be because the construction workers are for the most part migrants from the country side who have perhaps never lived in a decent apartment with electrical outlets, or have lived so simply that there was no need for outlets. Chinese apartments never have enough sockets and they are located in the most awkward places, often two metres high in the middle of the wall. Should you replace the PVC pipes in the walls with better quality? All of these decisions are made much more difficult because we were giving instructions and receiving advice in a language we have only a limited grasp of. I know now, because I learned from trial and error, that concrete is called *shui ni*—water mud—and that marble is *dalishi*, but so much other key construction vocabulary I bluffed my way through.

The original floor plan for the apartment was 135 square metres, two bedrooms, 2 bathrooms, a kitchen, and a nook. By building a wall and the loft we had created a third bedroom but the apartment lacked an office, and with the dining set in the living room things would seem a bit crowded. It was essential if we were to live there that we enclose the balconies on the east side and north-west corner of the apartment. My plan was for the long side balcony to be enclosed and divided in two with a wall. The north-east portion would be a laundry room, something unknown in Chinese apartments. Usually a washing machine sits obstructively in an already crowded bathroom or even in the kitchen. In some apartments I've seen the washing machine sit in the living room until it needs to be used and then it is dragged into the tiny kitchen or bathroom and the water runs across the floor and into a drain. Dryers are not common and clothes are hung out a window on retractable hangers, or anywhere in the apartment where there is space.

The front half of the balcony I hoped to be a dining room and sun room. The balcony in the north-west corner would become our office. Tony Xing, Mr. *Keyi*, suggested we use a company that specializes in windows and balconies. A plump young woman with an honest round face surnamed Yu, Xiao Yu —Little Yu—we called her, showed up with her boys armed with measuring tapes, and mimicking Tony Xing, said '*keyi*' and '*mei wenti*' to all our requests.

We paid twenty percent of the 40,000 RMB estimate to enclose the balconies and replace the crappy front windows and sliding doors in the living room and two bedrooms. The workers came out to begin and for the first couple of hours, everything was going well and the roofs were up and frames were getting drilled into the concrete. Suddenly, the power went out and Crazy Eyes Killer was downstairs yelling up at us. We were to stop all work immediately. The balconies, said Crazy Eyes, were not ours. We hadn't paid for them, had we? They were technically common property belonging to every-one in the complex, he insisted. Although it is true that we hadn't paid for the balconies, it was absurd to think that they were common property. If anyone wanted to access them they would have to knock on our door and walk through our living room. Besides, people all over China had filled in their balconies, including people in our complex. When I pointed this out, Crazy Eyes got me on a technicality.

'Those are all in phase one, this is phase two'

'So what?!'

'*Shi guiding*'. It's the rules.

Aggravatingly he followed this up with 'You are a foreigner. You don't understand. This is China'.

I hated that bastard.

In Canada one follows the rules because rules *are* rules. They were made (most of the time) for good reason and they are enforced and there are uniform and known consequences for breaking them. In Canada my friends wouldn't have told a foreigner that it would be no problem, screw the rules, and piss on anyone who tries to stop you. It was precisely because this was China that I attempted any of this. Although there were some Chinese who said we might not be allowed to close the balconies and several who suggested we just needed to wait a couple of years (out of the question if we were to live in the apartment), 90% of them, including the B&Q foreman, all my neighbours, and my best Chinese friends said 'do it and it will be no problem'.

'What are they going to do?' they said, implying there was nothing they could do.

Crazy Eyes said we could put up a roof, but could not enclose the space with glass. If we did he would call the cops and they would be ripped down at our cost. I desperately wanted to point to building 27 across the road with an already enclosed balcony and say 'what about him?' The problem was, it was Brad's apartment and I didn't want to cause him trouble. Of course, I knew that his apartment was owned on paper by Pengyou, who previously worked for the developers and had *guanxi*. Plus, Crazy Eyes had already freaked on Brad and forced him to undo some changes he made to his balcony railing at his own cost. Nor did I want to point out Blake and Sandy's filled in balcony next door to me. It seemed I was getting harassed for two reasons. I didn't have any *guanxi* and our balcony was right at the front of the development, easily visible to the whole town. Also, I was a foreigner, assumed to have bundles of cash poking out from all my pockets. Why not grab some? *'Kill the rooster to frighten the monkeys,'* they say in Chinese. I guess I was the rooster but Crazy Eyes was definitely a cock!

We laid low on the balcony front for a month or so and continued the work indoors, which was going painfully slow. B&Q, to save money, had sent just one crew and foreman out to do three jobs because we were located an hour from the city centre. Needless to say, it took three times as long as it should have, if not more. There were delays that were not their fault, like power and water interruptions, pipes freezing then bursting, and finally they needed the balconies done before they could continue. So I called Xiao Yu and told them to come and try again, working quickly, first on the back balcony, out of Crazy Eyes' sight, and then on the more visible large balcony. They were sure they could get it done in one day. An hour or so into the job, when everything seemed to be going so well, there was a knock on the locked door. Xiao Yu and her crew had decided to ignore it and they kept working, knowing full well it was the security guards from the front gate there on Crazy Eyes' behalf. Sure to his word the police arrived. Actually not police, they were some type of uniformed officers, who for all I know, may or may not have had any jurisdiction over these matters. I was told work had to stop or it would be torn down the next day and I would have to pay a huge fine on top of the cost to tear it down. Several neighbours and the B&Q foreman all got in there shouting away on my behalf. Crazy Eyes Killer acted the arse as usual, ranting and raving, his eyes bulging out of his head. I tried my best to convey to the officer that I had been told by all my friends and two building contractors that this was okay and that I had paid 40,000 RMB which I couldn't get back and besides, look around, this is happening all over China, and they knew it. He left me his final thoughts: Crazy Eyes and I had to come to some kind of agreement.

Aha! It was the perfect set up for bribe number two. Crazy Eyes led me to his office and pulled out papers written in Chinese that I couldn't read, apparently proof that people had applied and paid for the right to fill in their balconies. I was told that I should pay 10,000 RMB for this right. It was outrageous, but I didn't know how to proceed. My neighbour and friend Sandy, wife of my friend and colleague Blake, was chatting with me about the situation.

'Do you want me to call Pengyou?' she asked.

'No, I don't want to involve him,' I said. I had called on him enough over the years. I decided then and there to pay the bribe/fee and get this mess over and done with.

'I'll just call him and ask him what he thinks,' said Sandy.

Little did I know, and apparently neither did Sandy, that this phone call led to Pengyou wining and dining and singing karaoke all night with Crazy Eyes and the big bosses on my behalf. The next day Pengyou called and said I could pay just 2000 RMB and it would all be settled. I can't really explain how I had been resigned to pay five times more the day before but now didn't want to pay anything. I may have been influenced by my neighbours who continued to insist that they weren't going to pay anything. It was at the end of the day, sitting in our car about to head home, Sara and I, with Blake in the back, when I got the call from Pengyou asking if I was ready to pay. In retrospect, this was a key turning point in how all this went down. For whatever reason, after a brief discussion with Sara and Blake, I said that I didn't want to pay, at least not right that instant. I was about to drive the 25 km home to our kids who were waiting for us for supper. Surely this wasn't that urgent. At no point in this conversation did Pengyou suggest that this was a bad or stupid decision on my part. He certainly didn't make clear that there would be serious consequences.

The next evening I got a call from Pengyou's wife, an old friend of mine. She was very upset, more so than I had ever seen or heard from her. She explained the lengths that Pengyou had gone to help and now, because I had refused to pay, he had lost all his *mianzi*—his face—with Crazy Eyes and the bosses. He had been crying all day about it, and damn it, my inconsiderate actions had caused pandemonium in her family. She informed me that Pengyou would no longer be able to help and that I was not to call on him again. I apologized as best I could and tried to explain what had happened; I felt absolutely sick about it. Could this be explained as a simple cultural misunderstanding? If the phone call had not been made by Sandy, a bright and capable Chinese negotiator, I could accept that answer but I am still perplexed about it to this day.

Priority number one became patching up my relationship with Pengyou. I called him and we met in his jeep the next afternoon. I explained myself, said 'Baoqian'—the highest form of sorry—as often as I could and presented him with a bottle of scotch. We parted amicably but he said there was nothing he could do now. I would have to talk to Crazy Eyes myself.

Crazy Eyes' eyes were popping out his ugly head when he screamed that it was now going to cost me 30,000 RMB. Sara convinced me to get a decent translator to help and I finally agreed. I didn't want to ask Sandy since she had helped me enough and had her own balcony issues. So, on Sara's advice I called a female Chinese acquaintance who spoke excellent English and had good *guanxi*. I have no doubt that she could have helped but was unavailable that day and I was anxious to get things over with, and being a stubborn fool I decided to see the big boss myself. Big Boss was very amicable and I told him how much I loved China and Jinshitan and really wanted a home for my family there. I told him I could understand paying a fine because I had erred by believing my friends and I had been stubborn, but 30,000 was simply unreasonable. I stressed that I was a simple teacher, not a highly paid manager of a multinational corporation like many expats in China. He was agreeable and pleasant but in the end he said that I had to talk with Crazy Eyes.

Crazy Eyes and I tried to be civil walking up onto the offending balcony to discuss the situation. He came down to 20,000 RMB, ten times what I could have paid a couple of days earlier. I went home and thought about it and talked it over with Sara. It seemed now that we had no choice. I justified paying it by telling myself that the money was worth it when you calculated the cost of the added living space by square metre. It was in fact very cheap when thought of this way. But more than that, it was worth it for ending the epic struggle that had taken its toll on me emotionally. I was paying for peace of mind and to just get it over and done with.

Two weeks later a little bird told me that Pengyou had received half of the bribe. I'm still not sure what to believe. Pengyou helped me so many times over the years and I do consider him a *pengyou*. I don't believe his help was ever intended as a way to make money for himself. Any possible kickbacks would have been meagre. But could he have been given back some face with a cash payment from Crazy Eyes? I will never know because to ask him would be highly insulting. Either way, I hold no hard feelings and hope it is the same for him. The whole incident speaks to the difficulties of 'doing business' in China, especially for a *waiguoren* who doesn't understand the cultural nuances.

Sara with Alice and her mother on our balcony, Manjiatan.

In the end, I did secure a written agreement allowing me to enclose the balconies and was awarded 10,000 RMB compensation for the building being finished late. It was a small victory but it felt good after taking such a beating in the many apartment battles. Ultimately, now when I sit in my gorgeous sun room on a clear Sunday morning, the sun shining in, and I look out over all of Jinshitan, I think it was worth every second and penny of the hassle.

Stop the press!

Just as I was finishing this book, a man approached me outside my apartment asking how much I had paid Crazy Eyes for the balcony. It seems that others had also been forced to pay and now a residents' association was forming to fight back. They are going to take legal action and it seems this story is not yet finished. In addition to being pleased about the prospect of getting some money back, I was delighted to see a grassroots, democratic organization take form. Perhaps the rule of law is slowly making an appearance in China after all.

As much as I love our new apartment, looking back on our previous homes, it is clear that home is wherever you make it. On our summer trips to Canada, at a certain point, usually after about a month, the kids always ask 'when are we going home?' They mean, of course, our Chinese home. In each of our apartments in China we have always felt *zai jia li*—at home.

The Blob's Nest, Manjiatan.

Manjiatan

For the purpose of comparing Manjiatan with your home town try this: Put your book down and look out the window at the street, observing who comes and goes, and by what mode of transport. I sat on my balcony and looked out at the entrance of the new complex across the street where hundreds of displaced farmers had been resettled in the spring of 2009. Here's what I saw in a five minute observation:

2 cars (one VW Jetta, one Chery—a Chinese brand)

3 bikes (1 with two brooms sticking out behind, 1 with broom and shovel)

1 Truck (with a 3 metre bed laden with fishing floats)
1 tractor pulling a trailer and driven by a woman in a pink head scarf
2 vans (one 13-seater, one 7-seater bread van)
1 three-wheel tractor/pickup hybrid
6 motorcycles (125 cc)
1 motorized scooter
17 pedestrians

Let's take a walk through town.

Just outside the entrance of my complex I come to a bus stop where motorcycle drivers hover like parasites, waiting for the feeding frenzy when the bus discharges its passengers. The moto-taxi drivers edge closer and closer to the bus doors so that when the passengers disembark their escape route is blocked. In a desperate yet good-natured game, the drivers jockey for position, cutting each other off from the potential fares. Ignoring them, most passengers silently walk around the obstacles and cross the main street and enter the market area. Each Wednesday and Saturday morning the market swells and spills onto the side streets as farmers from the outlying areas set up shop on the curb side. The market is noisy but the first sounds are of honking horns and the *putt-putt-putt* of the three wheeled tractors, which still start by hand cranking the engine. With each *putt* the farmers' blue tractor-trucks belch a dark cloud of diesel smoke. Holding my breath as best I can I dart through the smoke and across the road.

It is summer time and the first vendor, a middle aged woman keeping the sun off her face with a bright pink head scarf, has laid grapes, nectarines, and peaches out on the sidewalk. Next to her stands a man in a straw hat, with 'Marlboro' emblazoned on the front. The Marlboro Man hovers over a giant honeycomb. When I ask '*duo shao qian?*'—How much?—he replies '800 RMB,' over $100. How much for just *yi liang,* or 100 grams? 5 RMB, or 80 cents.

A farmer's tractor parked in Manjiatan.

Just then a man walks by with a pole over his shoulders, from which hangs on either end baskets of fish, no doubt caught by himself or his sons. A blue tractor overflowing with potatoes has a healthy crowd around it; the price must be good. Eggplant, which curiously enough, is what the Chinese say when they take photos—'*qiezi!*'—because it sounds like 'cheese,' is heaped up in mounds. Beans and mushrooms follow not far behind. A row of a dozen old men sit on a ledge with their canes resting on their laps. All wear hats, some in wide brimmed white hats, and others still wearing the blue caps of the Cultural Revolution era. Their creased and craggy faces squint in the light and they watch me as I stroll past. I get the sense they would like to ask me the usual question— *Ni shi na guo ren?*—about where I come from but they lack the energy to bother. The *lao tou*—old heads—come down each morning and sit all day, talking and watching the action on the street.

Turning down a laneway behind the main market building, a woman runs a machine that turns sesame seeds into paste and oil. Soon the fruit and vegetables give way to seafood. Amid Chinese versions of 'cockles and mussels, alive, alive o!' I take stock of the excellent assortment of *hai xian:* seaweed, jellyfish, numerous varieties of fish, squid, miniature crabs, prawns, mantis shrimp, and several species of shellfish, all cheap, fresh, and tasty. It was several years before I even asked how much the mussels cost and I was shocked to find them considered cheap farmers' food: about 80 cents/kg!

Turning into the market building, the path is blocked by a beggar, stretched out and missing a leg, a few *jiao*— dimes—spread out on a cloth in front of his face. Beyond the beggar, a legless knife vendor sits in a wheel chair, his knives on display on a tray on his lap. Across from him a knife is being sharpened by a man who manually spins a grinding stone on a short wooden bench. Then, a woman from Yunnan province—or perhaps a local dressed as a Yunnanese—selling *Pu'er* tea. At the next tiny intersection, barbeque ducks hang, some baked behind glass, others in a cylindrical metal kiln. At 19 RMB a duck they are hard to resist, but experience tells us they are quite fatty and there's not much meat.

Inside the market building a more modern-style grocery store, with posted fixed prices, sells everything from pots and pans, to little plastic bags of milk, to Dove bars—for years the only chocolate found in China that doesn't taste like wax.

Heading out the front door, pickup trucks and three wheel carts working as cargo taxis wait for business. Next door, the bath house belches black smoke, all its hot water generated from a coal burning boiler room. Out front, women carry plastic baskets filled with shampoo, soap, toothbrushes, and combs...everything they need in the bathhouse. Most go because they don't have decent washing facilities in their homes; some go just because they like the relaxing rituals of getting an exfoliating scrub or a soak in a hot tub. A visit to the local bathhouse will set you back about two dollars.

Heading south towards the water the road turns a corner and the elementary school and middle school give displays of Communist and nationalistic propaganda each Monday morning during the flag raising ceremony. At 10 am each day the entire student body assembles on the dirt field and carries out group exercises in perfect unison, or sometimes a marching drill, and less frequently a massive show of *tai-jichuan*—tai chi.

Between the sidewalk and the brick wall that separates the school from the rest of the world a three-metre wide slope houses tomorrow's supper. A lonely goat bleats in vain and when I ride my bike to work the next morning I will see its severed head on the ground, its hide drying over a chair, its carcass steaming. I'll do my best to avoid riding my bike through the stream of blood that spills onto the road. The same scene is repeated a hundred metres further down the main street.

It's an odd choice of a location, but there is a makeshift outhouse built onto the brick wall beside the sad goat. Children scream and chase soccer balls on one side, while men urinate against the other side of the wall, in clear view of all the passers-by.

On the west side of the street trucks of various sizes—pick-ups, three-metre and five-metre trucks—gather for the day hoping someone will need to transport a load of something. Across from the trucks is Xi Cheng, a restaurant serving ethnic *Chaoxian*—Korean—food. I often go for lunch with friends, ordering a *banfan,* known in Korean as *bibimbap*, a delicious rice and veggie combo served in a burning hot crock pot and topped with a half cooked egg (stir it quickly and the egg cooks). It was here that I first ate dog meat and when we took my mother-in-law for lunch she was forced to use chopsticks for the first time in her life—there are no forks available in Manjiatan, that's for sure.

The rest of the main street, which stretches for no more than a few hundred metres, is mostly shops selling odds and ends, many full of men smoking and playing cards, Chinese chess, or *ma jiang*—mah-jong. In the evening barbeque stalls set up on the sidewalks and beer is swilled while patrons gnaw on lamb kebabs, spicy chicken necks and heads, barbe-qued corn bread, and hairy beans.

To the west of the main street a few rows of low rise hous-ing mingle with factories and workshops, building and repairing boat engines, until the buildings give way to farm land. To the east, several hundred apartment blocks stand in identical rows. In the back the relocated fishers tie their nets on the sidewalks and the old women cook communally outside in woks or steamers placed on old oil barrels. They stoke their fires with dried grass, corn stalks, or scrap wood. Inside, their apartments are bare concrete floors and walls. Many are too poor to pay for heat or buy gas for their stoves so they cook outside for free. But they don't seem desperate; rather, they look comforted in their community of thrifty *lao tou,* cooking as they did previously in their country homes.

Locals prepare corn for winter, Manjiatan.

I can't help wonder what they really think of their new urban lives. All around us the fishing and farming villages are being razed to the ground to make way for more development. Some residents try to resist but in China this is futile. No one listens and they don't get any sympathy from the young and urban Chinese, who can't understand why anyone would want to live in a farmhouse with an outhouse and water pulled up from a well. As I ride my bike or drive through the newly demolished villages, the half standing buildings speak sad stories to me.

There is a cruel irony present in one, its front wall smashed, roof ripped off, revealing five posters equally spaced across the house. The posters, diamond shaped with red writing, all read 福, pronounced *fu,* meaning luck.

The relocations are forced but do include compensation. In exchange for their country home with courtyard they receive a concrete shell apartment and several thousand *renminbi* in cash. One elderly couple that I met around 2001, while on a walkabout with some students during a unit on urbanization, provided a picture of how bleak it can be for those who are forgotten. At that time, many had been forced out of their homes but new apartments were not ready for all of them. A makeshift shanty sprang up, with crude brick houses assembled from the rubble of dismantled villages. The residents lived without water or electricity. The couple invited me and my two students, both teenaged girls, into their home. They had a kerosene lamp, and a bed. The walls were barren save a solitary scroll with the character 忍 —*ren*, to endure or persevere. My students were very moved by their story, previously unaware that such a sweet elderly couple could be abandoned to a life of dismal poverty like this, just around the corner from a booming beach resort.

Manjiatan's new skyline, 2010.

The couple told us how they didn't want to leave their home but had no choice. They could understand and accepted that their country needed their land for development and progress but they were angered that the officially stated 12,000 RMB compensation turned out to be a mere 3,000 (less than $500) by the time it reached them. How long would they have to live like this? Within a couple of years the shanty was demolished and everyone was put in their new homes. Some even got rich off it. One fellow I know came from a family that lived on a large parcel of land near the sea. The compensation scheme provided one apartment for each small farm house. Those who had larger pieces of land appropriated were granted more apartments. In this case the family received seven apartments! These could be sold or rented out for profit.

Jordan, Cosmo, and Hanna explore a demolished farmhouse.

Another interesting dimension to Manjiatan was brought about by the privatization of the local hospital. When it went private it launched an advertising campaign in Russia. As strange as it may seem to most Westerners, who fear the medical system in China, many Russians are flocking to the little town of Manjiatan for some good ol' fashioned TCM— Traditional Chinese Medicine. The second floor of the once grotty hospital is furbished with pinewood panels and healing rooms have Russian language signs affixed to the doors. I can attest to the quality (and good value) of the acupuncture. One day I had hurt my back and couldn't stretch out of a hunched position without squealing in pain. Twenty minutes of needles being poked and twisted in my back and legs, followed by a twenty minute massage by the doctor had me walking straight, and pain free too. This all for a couple of dollars!

I can fully understand why the Russians would come for this kind of treatment but they are not all here for Chinese medicine. More and more of them are coming for plastic surgery. On one of the walls in the hospital in the 'Russian ward' there hangs a poster that details a variety of shapes of lips, eyes, noses, and chins, each with a name. I would be a little wary of letting a small town Chinese doctor cut open my face, especially for reasons of vanity. It sounds like risk taking to me but I guess the price is right. The Russians also get to spend their recovery time on the beach, a short walk from the hospital. For a frosty Siberian this may seem like a 2-for-1 deal that you just can't pass up.

The town of Manjiatan is situated a couple of kilometres from a long, pebble-strewn beach that has been attracting tourists for some years now. Jinshitan, or Golden Pebble Beach, is surrounded on either end by impressive coastal erosional features, the kind you learn about in physical geography textbooks: caves, stacks, stumps, and headlands. The Chinese love to name physical features, consequently, in Jinshitan a traveller may see Beethoven's Head or a Dinosaur Meeting the Sea.

The government designated the area around the beach a 'National Holiday Resort'. As beautiful as the seaside scenery is the area remained largely undeveloped until very recently. Visitors from a decade ago would not recognize it today. The government has actively promoted development along the themes of education and recreation. Numerous schools have sprung up joining the Canadian-curriculum high school I work at: an art college, a model school, a dance school, the Shenyang music school, the humanities department of the Dalian Nationalities College, and most recently, an American international school to accommodate the children of the hundreds of families shipped out to set up the world's largest computer chip plant, owned by computer giant Intel. Several years ago a massive investment deal resulted in a huge theme park being built. Modeled on Disneyland, *Fa xian wang guo*, or Kingdom of Discovery began attracting tens of thousands of tourists, able to reach Jinshitan easily with the construction of a light rail line that terminates beside the theme park.

Now that Discoveryland has opened up in Jinshitan, in addition to bandaged-nosed Russians, the streets of Manjiatan also see Thai and Ukrainian dancers, Australian stunt drivers, and Romanian acrobats walking around. Although far from being cosmopolitan, Jinshitan and Manjiatan are no longer 'the end of the world' as my mother experienced in November of 1998 when our pleasant stroll down to the beach was sabotaged by the biting Siberian winds.

6

On the 'family car,' Dalijia, Liaoning.

I'm a Chinese Driver

Growing up in Vancouver, a city with a strong Asian presence, we often referred to 'Chinese drivers' whenever we saw an Asian face behind the wheel of a car that was driving poorly. Perhaps a tad racist we kids thought it was kind of funny. Now I know why Chinese drivers drive as they do, and I've become one.

In the post-war years most Chinese immigrants to Canada and the West were actually from Hong Kong, a very densely populated city with an incredibly well developed public transit system that is the envy of the world. An excellent subway, frequent buses (an awesome experience is to ride a dou-ble-decker bus as it careens through the flora and winding roads between Central and Stanley or Aberdeen), the Star Ferries linking Central to Kowloon, and the most amazing and ingenious of all, The Escalator, actually a series of escalators that links Mid-levels with Central. It would take my cousin, an investment banker in Hong Kong, 12 minutes to 'ride' The Escalator from Conduit Rd, the highest up the mountain to Exchange Square, the hub of banking and trading in Hong Kong. Until 10 am The Escalator went down, after which time it reversed and took people up. With transit infrastructure like this who needs to drive? Besides it's not like you can make road trips, the whole place is only 80 km². So these folks aren't really Chinese drivers, they are learners. That 45 year old immigrant woman is a less confident version of a 16 year old Canadian girl. Oh, and she grew up with traffic driving on the left.

Sara and the kids at the Escalator, Hong Kong.

A section of the Escalator, Hong Kong.

Mainland China is a whole different story though. Invariably foreigners are shocked by the driving. Taxi drivers in VW Jettas and Santanas compete with *Nouveaux Riche* in black Audis, BMWs, and Mercedes to see who can drive the fastest. 140 km/hour is not fast here, 160 km/hour is fast. I have yet to see anyone stopped for speeding. In fact, when we arrived you couldn't find a posted speed limit anywhere. They've since appeared in some places but are ignored. Take for instance No. 7 Middle School located on a major road in Kaifaqu. When school gets out in the afternoon it's a throng of cars picking up kids, crowding the streets and crossing the road haphazardly. Cars speed by them, most doing about 70 km/hour, many 100 km/hour. Nobody slows down. One day I noticed new signs.

'School ahead, slow down. 30 km/hour' they warned in Chinese and English.

'Progress,' I thought to myself. It's been two years since then and I've yet to see a single car slow down. Ironically, the nearby intersection is a favourite hangout for the police, who sometimes harass people who have stopped at the light and check their papers. Meanwhile, cars whiz through the marked school zone past the police.

'Speed kills,' we like to say in Canada, but that's only partially true. If everyone is flying along at 140 km/h then it is generally not a problem. You've heard of the Autobahn right? The problem on the Chinese roads is that while Mr. Businessman drives 140 km/h, Old Farmer Wang cuts across three lanes of traffic on his Flying Pigeon bicycle (no, he doesn't look first), three spaced-out girls with Rod Stewart hair walk haphazardly on the road (no, they didn't look either). At the same time Mr. Black Audi is passing on his left a three-wheeled tractor going about 15 km/h, and in the shoulder a 125 cc motorcycle with a helmet-less driver, his wife behind, and their precious child wedged in between them, swerves to avoid the unmarked pink scarf clad old woman hired to sweep the streets who is making extra large sweeping motions with her primitive corn stalk and willow branch broom. Oh, did I forget to mention the geezer doing 10 km/h on a rickety cart pulled by a donkey? Yes, he is still on the road in China too.

All of these vehicles will pull out from perpendicular crossroads without warning. Some will cut right in front of you and slow down; others slowly merge into the far lane, too lazy to use their steering wheel more effectively. Still others, aiming to actually cross the road, will creep out at a medium speed so you are not ever sure if they are going or not.

In 25 years of living in Canada I've never seen a dead body. In China I see one or the evidence of one—a pool of blood, a lonely shoe on the road beyond a broken motorbike—at least once a month. Who on earth would want to drive on these mad, chaotic streets? I, for one, did.

The decision to start driving in China was liberating. It gave us freedom, put us in control of our destiny, and removed the single greatest source of stress on the expat in China's life: Taxis and taxi drivers. I found out quickly that although it seems like chaos, there is a style, and patterns of driving can be learned and understood. Furthermore, there appear to be rules. For example, in Canada when one wants to turn left they wait for a suitable break in traffic, a break sufficiently long enough so that oncoming cars won't have to brake. If traffic is bad that means waiting until the light turns amber and at the last second making the turn. If you're the second car waiting to turn you may be able to piggy-back on the first car and get your turn in. If your timing is not right you risk being honked at or given the one finger salute.

In China, on the other hand, you don't need to wait for a sufficient break in traffic, or perhaps it is better to say that a 'sufficient' break in traffic in China is much shorter and would be deemed insufficient in Canada. Drivers in China have developed a real balance between aggressive and defensive driving so they are ready to slam on the brakes or swerve, and rarely do they give the finger (but if they do it is the index finger complimented by *biao*—idiot, used only in Dalian—or perhaps *cao*—fuck—and if really bad they add *ni ma*—your mother).

If you are waiting at a red light you will start your left turn just as the light turns green, thereby pre-empting the on-slaught of oncoming traffic. Once the first lunatic looks like he might successfully make his turn all subsequent turn-ers-in-waiting piggy-back on the first car. Sometimes the left turn gang looks like a veritable caravan. The would-be oncoming traffic inches up further and further into the intersection patiently yet impatiently, but with no horn honking, until the caravan passes. Then they let 'er rip. If you are slow off the start that's when you'll get a honk. The Chinese drivers allow you about one millisecond before they lay on the horn. After driving this way for eight years much of it now seems quite civilized, even courteous, such as letting the left turners go first. To be fair, I suppose they don't really let them go first, instead they force their way across.

Other patterns of the road include a right of way system for more expensive and/or larger vehicles. That doesn't neces-sarily prevent the little guy in his moto-tricycle from going for it though.

My driving experience in China started not with a car but with a motorcycle and sidecar, generically called a *san lun mo tou che*—three wheel motorcycle—in Chinese. The Chinese police have been driving these bikes for years and on my early trips to Beijing I noticed a number of older, very cool looking models, some of them souped up and often driven by for-eigners. I later found out that these bikes are called *Chang Jiang 750*. *Chang Jiang* means Long River and is the name the Chinese use to refer to the great river known to Western-ers as the Yangtze. The 750 refers, of course, to the engine size, 750 cc.

The *Chang Jiang* have a long and interesting history. They are essentially BMWs from the 1940s with some minor modifications. The story goes that prior to the outbreak of WWII, BMW was producing their classic bike the R-71 in Russia (or what would become Soviet territory after the defeat of the Nazi regime) and after the war the Soviets continued their manufacture, modifying the bike slightly and renaming it the M-72. Today's Ural and Dnepr brand bikes are still in production and can, like the *Chang Jiang,* be considered offspring of the original BMWs. In the 1960s, just before the Sino-Soviet Split, a cooling of relations between the two Communist giants during the Khrushchev years, the Russians brought some of the original BMW tooling and set up a motorcycle factory in China. The bikes were to be used by the PLA—the People's Liberation Army—and the police. The *Chang Jiang* were improved with an electric starter and some come with a reverse gear, which is nice when you've jammed yourself in a tight parking spot, because these are heavy bikes. Otherwise, they are pretty much as they were. They are not finely tuned machines and basically continue to operate on 1940s technology.

An Internet search in late 2000 revealed that they were still being produced in Southern China's Jiangxi province by a company that was known for aircraft production. China Nanchang Aircraft Manufacturing Corporation was shortened to *Nan Fei,* in the Chinese tradition of abbreviating by using the first character of each word that you want to combine. *Nan,* from the city name Nanchang, and *fei,* meaning to fly, the first character in aircraft. Armed with this information I began covertly plotting a stop in Nanchang for our 2001 Chinese New Year holiday. I say covertly because Sara, like all sensible women, would likely not agree to a holiday detour to a no-name, heavily polluted, industrial Chinese city that had no interest whatsoever to travellers except for those who knew of its Communist history. I can't say I blame her either. Our holiday was to Thailand that year, but to get there we trained to Guangzhou then flew from Hong Kong to Bangkok. On our return I still had to arrange the Hong Kong to Dalian leg of the trip. This was my opportunity. One of Sara's funny quirks is that, despite being an intrepid and experienced traveller with a background and degree in geography, she never takes an interest in how, or sometimes even where, exactly, we are going—I guess she just trusts me. So I was able to fly the family, which included two year old Hanna and three month old baby Cosmo to a city with no tourist appeal whatsoever, without my wife even knowing anything was amiss.

'So why are we going to whatever this place is called exactly?' she eventually asked on the plane.

I can't remember what my answer was, probably some ridiculous story about availability of flights and also, perhaps, maybe, there happened to be a motorbike factory I wanted to check out.

Nanchang turned out to be interesting mainly because it was still very much Old China. It was covered in filthy grime and smelled like coal. The streets were crowded with people and bikes. Everyone seemed old. Where were all the young people? They had likely migrated in droves to the newly prosperous cities on the coast like Shanghai, Guangzhou, Xiamen, and Shenzhen. The ageing population of Nanchang was in stark contrast to the youthful crowds in Dalian, where we lived.

We got settled in a hotel room and I slipped out, flagging a taxi in the street. I didn't have an address but figured the Nan

Fei company was sure to be known. The driver did know it and ten minutes later he told me we had arrived. I looked out the window but didn't see anything that looked like a factory or that said Nan Fei.

'*Nar*? Where?'

'*Zhe li*. Here,' said the driver and with his hand indicated that the whole neighbourhood was Nan Fei.

I got out and walked the streets asking locals but got the same response. The whole district seemed to be called Nan Fei.

'*Wo zhao yi ge Chang Jiang san lun mo tou che*'—I'm looking for a Chang Jiang motorcycle with sidecar.

Nobody on the streets had any clue and I seemed to be walking aimlessly from corner to corner asking people the same question and getting the same blank stare. Finally someone led me to a shop that sold bikes and they had brochures with *Chang Jiang* bikes of various models. Excellent, I was making progress. They said sure, I could buy one. They told me to call a number on the pamphlet when I got back to Dalian. But I wanted to see the bikes and the factory, I told them.

'*Bu keyi*'.

Somehow, after a few phone calls *bu keyi* became *keyi* and I was taken a few blocks down the road to a large hanger. I never could have found it myself and it wasn't well marked, at least not in English or pinyin. Inside, the hanger was empty except for two rows of *Chiang Jiang* bikes at the far end covered in two millimetres of dust. The manager seemed incredulous that I'd be interested in these bikes. Somehow he hadn't clued in that foreigners thought they were awesome. They came in two colors, army green or black. I got all the details necessary to purchase, and extremely satisfied, returned to the hotel.

'Okay dear, we can leave this hole now. Thanks for putting up with my obsession'. Sara was a good sport about it but was still a bit sceptical about buying a motorbike.

On our return to Dalian we found that an Australian friend had managed to order one of the *Chiang Jiang* bikes through a bike shop in the town where he worked, Wafangdian, an hour and a half north of Dalian. He paid about 18,000 RMB —$3000—and his bike looked great and even had a real license plate, something I would later learn was a challenge to get. A second friend, a German named Robert, was really keen to get one and using my contacts with the factory arranged for two bikes to be delivered to Dalian.

We paid 12,000 RMB for these beauties. When they arrived we went down to the train station in nearby Jinzhou and drove them home. What a fantastic feeling! I had never really driven a motor bike before although I was familiar with the gear shifting system from riding four wheel drive ATCs. I couldn't help but start singing Steppenwolf's *Born to be Wild* when I 'set out on the highway'.

Despite my lack of experience on a motorcycle, having a sidecar meant I wasn't likely to fall over by myself, although I did learn pretty quickly that there are some peculiar tricks to learn when riding with a sidecar. The first day I took Sara out, she was on the back, not in the sidecar, when I hit a curb with the sidecar wheel. The sidecar was thrown upwards and Sara was tossed half-off the bike and bruised her shin badly. She was not too impressed. Later I found out that turning too abruptly would cause the sidecar to flip up which is pretty cool if you are Steve McQueen and planned to do it, but I nearly killed myself once and quickly learned a lesson.

Within a few weeks I was comfortable driving and it jokingly became our 'family car'. The spring of 2001 was so much fun. Sara rode in the sidecar holding baby Cosmo, then just a few months old and Hanna sat at her feet on a short plastic stool. Sometimes we added someone else on the back and off we'd go exploring the countryside, often ending up at one of four Buddhist and Daoist temples around the largest mountain in the vicinity, *Daheishan*—Big Black Mountain. I can't stress enough how the freedom and sense of independence, adventure, and discovery that it gave us drastically improved our quality of life. Other times we got together for short road trips with David and Robert and their families, a gang of three *Chiang Jiang*. Very few expats in Dalian drive themselves; most either rely on taxis or have chauffeured cars and therefore miss out on so much.

Hanna with a Daoist nun at a temple near Jinshitan.

A bureaucratic hurdle remained: We had been driving our bikes around without a license plate for over a month. This might sound outrageous to Canadian readers, but in China you will see several cars everyday without plates. However, our bikes got a lot of attention. It had been years since these old models had been used by the PLA and police and many locals crowded around and asked me the make and model, curiously many of them assuming it was an import. When I returned to the street from lunch in a restaurant there would be a guy sitting on the bike smoking or perhaps children playing, or even peeing in the sidecar. It was bizarre; they seemed to think it was public property. We, and the bikes, were on show. I drove with trepidation past police monitoring intersections, but they almost always smiled when they saw me. One day I got a message at work. The local traffic police had called the school's security chief, a former policeman himself.

'Tell the guys with the bikes to get license plates. If we see them again we will confiscate their bikes' was the message I received. Awfully nice of them to send the warning like this, I thought.

The problem was, we soon found out, the greater Dalian municipality had suspended the issue of license plates for motorcycles. I guess they didn't want their streets overcrowded with noisy bikes like in Southern Chinese, or worse, Vietnamese cities. Cars were prohibitively expensive in China in those pre-WTO days and motorcycles were a cheaper alternative for the masses. We asked around at all the motorcycle repair shops and indeed, it was true, but they could arrange fake plates if we needed them.

My dilemma came up in an informal conversation with some boys in my grade 12 PE class. One boy said his dad could help. I told him not to bother his dad. I wanted to avoid a conflict of interest situation. The boy was struggling at school and I could just imagine his dad asking for a favour in return. As it turns out, the boy did tell his dad about my predicament. His dad was Mayor of the beach resort district where my school was located and he arranged a meeting with the local traffic police chief. The chief was very friendly and wrote a letter which I was to take to the motor vehicle branch office in Dalian city. Robert, my German friend, was holidaying in Europe and asked if I could take care of his registration too.

The next step was to get the bikes down to the motor vehicle branch, conveniently surrounded by the city's largest second hand car market. This way if you buy a car you can get it inspected, registered, and on the road right away. The registration process involved going to various counters on various floors to be told each time *bu keyi*. Each time I passed over the letter from the police chief. It worked wonders and my papers were nearly all stamped until the last counter. The branch authority was called out, he glanced at the letter and said no. I pleaded with him to call the number on the letter. Reluctantly he did and soon I was on my way. There were just a few more formalities.

The first was choosing the license plate number. Numbers are very important to the superstitious Chinese. The best number is eight because its pronunciation (*ba*) sounds similar to *fa*—to be rich—as heard in the Chinese New Year greeting *Gong Xi Fa Cai*. Four, pronounced *si*, is bad luck because it is a homonym for death. Other numbers too are thought to be good, bad, or neutral. To prevent people from harassing the issuing authority for a lucky license plate there is a machine, much like a slot machine, where you press a button to automatically generate a random number. I thought this was a great idea but they must not do it everywhere or all the time because when you see extremely lucky license plates, such as 888888 or 111111 or 666666, they are invariably attached to the most expensive cars, often from smaller cities than Dalian. This you can ascertain because the license plates in China indicate both the province—by a Chinese character—and the city, by a letter of the alphabet, A representing the capital city. My license plate reads 辽 B265438. 辽 for *Liao*, the first character in *Liaoning* province and B for Dalian, the second largest city in the province. Motorcycle license plates are all yellow but on cars the colour of the plate also indicates if the car is owned by a regular citizen (blue), government, police, or military (white), or a foreigner (black). Due to the policy of limiting motorcycle plates they are valuable and my front plate was stolen off my bike while I was away on holiday.

The final step was to attach the plates and have a photo taken of the bike with the plates on. The next day I returned to pick up the two bikes and a green registration book and a card-sized booklet with a photo of the bike in it. Nobody has ever stopped me or asked to look at these documents.

For eight years I drove around Kaifaqu and Jinshitan thinking I was the only one around with a *Chang Jiang*. One day in 2009 a colleague happened upon an army surplus store in an underground market in Dalian's Victory Square. The owner, Da Duo, was a *Chang Jiang* enthusiast and was keen to sell his beautifully restored bikes to others to make a profit, but more so to build up a network of *Chang Jiang* owners that he could go riding with. When I saw one of his bikes for 10,000 RMB, with a polished engine and fine chrome parts, I couldn't resist; I bought another one. Da Duo was a PLA soldier in his younger years and so he and his friends were able to use their army *guanxi* to get a supply of the old bikes. They restored them at an old tool and die factory in an early industrial part of the city. The place had a magical 'Old China' feel and Da Duo kept up appearances by adorning the walls of his workshop with communist era images.

Mao wearing motorcycle goggles, Da Duo's workshop.

Soon several other friends were introduced to Da Duo and bought bikes too. Before we knew it there was talk of getting matching leather jackets and calling ourselves the Bethune Bombers. Large group rides were organized on Sundays and we toured through cherry blossom covered hillsides and along the spectacular Jinshitan coastline. I never imagined I would join a biker gang, let alone in China.

The Bethune Bombers in Jinshitan.

In 2004, our kids were school age, and Sara decided to start working part time at the school I work at. Her daily routine now meant dropping off Hanna at her school, a short walk from our apartment, then taking Cosmo to his school, which required a bus or taxi ride, followed by a 25 km taxi and light rail combination to our school and then perhaps repeating the procedure on the way home. Taxis are cheap but all together this routine was adding up and the stress it caused was also a factor. Sara decided it was time to buy a car.

Since China had joined the WTO in 2001 tariffs were dropping on imported cars, but they were mostly still out of our price range. As foreigners who didn't own a home in China we were ineligible for loans or financing. We were in the market for something cheap but I also wanted something reasonably big, mostly for safety concerns but also because it needed to have a lot of storage capacity. I was playing hockey in the city every Sunday night in those days—more on this in a later chapter—and shared a taxi with other guys to save money, stuffing our gear in an overloaded trunk. If a car couldn't fit four teammates and our hockey equipment I wasn't interested in it. I have always been a bit of a cheap-skate, so when I saw a mid-size SUV for 59,000 RMB I was pretty excited. It was made by a Chinese company from Hebei province called *Zhongxing*, known mainly for pick up trucks, and it seemed to be modeled on a mid 1990s Toyota. I took the *Admiral* for a spin but it was a disappointing drive, not very smooth and had no jump. The dealer suggested I try the next model up, the mid range *Cruiser*. It felt much better. To be honest, I was in my early 30s and had never owned or even driven a new car. All my previous vehicles had seen better days. My driving portfolio included a 1972 Toyota Celica painted only in primer and bought for $250, a 1974 Volvo handed down from my dad, a 1972 VW Westphalia camper held together mostly by duct tape, a 1978 Dodge van that I lived in during my youthful tree planting and mushroom picking days, and the best of the lot, a 1984 Volvo station wagon that puffed black smoke. So I have to admit that I was impressed with the new car feel and smell of the *Zhongxing Cruiser*.

The Hulk filled with kids and pumpkins, Big Black Mountain.

'Whatever you think, dear,' was all Sara had to offer when we discussed it.

In late September, we bought the car. I went to the bank and withdrew 72,000 RMB and paid cash for it. This time, thankfully, the dealer took care of the registration and our black license plates showed up within the week. We named it 'The Hulk' because it was big and green.

In early October the so-called 'golden week' holiday celebrates the founding of the People's Republic of China, National Day, October 1st. I was itching to make a road trip and had grand plans for Inner Mongolia or the Russian border. Sara thought we ought to be less ambitious for our first trip with the new car. We settled on a triangular three day trip in Liaoning province. Our first destination was Dandong, the frontier town on the Yalu River across from North Korea. We had visited Dandong twice before and enjoyed the slow pace of the low-rise Korean influenced city. The drive up was smooth and uneventful. The new *Dan Da* highway was superb. Our last trip had taken four hours from Dalian but this time it was only 2 ½ hours, driving 120 km/h the whole time. The hulk drove well at that speed but any faster seemed a bit of a stretch for the four cylinder engine.

We enjoyed the usual Dandong experiences: Walking out on the half-bridge (half was blown up by US bombers in the Korean War), taking a speed boat trip within metres of North Korea, and visiting the Museum of US Aggression (AKA, the Korean War museum). This time we also visited the Easternmost section of the Great Wall, a beautiful section that stops right on the North Korean border. Never mind that it was recently rebuilt (some suggest built for the first time, but apparently there are Ming dynasty records of the wall) and that Chinese guidebooks made no mention of it at the time. It was awesome and the kids enjoyed themselves so much, charging along the wall in an imaginary fight, their imaginations enhanced by the Disney film Mu Lan. I snacked on BBQ silkworms and we returned to Dandong for the night.

The next morning we were on our way out of town when I had to turn left onto a one-way street along the river. Traffic was thick and I had to concentrate to seize the opportunity when there was a gap in between cars. I saw a chance and hit the gas. Just as I was pulling out I turned my head in time to simultaneously hear a thud and see a middle aged man fall across the hood of The Hulk and then flop onto the road.

The crazy bugger was cycling the wrong way down a one-way street! Sara and the kids were in a panic and I jumped out to assess the situation, my heart pounding. The man was okay, thank God. I had only just pulled out and he was not going too fast on his single-gear Flying Pigeon bicycle. I was very concerned about him and offered to take him to the hospital. He declined, saying that he just had a minor bruise on his hip and elbow. He was most concerned about his bicycle, the Flying Pigeon that lay half under The Hulk. I got back in the car, gave a quick synopsis to Sara, and backed up off the wheel of the Pigeon. A crowd of people had formed, dominated by a group of female street sweepers. Now the game began in earnest.

When a car accident occurs in China the two parties leave their vehicles exactly as they were and get on their cell phones to call whoever they know who is connected to a police officer or insurance agent. They may be blocking a major intersection but until the police have determined who is to blame nobody moves. This can take considerable time, with the two parties shouting and arguing at each other. I have witnessed more than a couple of these incidents turn into shoving matches. The police act almost as a judge in a civil court case, determining who are the rightful plaintiff and defendant and suggesting compensation. I really didn't want this to turn into an all day affair so I quickly asserted that the cyclist was in the wrong, but that I would happily compensate him for his bike. These bikes cost about 350 RMB brand new and his was an old beater. In fact, only one wheel needed replacing, the majority of the bike was fine. I offered him 300 RMB and a trip to the hospital. He didn't want the hospital trip, only cash. Miraculously, the street sweepers agreed with me and badgered him to accept. Obviously it was a good deal for him in their eyes. He kept arguing and I was getting concerned the crowd would attract the police, which would mean our day was ruined. I pulled out 400 RMB, more than the cost of an entire replacement bike.

'*Hao, hao, hao*! Good, good,' the crowd said in unison.

The man grudgingly accepted, still playing the role of victim. I hoped in the car to hear my kids, in tears, asking 'Are you going to go to jail daddy?' Nope, but I did have a pain in my chest for the next two days!

The rest of the trip went without a hitch. We drove next to a fantastic Karst cavern system at Benxi, then to the provincial capital, Shenyang (formerly Mukden), where we visited the Qing dynasty's original Manchu Forbidden City. Sara couldn't read our Chinese-only maps so we did have a few interesting exchanges between driver and navigator as we entered the city. The following day we attempted to drive out to some

Mongolian grassland but turned back due to bad roads and were back in Dalian by evening. The Hulk survived the first road trip with only a small scratch on the fender.

The next May, when we had another week-long holiday for International Labour Day, my dad and stepmother were coming for a visit, arriving in Beijing.

'Why not drive to Beijing to meet them?' I suggested.

China's new and rapidly expanding network of toll highways linking the major cities is excellent and we made good time driving up the *Shen Da*, then heading northwest at Panjin, cruising easily past large turbines in wind farms, then west across the vast *Liao* delta wetlands. It was the first time I had seen these wetlands because normally we fly over, or travel on a night train.

Our plan was to stop for the night at Shanhaiguan, where the Great Wall meets the sea. Shanhaiguan had been our first trip as a family in May, 1999 and both Sara and I had fond memories of the quaint, walled town, and for Sara, nursing baby Hanna on the Great Wall was an unforgettable experience. We had hoped to get there before dark. No such luck.

As previously mentioned, the main toll highways are excellent but the smaller roads, and especially the rural roads, are often brutal, pot-holed, and dark. We found the turnoff for Shanhaiguan easily but once off the highway it was trial and error in the dark. The hazards of rural driving at night are numerous: Dogs, bikes, pedestrians, cattle, and tractors all litter the road. Another hazard, and this is true in the cities as well, is that man-hole covers are frequently missing. Every time the government road crews replace a man-hole cover or sewage grate it is immediately stolen and sold for scrap metal. In some places they have had to switch to cement covers and grates, but these don't stand up to pressure as well as the metal ones and quickly disintegrate. So far I haven't driven into one, cross my fingers, but I have seen cars stuck in these gaping holes. In a slightly more humorous case, an American friend fell in a sewage hole while walking at night in Kaifaqu. Yuck!

The roads are not lit and when lights do appear they are from oncoming traffic. The Chinese drive with their high-beam headlights on at night so when there is traffic, instead of adding helpful illumination of the road's hazards, they inadvertently blind you temporarily. It is absolutely mad-dening. On rural roads when there are road signs they never include *pinyin* (the Romanization of Chinese), so unless you can recognize the Chinese characters you can't read the signs. It took about twenty minutes to find the town. Sara had used the dreaded L word, lost, and now the kids were in a weepy panic. We *were* lost but I screamed into the back of the car to be quiet and calm down and uttered a few nasty words towards the navigator's seat. Sara is very adventurous but she doesn't do well lost on a dark Chinese country road with tired and hungry kids. Go figure.

Once at the town centre we were able to find our old fa-vourite, the Jing Shan Hotel, a traditional Chinese design located just beside the Great Wall at The First Pass under Heaven. The hotel looked closed, but then again, so did the whole town. It turned out that the town was without power that night, which explained why it was so dark and difficult to find our way into the walled town. Without power the hotel restaurant was closed. The staff gave us a couple of candles and we dined on peanut butter sandwiches (Sara always travels with peanut butter, thus the kids can always be satisfied if we can't find suitable food). Sara decompressed and I revelled in the adventure, with a quiet beer in the dark.

The drive the next day to Beijing was easy until we had to navigate our way through the city. Beijing is sprawling and getting bigger and busier everyday—seventeen million and counting at present. Except for key landmarks like Tiananmen Square, I don't recognize anything from my first visit in 1994. We were staying at our friend Suzanne's apartment, but she was away on business so we couldn't call her for help. I swear that her emailed directions were wrong but I am a man and I recognize that it could have been my mistake, but without proof I'll never admit it. Beijing has a series of ring roads and we must have taken the wrong turn on the third ring road and ended up on the wrong side of the mega city. Eventually admitting defeat, I pulled over, flagged a taxi and paid him to lead us to Suzanne's. After that we just took taxis around Beijing. I didn't want the stress of trying to drive the strange streets and with traffic flowing at a meagre 15-20 km/h much of the time it's no place to navigate by trial and error. The drive back to Dalian though, with a stop at the Great Wall for my dad and step mum was smooth and easy. One bizarre sight was seen as we passed a large truck with flames shooting out the side of its fuel tank. I'm not sure how it didn't explode. Anyhow, it just kept driving.

Did I mention that I didn't have a driver's license? Of course, I did have a Canadian driver's license, just not a Chinese one. The Chinese have, up until just recently, refused to accept either foreign driver's licenses or the near universally recognized International Driver's License. Considering we now owned a car I thought it was time to get one.

Step one: Go to the police station and show your Canadian license. I did that in Kaifaqu, where I was given an address of a police station in Dalian city. A thirty minute taxi ride got me there where I paid fifty RMB to have my license translated, taking only about fifteen minutes. Sara had gone through this process already and I knew that it could not be done alone. I needed to have a Chinese friend to 'translate,' which in fact meant to cheat for me on the exam. I asked Pengyou if he would help. He was working as a taxi driver in those days so I figured he knew what was up. He suggested that we could do everything in Kaifaqu and that there was no need to go to the city as Sara had done.

On our first trip the office was closed for some unknown reason, on the second attempt their computer system was down. The third trip saw us make some progress. We were told to head down to the hospital for a medical check. Always a little uneasy in a Chinese hospital, I was relieved to find that the medical check consisted of a doctor sitting at a desk asking me my height and weight.

'How many?' I think he asked, holding up a couple of fingers. And with that I was deemed medically fit to drive in China.

Back to the driver's office we went, to find it closed. On the next visit we made it to the testing centre. Because I had a valid foreign license the actual in-car driving test was waived, but I had to take a written test. The test was a hundred multiple choice questions answered on a computer. The questions were in Chinese only, which is why I needed a 'translator'. To pass you must get 90% correct in only 45 minutes. Essentially this means there is not enough time to have the questions translated into English and then your answers translated back in Chinese. So the 'translator' cheats and answers the questions for you while a façade of translation is set up for the authorities.

Pengyou was worried that he might fail because it had been years since he had written the test and it is notoriously hard. He offered me the option, which he seemed to prefer, of paying a thousand *renminbi* to a police officer friend. I didn't want to buy the license; I thought we should try to do it at least semi-legitimately. We waited in line for an hour or so then we were led into a room with about twenty computers. We sat down at one and started the exam. At first Pengyou attempted to translate but he doesn't really speak English (funny choice for a translator eh?) so he just told me in simple Chinese what the questions asked. It soon became clear that we weren't going to be able to finish in time. About fifteen minutes into the exam a police officer on duty in the exam room recognized me and began asking Pengyou questions.

'Is he the guy who lives in Song hai li? Does he have two kids? He has that black *san lun motuo che*, doesn't he?'

Uh oh, this guy lives in my complex and knows I've been driving a motorcycle for three years without a license. Was he going to cause a stink?

On the contrary, the officer stood behind us and read the questions over our shoulders and discreetly indicated the correct answers. A little while later, when the head of the examination department did her rounds, she stopped and talked to my cop-neighbour and now friend. After getting the whole story (he's a Canadian, has two kids, a teacher, can speak Chinese, has lived here for many years...) she nodded to me with almost a smile and began helping us answer the questions. Getting near the end of the exam, with the time limit fast approaching, she told Pengyou to stand and then she herself sat down and went through all the questions, scanning from beginning to end, changing our answers as she saw fit. When it was time we hit the submit button. Voila! Exactly 90%. Perhaps it is hypocritical but I've always been pleased that I didn't pay off anyone or expect any help and, of course, I had a Canadian license and completed driver training successfully when I was sixteen in Canada. I must have good Karma, I thought to myself. The story somehow captures the absurdity of China's bureaucracy though.

The final step was to take my medical check results, my exam score, my passport, my residence card, and a copy of my employment contract (showing that I would be in China for at least another year), to the main branch of the drivers' testing centre in Dalian proper. At this point I felt I had used up more than enough of Pengyou's time so I set off on my own. Waiting in this line, then that line, I eventually found myself being scolded quite severely by an officer who insisted that, as a foreigner, I should have done my exam there, and that I had no right to do it at the Kaifaqu branch. In broken Chinese I attempted to explain that the Kaifaqu branch has a five metre-long banner that reads 'Designated Driver's Education and Testing Centre for Foreigners,' but to no avail. I returned home and told Sara what had happened. She reiterated her belief that from the beginning I had gone about the whole thing foolishly. I should have called Ella, a wonderful and very capable former assistant to our friend Suzanne. Ella was fluent in English and very good at negotiating with the Chinese.

I called Ella, who happily agreed to help, and I met her at the test centre one day when I was able to leave work early. Apparently, we would need to smooth things over with the head honcho but he either wasn't there or wouldn't talk to us.

We tried again another time and Ella did her best to convince him that I had done nothing wrong, the Kaifaqu branch was responsible for any wrong doing. And with that it was concluded that I should return the next day to pick up my license which I did myself the next day. My name on my driver's license was 孔锐迪, pronounced *kongruidi,* and vaguely resembles my surname. That made me chuckle. All told it had only cost 200 RMB, but it had taken thirteen visits, two translators, and two friendly cops to become a Chinese driver.

I suppose the final chapter in the saga of becoming a Chinese driver was written in Canada. My British Columbia driver's license expired on my birthday in 2001. In the summer of 2002, while on holiday in Canada, I applied for a renewal. The clerk at the motor vehicle branch asked if I still resided at the same address, which, because I moved around so much in my twenties, was my mother's address in Vancouver.

'Yes,' I lied easily. I was staying there, after all.

In 2008 when it was due for renewal again I returned to the same branch expecting the same question. Instead, I was asked if I had a valid driver's license from any province or country other than BC. I was caught off guard.

'Uh...yes, I have a Chinese license,' I stammered, knowing there and then this was going to be problematic.

'Why do you have a Chinese license, sir? Are you a resident of China?

I knew I was in trouble and I explained that I live some of the year in China but that I own a residence in BC. This was actually true, we had bought a cabin in BC's Cariboo region in 2004 and technically it was zoned residential, even though there was no running water.

'Can you show proof of your residence?' asked the clerk.

'Like what?'

'A phone or hydro bill with your name on it and a BC address. Either will do'.

Damn. Unfortunately I cancel my phone line at the end of each summer to save money and my power bill I receive online. I had no proof.

The clerk assured me it would be no problem. I could drive for six months in BC with my Chinese license. The problem was, I explained, that my Chinese license was locked in my car in Dalian, China.

'I've got to drive up to the Cariboo with my wife and kids tomorrow, what am I supposed to do?' I pleaded.

The clerk didn't give a damn, confiscated my expired license, and sent me on my way. It's funny how I had driven without a license in China for years and never really worried about it, but in Canada I was absolutely paranoid. What if I had an accident? Would the insurance be valid?

I went back to my mum's and told the family the bad news. Sara was mad. My mum, always optimistic, suggested trying again at a different motor vehicle branch and lying this time. So off I went to downtown Vancouver's Robson Square, took a number, waited for an hour, only to be publicly humiliated. It seemed that the clerk raised her voice several decibels when she asked the question:

'Is there any reason you know of why there is a flag on your license? I'll have to call Victoria'.

I could feel eighty pairs of eyes on me; after all, when you are waiting for an hour you have nothing better to do than eavesdrop on others. All the more interesting when someone is getting denied a license.

'I see you applied and were rejected at our West Point Grey branch earlier today'.

I explained my predicament again, the manager came out, and I explained yet again, and was denied. It was official. I hated Canadian bureaucracy more than the Chinese. They were being unreasonable in my eyes. At least in China there is always a *banfa*—a way.

In the end I was able to call a friend who, as luck would have it, was still in Dalian and had a key to our apartment. Also luckily, I had a spare car key in a drawer and I gave him instructions over the phone to find the key and then to find my license in The Hulk's secret hiding spot. I was then able to pick up my license from him in Quesnel, BC, three weeks later. In the meantime, when Sara wasn't behind the wheel, I drove cautiously.

One situation I did find humorous was buying beer and wine from a BC liquor store by credit card. Their policy was to ask for a driver's license as proof of identification and I would pull out my Chinese license which had my photo, but not an English name.

'Where's your name?'

'It's here' I'd reply, pointing to 孔锐迪.

I already mentioned in the story of hitting the cyclist in Dandong, that in China drivers leave their vehicles exactly as is when an accident has occurred. I can only assume that this is required to prevent insurance fraud. In addition to knocking down the cyclist, which didn't really damage The Hulk, we had a couple of other minor accidents. The first occurred when Sara was downtown shopping with friends. She was backing up in a parking lot and bumped into a raised flower bed that wasn't easily visible. The damage was minor, but we wanted it fixed.

When I bought the car the dealer had also sold me insurance. I had no idea what kind of coverage I had, I just remember hearing '*di san...*' and thinking that that must be third party liability and that I paid 2800 RMB—less than $500—for a year. So when Sara returned with the car I drove off to find the car dealer. He asked me where the accident occurred and I told him I wasn't sure exactly, except that it was downtown somewhere. He grabbed something from his office and told me to get into the passenger's seat. He jumped in the driver's seat and as we drove down the sidewalk, yes the sidewalk, he kept glancing around searching for something. I had no idea what he was looking for.

At the corner, he found what he needed. It was a cement planter about the same height as the damage on The Hulk. He suddenly backed The Hulk into the planter, making even more damage. What the f—is he doing smashing my car? I was so bewildered I couldn't even get angry. I've learned to trust the Chinese in these situations. He jumped out of The Hulk, pulled out a camera, and took a few photos of the scene of the 'accident'.

'*Mei wenti*'. No problem. 'You can pick up your car tomorrow afternoon'.

An old lady emerged from her shop to see what the noise was all about, assessed the scene, and returned to her shop after a lengthy gaze at the foreigner. Apparently this didn't concern her. The Chinese live an interesting paradoxical balance between nosing around in everyone's business and at other times not getting involved. They are gossipers, gawkers, and love to crowd around and yet they feel no responsibility to involve authorities or to step in when something is wrong. When you see a man beating his wife or mistress on the street or openly in a restaurant and nobody intervenes this is seriously troubling to most foreigners. In cases like this, when you are trying to get away with something, it is quite nice to enjoy such freedom from vigilantes.

I was pleased to find out there was no deductible. The next year when I foolishly hit the brakes in snow The Hulk spun 270° and hit a lamp post. To this day Sara thinks I was deliberately doing donuts in the snow, but I was actually trying to assess the car's handling on what I thought was a safe, empty, road. Either way it was a bit stupid but no worries, I dropped the car off and I can only assume that they found a lamp post and recreated the scene of the crime again.

One mystery to me is the cost of insurance. The first year it was 2800 RMB. Sara dented the fender and then it went down to 2000 RMB the second year. We'd been rewarded for being bad drivers! No wonder the Chinese drivers are crazy. The third year, however, it jumped to 3000 RMB and lately it has jumped even higher to over 4000 RMB a year. Lord only knows why, but one explanation might be that the second year coincided with an increase in competition in the insurance market as WTO related reforms were enacted. This coincided with a huge increase in the number of new Chinese drivers which could only mean one thing: More accidents. That, in turn, led to higher insurance premiums.

When I bought The Hulk, the dealer took me to a couple different offices to pay various taxes. I never had any clue what I was paying. That might sound strange, but after several years in China, and even still today, my Chinese proficiency was so low that I often bluffed and fumbled along, agreeing to whatever was said and trusting people based on intuition. I can't complain about The Hulk—you get what you pay for. But after four years it just wasn't driving well anymore, Sara had become quite concerned about its safety and we considered selling it. I was keen on a smaller car and had my eye on one called the Chery A3. The dealer could arrange for me to sell The Hulk. I was told I would likely only get 20,000 RMB for it.

The dealer called the next day and said he had found a buyer. The buyer was a policeman and when I went by to meet him he and his three cop buddies didn't even look at me. They were playing a game of tough guy intimidation. They wanted to bully me into selling for cheaper. I held firm but a couple of snags appeared. First, the policeman ran a check and found three outstanding parking tickets. I only knew about one, but Sara 'fessed up about the other two. Of course, when you get a piece of paper, all in Chinese, on your windshield you have no idea what it is, so you choose to hope it isn't a parking ticket. Besides, you don't know where to pay it anyway.

The cop agreed to take care of the tickets, which I am sure meant deleting them from the system and certainly not paying it himself, in exchange for a reduced price. Fine, I said and we met half an hour later to exchange the car for the money. He had just one last question.

'Have you paid the *yang lu fei?*'

I had no idea what a *yang lu fei* was except that *fei* was a fee or tax and that *lu* probably meant road. The dealer took me for a drive to an office a kilometre or two away. The minute I saw it I recognized it as an office where I had paid one of the initial taxes when I bought The Hulk. Damn! I knew this wasn't going to go well.

The *yang lu fei* was indeed a road tax I was supposed to have paid, 90 RMB every month. I owed nearly 4000 RMB in past taxes. That I could live with, but on top of that the overdue charges equalled 14,000 RMB. The grand total owing was 18,000 RMB, pretty much equal to the total value of The Hulk. I couldn't sell The Hulk and the *yang lu fei* issue remained unresolved for some months.

A few months later I happened to mention the story to a Chinese friend and she said she would look into it. She called me back a couple of days later and said she knew somebody somewhere and could take care of it for me for 5000 RMB. God Bless China!

Months after I wrote this chapter, another fiasco occurred. I was reinsuring the Hulk when the insurance agent pulled me aside and whispered something that I couldn't understand. From his body language, the whispering, and the fact that he had pulled me aside so nobody would hear, I understood that something was serious, perhaps seriously wrong. After some clandestine back and forth charades, I figured out what he was saying. My car was two years overdue for a safety inspection. As readers will recall, I bought the Hulk new and never considered that it would need a safety inspection, although in this case, being an inexpensive Chinese brand, it probably did warrant an inspection. Brad took his car in for the same inspection and was charged 200 RMB for being one month late. I can only imagine that my overdue fine will be in the thousands again. Once more, being an illiterate has proven to be *ma fan*—troublesome.

7

The author with his geography students, Bing Yu Gou

Piece of Crab

L iving in China was not the only new and exciting aspect of our adventure. This was my first 'real' teaching job as a certified teacher and working in China presents certain intricacies that test one's resolve. One of our Canadian bosses once challenged us to see these as adventures rather than irritants. Sometimes and for some people that is easier said than done.

Take, for example, when our plane arrived in Dalian that first day and we walked out searching the crowd with anticipation of a sign with our names on it. At the very least we assumed someone from our school would be there to meet us and would pick us out of the crowd. We were, after all, the only Caucasians on the flight. Sitting on the steps outside the airport, in sweltering August heat and humidity, Sara began to worry.

'Do you have a number we can call?'

'No. They said they would meet us'.

After nearly 45 minutes our Canadian principal came running up, panting and sweating, drenched in his shorts and t-shirt. He had been playing cards with the Chinese woman from the foreign affairs department and the school's driver.

'Sorry,' he said.

On the bright side, at least my boss was a casual guy.

I didn't know exactly what to expect my first day on the job. The students hadn't arrived on campus yet and neither had two of the five teachers who had been hired from Canada. We got a quick tour of the facilities. They seemed decent enough considering China was a developing country, but I was concerned how I would teach in the heat and humidity without at least a fan, never mind air conditioning.

'Can we see our classrooms?' we asked.

'Maybe...if we can find the keys'.

'Can we see our office and work space?'

'Yes...but we don't have the keys and the doors are locked'.

'Can we have a look at what textbooks are available so we can start planning our lessons?'

'That's difficult because the textbook room doors are locked'.

I learned that first day that the guy with the keys was one of the most important people in China. If I ever got hold of a key

I immediately went into town to have it copied. My key chain soon resembled a janitor's and all my work pants were worn through at the front right pocket from the mass of keys I carried with me. When the students arrived they taught me how to break into locked rooms using their cafeteria cards. This resulted in dirty looks from the Chinese staff but it was necessary on more than a few occasions.

Once when I had gone through all the proper channels and booked the library for one of my classes we arrived to find it locked. The doors were held together with a bicycle lock. I examined the lock and noticing that it looked rather similar to my own bike lock so I pulled out my own key and gave it a try. It worked and I let my class in. When the Chinese librarian returned from her lunch break, a good ten minutes late, she demanded to know how we had got in. With a straight face I lied and said that I had found the doors unlocked. I felt terrible about lying to her later, especially when I got to know her. She is a wonderful woman but at the time I felt an overwhelming feeling of irritation that the library was locked, preventing my class from doing what we had planned, and picking the lock seemed an appropriate adventure.

With the classrooms, offices, textbook room, and computer lab all locked up there wasn't really much we could accomplish that first day. The principal was equally shut out and had no clue how to affect any progress, having been in China only a week.

'Let's go for a walk,' he suggested.

He and I headed down the road and ended up at the beach. The impressive shingle beach stretched for several kilometres and was dotted rather sparsely with a handful of bathers, pony- and camel-ride touts, and inflated inner-tube vendors. The beach was littered with trash, spoiling an otherwise decent scenic spot. Across the street makeshift restaurants offered barbequed meat skewers and local seafood dishes. We sat down and had the first of several bottles of warm beer. Cold beer, we had already learned, was a rarity in China. The locals seemed to prefer it room temperature. Looking on the bright side, the price was amazingly cheap. A large 640 ml bottle of Keller Beer, brewed locally, cost 1.8 RMB, about 30 cents!

I hadn't expected to start my first day on the job drunk at the beach but with the principal's active participation and encouragement that's pretty much what happened. We soon attracted a small crowd of interested onlookers including a policeman on a motorcycle with sidecar, the more modern version of the Chang Jiang I later bought. My Chinese was very primitive then but I managed to communicate a few basic sentences. The combined effect of the beer and the hot noon sun had left us wondering if we could make it back to work. The two other Canadian teachers, Linda and Kathy, must have wondered what happened to us. The policeman offered to give us a ride and I sat on the back while my boss rode in the sidecar. We arrived back at the school with huge grins on our faces. Day one working in China had been more adventure than irritant. It was less so for Linda and Kathy who had been locked out and prevented from getting any work done.

Irritants soon replaced adventures and our Canadian principal quit after just five months on the job. He found out quickly that he had virtually no power. It was not that he was power hungry but to run a legitimate Canadian high school program a principal should at least have the power to order a few pens or notebooks. He simply couldn't take it anymore.

His replacement did a better job with the balancing act that was required but he too would snap at times. I recall the first staff meeting of the year when he announced that something or other was happening. He had assumed that his requests for work to be done over the summer had taken place but I had seen that in fact it hadn't and I spoke up and told him so. His fist flew down in a rage, crashing onto the lectern he stood at, and belted out 'Either I'm the God-damned principal or I'm not!' Something like that would happen at the start of nearly every school year. New teachers, freshly arrived from Canada, wondered what on earth was going on. The Old China Hands just laughed.

By the late 1990s Chinese society at large had changed considerably but many institutions retained aspects of the Communist era, some of which continue today. One of the first shocks for the Canadian teachers was the week-long military training that the students suffered through at the beginning of each school year. Military 'training' was really no more than marching drills practised outside under a scorching sun. Marching competitions are still held in the elementary schools. The Chinese teachers train the students to march in elaborate patterns, like the RCMP's musical ride minus the horses and music. The kids even learn to kick out their legs, Soviet style. Cosmo's class wins every year.

Another leftover in the schools is the Communist Youth League, which acts like a student council but without elections. I don't mind the Youth League but what really struck me as odd when I first arrived was the propaganda at school. I would have expected as much in public schools but my school was a private school, and to me it was a symbol of the transformation to a market-based, or capitalist, society.

Hanna leading her class marching. The sign says 'grade 3, class 3'.

School newspapers in Canada are filled with student work and are light-hearted affairs. Our school newspaper was a multi-edged tool that balanced Communist party propaganda and school promotion. I learned quickly that propaganda does not have a negative connotation in China as it does in the West. In fact, it is seen as a positive force in society. I recall the first sports day when teachers were encouraged to 'join in the propaganda'. It all seemed a bit ironic when at that same sports meet the students were awarded stars and stripes Budweiser hats as prizes. The speeches suggested we must 'Love the Motherland' while the prizes promoted youth drinking American beer.

School newspaper headlines, 1999.

From a teacher's perspective there is one absolutely fantastic aspect of working in China and that is the students. I worked in a private school where the students were from wealthy, well-connected families. The Chinese teachers said they were spoiled and disrespectful but to Canadian teachers, used to the rowdy crew of teenagers back home, they were a dream to teach.

When I entered the classroom, the class monitor yelled out a military command and the whole class rose to attention and called out in unison 'Good morning teacher!' This seemed odd and made us feel slightly uncomfortable. The teachers instructed the students to ease up on the rigid formalities. In retrospect that was a poor decision on our part. The student culture in the school has changed considerably in the last decade and some days when I enter a rambunctious class-room with boys practically swinging like monkeys from the lights I long for the good old days.

We also had to train the kids to stop calling us 'teacher' and refer to us by name. This habit came from their Chinese schooling where teachers were simply referred to as *lao shi*. If a name was used Mr. Wang became *Wang lao shi*—Teacher Wang.

The kids treated their Canadian teachers with so much respect. We seemed to represent their future dreams and aspirations—they all planned to study at universities in Canada or other Western countries—but unfortunately they didn't always show their Chinese teachers the same respect. Walking the halls past classrooms when Chinese classes were in session students could be seen slumped over asleep on their desks while the teacher carried on with their lecture.

I have a great deal of respect for many of my Chinese colleagues. They work exceptionally long hours compared to their foreign counterparts but don't teach nearly as much. There is a lot of down time and sleeping on desks but they are frequently expected to go well beyond the normal call of duty for a teacher. For the lack of respect from students, the long days and the superficial curriculum that many of them are stuck teaching they are rewarded with pay about one fifth that of the Canadian teachers they share office space with and face salary garnishment for all sorts of things. This is surely unlawful in a so-called Socialist state but the dictatorship of the proletariat doesn't require, or allow, unions, so there is little that can be done except to quit.

The discrepancy between the treatment and pay of the Canadian and Chinese staff often causes Canadians to feel very upset. Sometimes it is heartbreaking. One year, when I occupied a desk in the Chinese Dean's office, a Chinese female counterpart who sat across from me had the unfortunate situation where her father-in-law passed away. As is the case with many Chinese families, she had moved away to get this job and she could not get time off to return home for the funeral. She was distraught. To miss her father-in-law's funeral was awful but to be docked pay or fired—a very real threat, for taking four days off to train up and back to her hometown—was worse. It was her pay that was the very reason she made the sacrifice to leave her husband and family behind and come out to Dalian.

There are always those Canadians who want to 'do something' for their Chinese colleagues and friends but in the end little can be done. I have learned that the system, indeed the culture, can not be changed overnight and certainly not by a single or several foreigners working in a school. We too are expendable.

Indeed, I was nearly fired at the end of my first year in China. Relations with our Chinese boss were strained when he left the school in the charge of a woman who had no background in education, spoke not a word of English, and who had little concern for the 'foreign experts,' as we were officially known—we had an official red book to prove it. Our boss returned at the end of the year and met with us to discuss our concerns, but he upset us over two major issues. We were told we would all be forced to move apartments even though we had been moved forcibly just five months earlier and promised we would not have to move again. And then, only after being prompted by her direct question, he told the Chinese wife of our Canadian colleague that she was being let go for no reason. I couldn't believe my ears and when I looked around the room everyone had hung their heads, embarrassed and not sure how to react. I reacted strongly and said 'this is a slap in the face'.

The next morning my Canadian boss came in, slammed his huge fist down on my desk and bellowed 'don't you ever speak to the boss like that again!' Thankfully, my principal had gone to bat for me, convincing the Chinese boss not to fire me, which he evidently wanted to do for challenging him like that in front of the other staff. I learned a lesson and checked my emotions much better after that.

Strangely enough, just two years later when the Canadian administration was returning to Canada I was promoted to vice-principal. I heard the news from a Chinese teacher who greeted me on my return from summer holidays with 'congratulations!'

'For what?' I asked.

'You are the new vice-principal!'

I pranced around campus for the next half hour, elated at my promotion. I was only 28 years old and truth be told, wasn't qualified for the job but in China it is often a case of 'big fish in a small pond' so I accepted the news at face value. But when I arrived at my first Canadian staff meeting—by then we had grown from five to about 35 teachers—I heard the new principal say that they were trying to hire a vice-principal from Canada. And just like that I was demoted. To keep me happy the new Canadian principal threw me a bone: I was appointed Academic Dean, a position without a job description which I was to accomplish in the four hours a week that were taken away from my teaching schedule.

Most of the time, relations with our Chinese colleagues were good but occasionally things got weird. When I was working as Academic Dean, liaising between the Chinese and Canadian staff I was often approached by Chinese school leaders asking me to commit Canadian staff to extra work or projects. Most of the Canadian teachers felt exhausted from their regular jobs, not to mention the daily difficulties that simply living in a foreign culture presents—all of which seem to increase fatigue. The requests tended to resemble demands and everything was last minute. I explained time and time again that Canadian teachers expected and required adequate notice. If they were told last minute and felt pressured to do something they didn't feel comfortable doing then resentment would build. Morale is always an issue for foreign staff in China and I tried to get the idea across that better planning would result in happier teachers and better relations between the two cultures.

On one occasion a very persistent and demanding Chinese colleague who had got a bit power hungry came with another last-minute demand. I got upset and with a raised voice said something along the lines of 'how many times do I need to tell you that you can't treat the Canadian teachers like this?' We had just gone through the same thing a week or two earlier. When he responded with 'Oh, it's just a misunderstanding' I snapped.

'Misunderstanding?! That's what you Chinese always say. That's a lame cop-out and a piece of crap!'

The poor fellow had lost face. This interaction took place in our office with several Chinese staff members present. I was wrong to lash out, but I had been pushed too far. The next day I received a typed letter in my mailbox. The best line read:

> You hurt my feelings and insulted the whole Chinese nation when you called us a piece of crab.

Ironically, one of the greatest things about working in China has been the amazing friendships I have made with Canadians. In our early days in China, when our school and staff were very small we found ourselves hanging out with people that we probably would not have befriended had we met them in Canada. The isolation that comes from being a *waiguoren*—an 'outside country person'—encourages people with varied backgrounds and ages to mix socially. Without one another we would likely go crazy. So youngsters in their early twenties go for dinner with retirees and first year teachers play squash with their principal after work. The relationships that develop are intense because of the proximity to one another both at work and home and many times colleagues who share an office space also live literally across the hall from one another in their apartment complex. With few other family or social distractions the relationships that develop over a year or two seem stronger than those that have existed for decades. When I attended a wedding in Canada for a couple that had met teaching in China it did not go unnoticed that all the guests, save the family members, were colleagues the couple had met in China.

China attracts some odd people. Generally the foreigners we meet are more adventurous and open-minded than most Canadians and but often they are quirky too. Perhaps I too fall into this category of Canadians but some of the expats are down right strange; the kind of people who simply don't fit in at home but find that their peculiarity isn't immediately evident to the Chinese, many of whom are keen to make foreign friends. Some are out and out insane like the fellow who showed up and stopped taking his medication and within two days of his arrival publicly announced that he had found 'safe sex' in the local bathhouse and the following day

126

was found in a manic state, naked and confused, in the hairdresser's shop below his apartment. The police were called and he was physically restrained in the mental ward of the hospital until he was led onto a plane returning to Canada.

Others, although not insane, come to China to lead an alter-ego lifestyle. Awkward and unattractive men find girlfriends easily; men with a wife and grown kids at home find young local boyfriends; and in a rare but real circumstance a pedophile found safety in a society less protective and suspicious than Canada. All of this leads to some pretty bizarre circumstances, the height of which was an alleged male on male rape in which both the perpetrator and victim were my colleagues and peripheral elements of our social circle. Many in the community suspected it was more a case of buyer's remorse than actual sexual assault, but who knows.

Despite the nutty foreigners, the bureaucratic irritants, the freezing cold offices, and the ups and downs of staff morale, teaching in China has been a wonderful and valuable experience; an experience that allowed and pushed me to grow professionally and personally. Some people will tell you working in China is crap. With the right perspective I think it is more like crab. It is something that needs to be handled delicately, requires perseverance and patience, but ultimately is worth the effort.

Part two:

GALA

More precious than the common ceremony, the gala excites the Chinese leadership and common folk alike. On TV, in school gymnasiums, at the local theatre, there is always a gala performance of some kind or another celebrating something or other. The Chinese gala is polished and taken seriously.

I stand in a satin *zhong shan* suit with a microphone in hand at my imaginary book opening:

'With each page turned a dove is released (but really they are common pigeons). I hereby declare the subsequent chapters to be a gala, a celebration of harmonious adventures in China!'

8

The Dong Bei Ren logo, designed by the author.

Being Canadian

When you choose to become an expat you make a conscious decision to give up your way of life. For Canadians and many other Westerners, that means giving up a standard of living that is thought to be among the best in the world. The decision to live in China is one that baffles many of those who choose not to leave their comfortable life at home. Are we crazy?

Unlike the immigrant, the expat doesn't expect to give up their way of life completely or forever. Most expats go overseas for only a year or two and they react to their new environs in various ways. There are three general types of expats in China. The least frequent are those who totally immerse themselves in China, avoiding other Westerners, sometimes to the point that they actually refuse to speak English to foreigners when they meet in the street or in shops. These folks are odd, but I admire their determination to master the language. Many times these expats are actually students, although they may have taken a teaching job to help them make ends meet.

On the opposite end of the spectrum are those who have virtually nothing to do with anything Chinese. They don't learn more than a couple of words of Chinese, they have no Chinese friends, and in extreme cases, they don't even eat Chinese food. These people are here for the money and they count down the days until holidays, not so much for a break from work but because they can't stand their life in China, and they book the first possible flight out. This group is considerable in number and I can't stand them...er...I mean some of them are okay. To be fair, they are probably just people who haven't dealt with their culture shock or who left home for the wrong reasons.

The third group, to which I think I belong, integrates into Chinese society to varying degrees. We make an effort to learn and speak Chinese, some much more successfully than others, and we maintain a balance in our social life, mixing with both locals and foreigners. Some of these people stay only a year and leave reluctantly; others stay for years and many find a local mate. We can add also to this list the numerous missionaries in China, many doing honourable work, others just plain creepy.

Although I've strived to integrate into Chinese society, my Canadian identity remains a strong and vocal part of who I am. In some respects, it seems that living overseas even pushes one to celebrate their Canadianess more than they would at home. Our need to be Canadian manifests at our traditional holidays and festival times. At Canadian Thanks-giving, earlier than American Thanksgiving due to the early arrival of winter and harvest, we always have a big supper. In our early days in Dalian we would invite a few single teachers who made up our extended family in China. As the Canadian community grew, our suppers became Thanksgiving feasts, with up to ten Canadian and mixed families joining together. Often the large hotels in town would put on Thanksgiving dinners, usually in late November at American Thanksgiving, and many Canadians, especially those who were single or without children and who really craved a home-cooked Western meal would gorge themselves on turkey and pump-kin pie at these events. As our community of expat families grew, our gatherings got so large that they could no longer be hosted in our apartments.

In 2008 a colleague organized a Canadian Thanksgiving feast at Discoveryland, an excellent Disney-style amusement park. Nearly a hundred people feasted in a *faux* medieval chamber. Whenever these events are hosted by the Chinese there is an absurdity that emerges at some point. On this occasion it occurred just as we were finishing supper, when the entertainment arrived. Thanksgiving isn't about enter-tainment, is it? The Chinese hosts wanted to please and a troupe of Russian and Ukrainian dancers and singers ap-peared, surprising the Canadian organizer as much as the guests. Our dinner table suddenly morphed into a front row seat at a strip club. I practically got a lap dance by a scantily clad blond belly dancer. I was a tad uncomfortable to say the least, my daughter and wife beside me as a Slavic hottie gyrated in front of me. Now I had something to be thankful for, I joked. Apparently my friends, feeling my discomfort, were saying that they were thankful they weren't in my shoes. That was Thanksgiving, China-style.

Likewise, at Christmas we gathered together with the families in our apartments. Many expats working in foreign or multinational corporations take leave at Christmas, but the Canadian teachers at our school get only Christmas day off. We hurried home after work on Christmas Eve to prepare our supper. Our first Christmas, Sara, whose mother's side is Ukrainian, kept up her family's tradition of homemade perogies. She used the *jiaozi*—dumpling—wrappers sold fresh in the markets and filled them with potato and cheese. They were delicious. We enjoyed them together with our school's principal and the Chinese foreign affairs manager Alice, and her son Tong Tong. Tong Tong wasn't too impressed with the perogies and he choked on some bacon, spitting it up on our floor. In retrospect he may have just not liked it and spitting it out on the floor seamed a reasonable tactic.

As the years passed, our Christmas supper grew to include my family tradition of cheese fondue. We would, if were lucky, find Swiss cheese at Carrefour, a French department store that opened in Dalian city a few years after we arrived. Otherwise, we would ask a visiting friend to bring some from Canada. In 2004, a German food wholesale store called Metro opened in the city and we never went without cheese or wine again.

Speaking of cheese, well, I just can't live without it. Cheese was one of the very few things that I really missed. With a little creativity and effort in the kitchen, we found that we could reproduce many of our favourite dairy products. First of all, we learned from a friend that sour cream was the easiest thing to make, provided you had access to cream. Dear old Nestle had infiltrated the Chinese market, leaving small containers of cream in the better stocked shops. My appetite forced me to end my boycott of Nestle products—I guess I found it in my heart to forgive them for pushing infant formula in developing countries. Here's the recipe:

Sour Cream

1 cup cream

1-2 tablespoons vinegar

Pour cream in a bowl and stir in 1 teaspoon vinegar. Cream should thicken instantly. If it doesn't, add another teaspoon of vinegar. Keep adding vinegar until it thickens.

Jeff Laird, a friend and connoisseur of fine foods, exclaimed one Christmas Eve that it was the best sour cream he had ever tasted. In fact, we found that many times our home-cooked, improvised versions of foods we missed were better than the 'real thing' back in Canada. We didn't realize it until we returned to Canada on our summer holidays. Much of the store-bought food tasted fake and overly processed.

Another friend introduced us to home made Feta cheese. It wasn't real Greek-style goat cheese, but it was a reasonable facsimile. This, too, was simple. After some experimenting and Internet research, I found that I could reproduce several types of cheese all by varying the same simple process. Feta, cottage cheese or ricotta, cream cheese and other spreadable cheeses, and Indian style Paneer, were all easy to make.

Basic Soft Cheese

2 litres of milk

1-4 tablespoons vinegar

Salt to taste

Spices (optional)

Heat milk in a saucepan until hot to touch, but not boiling. Add vinegar in small amounts until the curds separate from the whey. Whey should be transparent and will resemble a weak green tea. Strain curds from whey. Hang in a cheese cloth (or tea towel) until the desired moisture is achieved. Add salt to taste. For Feta and Paneer press into cubes. For cottage and ricotta, serve as is. For cream cheese, cream with spoon or hand blender until smooth.

It's that easy and Sara made the most delicious cheese cakes from cheese I made. Other improvised Western foods came from the market. For instance, I was buying fresh noodles in the market one day (a fine linguine substitute) when it struck me that the noodle ladies could probably make lasagne sheets. I explained what they looked like and her reply was 'just give me five minutes'. Sara's lasagne was delicious.

Halloween and Easter were always fun too. Trick or treating required contacting all the foreigners in the vicinity and asking if they would be willing to have the kids stop by for candy. It is quite a sight to see a group of thirty or more foreigners, dressed as goblins, pirates, and fairies, traipse through local residential neighbourhoods. The locals stare at us when we are dressed normally, on Halloween they are utterly confused.

'What festival is this?' they called out.

'*Wan Sheng Jie*' we replied, but few of them knew what we meant.

At Easter too, I would organize a chocolate egg hunt for the kids in the garden of our complex. You couldn't set out the chocolate too far in advance or they would all be eaten by the local kids. Old grandmothers could be heard encouraging their grandsons to join in the hunt.

'The foreigners are giving away free candy. Go and get some!'

Actually, parents paid a pretty penny for each child to participate because the eggs and chocolate were not cheap, and were hard to come by in Dalian. During one of our first years in Dalian, our Australian friend David organized a hunt in their housing complex, the Beverly Gardens. He had organized chocolate bunnies to be sent out from America and there were only just enough for the several children there. Sara and I helped set out the bunnies and when the kids found them, they had all melted in the sun. We felt so bad about it, knowing how precious they were.

Usually our Easter egg hunt would end with 20 to 30 kids and their parents—Canadian, Chinese, American, German, and Japanese—all together in the playground, the kids playing and the parents enjoying coffee from a Thermos, or a home-baked muffin. If we were lucky, somebody had brought cinnamon buns from Dalian city's best coffee shop, I-55. They weren't hot cross buns, but beggars can't be choosers.

Our Canadianness manifests in other ways too. In our first year in Dalian I was teaching PE and our principal, when he went home for the October break, brought out some hockey sticks. We had the school's workers fashion goals from scrap metal and local fishing shops sold us netting. Ball hockey in Dalian had taken off. Although it could never compete with basketball and soccer, hockey soon became a passion for many students.

It was interesting to see how many girls took to the sport, finding a relative advantage because neither the Chinese girls nor boys had any experience with the game. Soon homeroom classes were competing against each other and some classes would challenge the teachers. In 2003 two teachers started a weekly hockey club and before long we started to see students strutting around campus with their own hockey sticks. The Korean students, for whatever reason, took especially to the game and they would bring back sticks from South Korea on their holidays, all the best known brands: CCM, Easton, Koho, Reebok. Although the students' enthusiasm for hockey delighted us, we were very much focussed on our own teacher hockey games.

Early on, teachers' hockey established itself as an institution at our school. We played religiously every Tuesday and Thursday, from 3:45 to 5pm or later, depending on the natural light. In 2003, when a new crew of teachers arrived who all lived in the school-provided apartments on campus, we held a best-of-seven series between the Jinshitanheads and the Kaifaqu Canucks. The Kaifaqu players swept the series in four games, but it wasn't without controversy. The school had built, on our request, a small ball hockey court and, because no other facilities existed in the whole city, our workplace also became our recreational facility. One of the challenges, but also the benefit, of living in China is that the line between work life and social life is blurred. On the hockey court, we faced this challenge continuously, and I think, for the most part, we've done a terrific job of behaving well. During our first 'summit series' however, things got a bit ugly. When you give men sticks and allow them to chase the same ball there is bound to be some conflict. On this particular day some words were exchanged between a forward and the opposing goalie, the result being the player slapping the goalie across the face. In Canada in a recreational league this might not be noteworthy enough to make it in to a book, but considering that our students lined the fence, cheering us on, it was a poor decision on the part of the offending player. When tempers cooled there was a half-hearted apology and the games continued. We take our ball hockey seriously.

Unbeknownst to us, watching from a window in a nearby building, where he was teaching late afternoon ESL classes, was a new teacher named Craig Engleson. Going mad with frustration from not being able to play, he would the next year create an annual tournament which grew to include student, men, and women teachers' teams that swept much of the campus up in a fever.

Perpetually misunderstood and getting himself into trouble, Craig is a creative genius and one of the best friends I've made in China. We are kindred spirits, he with his crazy ideas and creative genius and I with a will to get things done, both believing that anything is possible in China and that a dumb idea and some determination can make for a beautiful thing.

My introduction to Craig went something like this: Phone rings.

'Hello there, this is Craig Engleson calling. I've heard you are the guy to call about embroidery'.

'Uh...embroidery?'

'Yes, you know, embroidered patches and the like. I want to get some ping pong patches made for a cardigan'.

'Ping pong patches? For a cardigan? You mean a cardigan sweater?'

Jeez, who was this guy? Little did I know he would become my office mate, my goalie, and an inspirational friend. If a man in his early thirties making patches for a cardigan sounds weird, imagine the sight of twenty grown men all wearing matching cardigans, smothered in colourful patches, all designed by Craig. That's the contagious enthusiasm he generates.

Because of his passion for curling, he was once jokingly referred to as Schmirler, a reference—with no disrespect intended — to the deceased Canadian and world curling champion, Sandra Schmirler. On our work intranet this was misspelled 'Smirler,' and henceforth Craig became Smirler, or just Smirls.

Smirler's first contribution to our community was the Dong Bei Cup. *Dong Bei* means north-east in Chinese and refers to the region of China formerly called Manchuria. The *Dong Bei* people have a distinct identity, which was expressed in a quirky but popular song and animated video. The first year of the Dong Bei Cup I designed a logo for the tournament using the *Dong Bei Ren*—the Manchurian—from the music video sitting on a donkey cart with our Stanley Cup-like trophy, the Dong Bei Cup. Each team wore T-shirts with the Dong Bei Cup logo, but in different colours. In each subsequent year

Smirler used the *Dong Bei Ren* image to create new logos. The T-shirts were such a hit that teachers, both former players and spectators, would email after they had returned to Canada asking for the latest Dong Bei Cup T-shirt to be sent out. The shirts and logos also got the attention of Ray Plummer and Yoko, two key organizers of hockey in Beijing, and we designed a logo for the second annual China Expat Cup, a tournament for expat ice hockey players, which was won by our team, the Dalian Ice Dragons! Beijing International Hockey then commissioned from us another logo for jerseys for teams they were sending to international hockey tournaments in Bangkok and Pyongyang, North Korea.

One of the great things about living in China is that virtually anything is possible, and a project that might take weeks to complete in Canada can be accomplished within hours. Someone had discovered a granite factory not far from our school. Owned by a Japanese company, its name was Fukunei, which we gleefully called 'Fukin' eh's'. The first year Smirler had commissioned the Dong Bei Cup from a local wood-worker and metal worker. The second year, wanting to expand the trophies to include an MVP, top scorer, and a top goalie, we went down to Fukin' eh's and had the trophies made out of granite. The third year, the tournament had expanded to include the students' matches as well. The day before the final game, we had no trophies that girls would likely win.

'Let's head down to Fukin' eh's,' I suggested to Smirler.

Twenty four hours later our trophies were ready, although an hour before game time they were still being polished and the plaques weren't yet glued on. One of the best trophies was named after a teacher who had never played hockey before coming to China but had so much heart, on and off the court or ice. He too was an enthusiastic supporter of Smirler's crazy projects and himself had many a granite project made at Fukin' eh's. Ironically, the Kissinger Trophy was delicate, its thin granite hockey sticks have all broken off, whereas the real Kissinger could never be broken.

Smirler had a couple of other projects with Fukin' eh's. One was granite bocce balls and roughly twenty people ordered sets of grey and black balls. Playing bocce on the weekends was sport on more than one level. Grassy areas in China are generally not considered places for the public to use, even in parks, and this goes against the fundamental Canadian desire to walk, play games on, picnic, or just sit on grass. Sooner or later, a security guard of some kind or another would interrupt the bocce game to order us off the grass. Half the game was bocce; half was avoiding the grass police.

The greatest of the granite projects, however, involved a great originally Scottish, but now Canadian tradition—curling! Each curling rock was hand cut and polished and no two were alike. They cost 320 RMB each to make and together Smirler and I went on a fundraising campaign at work. We burst into the staffroom everyday at recess selling 10 RMB 50/50 draw tickets and campaigned especially hard at staff meetings. One gimmick I came up with was the 'Scott Tournament of Darts' where people threw darts for a chance to win money. Of course, like most arcade games, it was nearly impossible to win. Only the bull's eye received a payout, 100 RMB for the center and 50 RMB for the outer ring, while any other dart resulted in the player paying whatever they score they hit. Now that was a money maker! Another game involved sliding Frisbees across the staff lounge floor in a simulated indoor curling game. It cost 10 RMB to play, the winner took five and five went into the kitty. It wasn't long before we had enough money for 24 rocks.

Smirler's master plan culminated in a New Year's Eve midnight bonspiel on a frozen pond. At the last minute, we realized we would need lights on the pond but there was no source of electricity around. Just as *jin ma* market was shutting down for the night we managed to find half a dozen kerosene lamps.

What ensued next was hilarious. The word for oil in Chinese is *you* and all forms of oily substances are a variation of this word. Petroleum is *shi you,* gasoline is *qi you*, and butter is *huang you*—yellow oil. We asked the vendors what kind of *you* we would need to run the lamps. They said *mei you* and we started laughing immediately because kerosene was a homonym for 'don't have' or 'not available,' one of the most commonly heard words in China. With our penchant for screwing up the tones of Mandarin, and not able to distinguish the tones when spoken to us, we knew this was going to be funny or frustrating, or perhaps both.

Here's the problem. To ask 'do you have...?' you say *'you mei you?'*—have no have?

We approached people in the market asking *'you mei you mei you'* which to them must have sounded like 'have no have no have'.

We got blank expressions, a wave of the hand, or the common *'mei you,'* which normally means 'don't have' but in this case could be a repetition of the word kerosene, as if to clarify what we were asking for. It turned into an Abbot and Costello Who's on First routine. Eventually, we found a gas station that sold kerosene but only in huge quantities. We had to buy gallons of the stuff.

It turned out to be a very memorable New Year's Eve, with lamp-lit curling and skating in minus ten degree temperatures. In the middle of a sea of Canadians celebrating the New Year, two Uyghurs, Turkic speaking Muslims from China's far west, barbequed lamb kebabs and sold them to us for one RMB each. Ahh, a slice of Canadian heaven in frozen Manchuria.

Local men curling with our rocks in Dalian's botanical park.

Another slice of Canadiana that Smirler brought to China, this time in a non-granitic form, was crokinole, a game originating in rural Ontario some 140 years ago. Crokinole is played by flicking wooden disks, or chips, on a round wooden board. It's a cross between curling and shuffleboard. In

Smirler's original design he had the Chinese characters for north, east, south, and west painted onto the boards, giving them a Chinese touch. He had numerous boards made, all beautiful with jade pegs, and he organized the Chinese Championships of Crokinole. He notified the organizers of the World Championships of Crokinole, held each year in Tavistock, Ontario, who found him after Googling crokinole and finding his blog, and they enthusiastically agreed to recognize the tournament and reserve a berth in the World Championships for the Chinese Champion. I am pleased to report that I am the reigning Chinese Champion of crokinole four years running, with a yet-to-be claimed seat at the World's in Tavistok, Ontario.

In early 1998, my mother-in-law knit me an old style Vancouver Canucks jersey, the hockey stick design. At that time the old-school logo hadn't yet made its comeback, but the response I got from people on the street in British Columbia indicated that it was very popular.

'Phat jersey dude, where did you get it?'

'Did he just call your sweater fat?' wondered Sara.

One guy on Granville Street in Vancouver offered me $250 for it.

'Sorry, it's custom made and not for sale'.

Once in China, however, all that changed. Ian, a colleague and hockey player, asked to borrow my sweater to have it copied. He took it to a woman who had a small shop that sold wool. She would come to be known in our community as

145

'Sweater Lady'. Next Eddy borrowed it for the same reason, then Smirls.

Smirls became Sweater Lady's best customer. He and several other guys started taking designs of classic hockey jerseys to her. I got in on two of these, getting a '72 series 'CCCP' Russian jersey and a 1948 RCAF Flyers, the Olympic champs that year. Some of the guys got out of hand, making more than fifteen different jerseys. Smirls' inclination to wear cardigans got a big boost from his acquaintance with Sweater Lady. He now has a different cardigan, each adorned with buttons and patches, and each with a theme—curling, hockey, football, you name it—for each day of the week, for a two week rotation. My God, not even Mr. Rogers could imagine a fortnight of cardigans!

Sweater Lady must have a pretty funny impression of Canadians. We are very particular about what colours and how many and how big the stripes should be. Sara even commissioned matching Cowichan style toques for me and my son. They were modeled on my lucky toque that has travelled around the world.

We have managed to recreate many of the Canadian experiences that we want ourselves and our children to have, but there remains one serious lack: organized sports for youth. China doesn't have community parks like we find in Canada, with grassy fields for baseball or soccer teams to play on. Nor do community centres exist. Music, art, and dance classes are all available from private tutors or small scale private schools, but there is nothing for the athletic child. As Smirler's son got older he talked of trying to create a youth soccer league. The problem was we had nowhere to play. We considered various venues, such as school gyms or their artificial turf or concrete fields, but I came to believe that we needed to find and rent a space that was ours, otherwise we would perpetually be frustrated by changing timetables of Chinese management. One day, it dawned on me while visiting a friend who lived in a well-to-do housing complex that the complex's abandoned gym would be perfect.

With the help of old friend Ladon, who knew the 'owners,' we attempted to negotiate a deal. It was a classic case of how things often work in China. The 'owners' of the gym aren't in fact the owners, but they likely know the owner. The two brothers, who we refer to as The Doofuses, appear not to work at all and yet are very affluent by Chinese or any standards, living in a detached house and driving BMWs. Ladon explained to Doofus my concept, which was to establish a non-profit community sports club, where member fees would initially cover minor construction costs and start up purchases and then simply cover rent and maintenance costs. The club is open to anyone who pays and wants to join. It is not exclusively for foreigners but it would be established to meet the needs of expats, especially the families who want to organize sports for their kids. The gym is located in a fledgling complex and Ladon suggested to Doofus that the club might attract prospective house renters. She also told them that their kids could join in, and in essence, they would be getting free English lessons while playing sport. Doofus thought it sounded okay. We negotiated a very reasonable rent of 1000 RMB a month but there was a stipulation. There would be no contract. Doofus, not being the real owner, couldn't say when the gym would be torn down to make way for more houses. We got verbal assurances that we could have the gym for at least a year and told we might be able to have it for five years, but no contract. Also, we couldn't make any structural changes.

The gym had been set up for tennis and two nets were imbedded in the green rubberized surface and tennis court lines had been painted. Having been abandoned for nearly three years, the open and broken windows enabled several families of pigeons to nest in the rafters. The pigeon guano would need to be cleaned out, the windows fixed, and all the water cleaned up because the roof leaked. We would have to fix that with our own money.

Except for the lack of a contract, it was perfect for us because it was ours to control. Using the 10,000 RMB from our hockey team's kitty that was intended originally to donate hockey sticks to kids up in Jilin or Qiqihar, I had a small roller rink built with plywood in one half of the gym, the boards built literally over the tennis nets, which remained in their original position. Hockey goals were welded and indoor soccer goals made for the other side of the gym. The goals and lines I painted with the help from a few friends, and I purchased fishing net from a local shop in our town and hand tied them to the goal frames.

The Dalian International Sports Club was born, and on opening day, March 15th 2008, we had about fifty kids show up, and we began weekly indoor soccer for two age groups, coached by several of the dads. The men started inline hockey two nights a week, which we continue with passion because it's our rink in lieu of real ice in Dalian. In the fall, Bill Colorado, a fellow teacher and father of three girls, and I began coaching a group of kids inline hockey. We were thrilled to find that the kids preferred hockey to soccer and our group quickly grew to nearly twenty 6-12 year-old hockey enthusiasts from Canada, the US, Sweden, Scotland, China, and Japan.

Around the same time that the gym was in the planning stages, I saw something amazing. We were driving down the main street in Kaifaqu, the busy *Jinma lu*—Golden Horse road—when Sara spotted a group of Chinese teenagers playing roller hockey on the sidewalk. They had found a patch of tiled open area in front of a library and were knocking around an old battered baseball, but they all had matching red Koho hockey sticks. I made a quick U-turn and stopped beside them.

'Who are you guys?' I asked, amazed to see hockey happening right in our neighbourhood.

A man appeared who I recognized as a hockey player from Heilongjiang province, who had dropped in on our parking lot roller hockey a couple of times. Li Wei was coaching these kids, who were all students from Kaifaqu #10 middle school, a designated 'sports school' located in the outskirts of the development zone. They had no facilities to train in and their practices were held on the sidewalk, just metres from the main intersection of town. I told Li Wei of my plans for the roller rink and once it was built they began practising there twice a week. To do our part to help build hockey in China I gave them a half price discount for using the gym, 100 RMB for three months of unlimited use.

Shortly after this time a group of dedicated students from our school got the passion for inline hockey and formed a team which Bill and I also coached. Coaching and playing with my kids and seeing the excitement and enthusiasm for hockey grow in others has been a truly joyous thing for me.

The parents are so grateful that something is finally available in Dalian for the kids. The Chinese parents are especially pleased and surprised that we volunteer our time, and that the fees are so low. Hopefully more of this kind of affordable community sports culture that we take for granted in Canada will spread out across China as it rapidly develops economically and socially.

You get the picture: living happily in China means getting involved in community activities and literally building from the ground up. It's a sort of do-it-yourself virtual world, where doing-it-yourself applies to practically every situation, even weddings and funerals.

In addition to being best man at a friend's wedding I have also officiated a friend's wedding, acting as priest. Although I never imagined myself having any 'power vested in me' to do such important work, it is quite an honour. At our own wedding, at Mui Ne beach in Vietnam, our friend John who was teaching in Taiwan at the time, flew down to officiate. It may seem to some people that these 'informal' and non-official weddings are something less than perfect or real, but to me they seem much more real and meaningful; traditional weddings now seem fake to me. Especially since young couples rarely attend church these days and have no relationship with the priest or official. Why would we want strangers so involved in such an important ceremony?

Unfortunately, weddings and happy events are not the only times the expat is called upon to organize. We were also unlucky enough to have needed to organize a memorial service for a friend; more on that later.

The 2005 Dalian Ice Dragons at #10 middle school, Liaoyang.

Buddha Loves Hockey

For me, one of the most tremendously satisfying experiences has been playing hockey in China with my team, the Dalian Ice Dragons, whose exploits are detailed in another, soon to be published, book. Hockey is one of the things that Canadians can relate to and when you meet hockey enthusiasts from other cultures you make an instant bond. Soccer and basketball fans are a dime a dozen in China and throughout much of the world, but hockey fans, or better yet hockey players, are a different breed. We understand one another in some indefinable way.

I remember riding the Trans-Manchurian Railway from Beijing to Moscow in 1994 and when Russians found out I was Canadian there was an instant connection. With the young, it was all talk of Pavel Bure, playing for my hometown team, the Vancouver Canucks, who had just lost to Nemchinov's New York Rangers in the Stanley Cup finals that year. For the older Russians, it was the good ol' days of the '72 series and there was widespread respect for Phil Esposito. In those days my favourite player was the Russian centre Igor Larionov, who then played for the Canucks before going on to play in Switzerland, then the Sharks, and finally the Red Wings. In Moscow, I sat down and joined a table in a fried chicken restaurant in GUM, the mall adjacent to Red Square, already occupied by two young Russian women because there were no other free tables. In excellent English, Olyssa, an ethnic Ukrainian who grew up in Kazakhstan, told me that I was a Sagittarius like her. Indeed I am, and we were precisely the same age. In our next exchange she asked if I played hockey and I said I did, but not well.

'My favourite player is Igor Larionov' we both said in synchronicity.

Wow, almost true love in Moscow, brought together by hockey and Igor Larionov. I never saw her again. I left for St. Petersburg the next day, but Olyssa sent me several letters with Russian hockey cards and old photos of Larionov.

Two years later, while backpacking across China, I met Buddha, a Mongolian from Siberia who was a diehard hockey fan, and also a Larionov fan. We shared a few bottles of Yanjing beer in a damp, mosquito infested dorm room in the basement of the Xing Hai hotel, south of Qian Men gate in Beijing. Buddha is a hockey fan, how cool is that! In my inebriated state I promised him I would give a cheer for Larionov and the Russian team at the upcoming World Cup of Hockey being held in Vancouver in September, which was only a few weeks away. I unfortunately couldn't get tickets but gave a cheer for Buddha to the TV screen anyway.

When I arrived in China for work in 1998, I had no idea there was any hockey played in the Middle Kingdom. In those days, the researching power of the Internet was still in its infancy and I was oblivious to the Chinese hockey scene. By early December I noticed that the small ponds around our school were frozen solid.

'Does anybody skate around here?' I'd ask the locals.

'It doesn't get cold enough in Dalian' was the standard reply.

It was infuriating because it clearly was cold enough. I vowed to bring out some skates from Canada the next year and get our students skating and playing pond hockey.

In those early years I was teaching PE and our school didn't have a gym. In the winter the sky was usually blue, but its appearance often betrayed sub-zero temperatures and howling polar continental winds that descended from Siberia. Skating and hockey were activities that seemed somehow more appropriate in those conditions then outdoor volleyball or soccer.

On our first summer holiday in Canada I annoyed the family by stopping at every thrift shop and sports consignment store hunting for old skates, and I managed to scrape up enough to get a considerable number of students on the ice at the same time. Skating and hockey were quite popular with a few of the kids and they began joining the several teachers who trundled down the road a couple hundred metres from the school to an abandoned field that was once dotted with villas. The villas were in a state of half-completion and

155

serious decay. The field was like a poor man's Bagan or Angkor Wat, reminiscent of an ancient civilization. In the middle of the decaying brick structures was a small pond, fed by a spring, just big enough for a 4 on 4 game of shinny. I have a beautiful video clip from those days, on which Linda Hilbrecht, our school's senior biology and chemistry teacher called a play-by-play.

> *Here we go...teachers versus students. The teachers... and some little kids... fighting for the ball, Jack Nan's up there... there's a little guy there... don't know who he is... oh... woops, stolen by... can't tell... JJ is down! Leo's up front, Primavera... here we go... lost the puck... making a move... and he's down... Conradi's got the puck... he's coming up, passing up... defence... taking a shot... Jack Nan... he scores!*

In the middle of this video the play-by-play gets sidetracked when two local kids slide through the middle of the game on a classic homemade Chinese sled—a piece of wood attached to two metal rails, propelled by metal spike poles.

The next year a new batch of teachers arrived when I was left the only one to stay on after our initial two year contract expired. This group was larger, growing in size with the school's growing student body. There were several fit, keen young guys on staff. They would make up the starting line on the original Ice Dragons.

One warm December school day at lunch, Darren Brown and I—the only two who believed that it was cold enough to skate that day—were playing a little game of shinny when the puck ended up right beside a hole that had formed in the ice. Darren was closest to the puck and inched forward to retrieve it but then retreated, citing safety concerns. I, perhaps twenty pounds lighter than Darren, figured the ice would hold and crept forward on my skates, slowly inching toward the puck. By the time I heard the cracking, it was too late. I was through the ice.

Hanna rides a Chinese sled on a pond in Dalian's botanical park.

Luckily the hole was near the edge of the pond and I fell in only to my waist or so, my skates scraping the bottom, as I flailed around splashing the freezing water up over my shoulders. I remember distinctly the extreme difficulty of unlacing my skates, my fingers and feet in a state of pre-hypothermia. Once he was sure I was okay, Darren started howling in laughter.

It was an uncomfortable walk back to school. As I entered the school building, making a squishing noise with each step I took, I could hear teachers' laughter echoing through the halls. I think they all knew I would go through the ice sooner or later. Luckily, I had a change of clothes in my office and was soon in my gym strip. If not warm, I was at least dry. Curiously, when I got home, Sara informed me that our daughter Hanna, just two years old, had told her that she dreamt that Daddy had fallen in dirty water.

It was shortly after falling through the ice that I had a fortuitous meeting in downtown Dalian with a young man named Wang Jun. I was out with two other dads and our kids at Labour Park. We rode the giant and incredibly scary Ferris wheel. A quarter of the way up the wind caused a loud cracking sound and I began to panic—what were we thinking, riding on this thing, maintained in China in an aging amusement park? After the kids had tired themselves out, and tired the dads even more, we walked out the back entrance of the park and came across a building with a large, puffy, blue roof. Inside we saw a former bowling complex, doors locked, several billiards tables, and most amazingly, an ice rink!

The rink was a half-rink. Literally, it was half of a small hockey rink, round at one end; the boards were flat and straight across where the centre red line should be. Glass surrounded the flat end at one side of the rink. The rink was very poorly lit, most of the bulbs had long ago burnt out. A no-name brand Zamboni sat parked in a corner. There were two goals stacked up against a wall. I'm not sure if I have ever been so excited to see anything in my life, barring my children when they were first born. Inside, we met Wang Jun, who recognized the hockey stick on my old-style Vancouver Canucks sweater. In Chinese, he asked if I played hockey and told me that there were a handful of hockey players in Dalian. We exchanged phone numbers and agreed to call soon.

No more than two weeks later Wang Jun called to invite me to get a line together to play hockey somewhere up north, in a place called Liaoyang. My Chinese was pretty primitive in those days—it still is I suppose, but it was really simple then. This meant that I really had no way to determine what to expect. Was it a tournament? Did they think we were pros? Who were we playing with? Against? I had no idea.

A hockey road trip in China! In retrospect the most difficult thing about the whole trip was convincing people to join me. Wang Jun had suggested we needed five people—and did we have a goalie? Eddy Kim and Scott Jensen signed up. They were decent ball hockey players and said they could skate, but didn't really have any experience playing ice hockey. Darren Brown, who has become one of the keenest hockey players in Dalian, said he was game. It would be his first organized game of ice hockey. As for myself, I played in goal as a kid, but always wanted to be a forward. I had played only a handful of times since I quit at age 15. But the passion for hockey was coming back.

Jeff Laird, perhaps the bravest heart since William Wallace, agreed to play goal. Goalies are brave at the best of times but Jeff was going armed only with home-made foam ball hockey pads, a baseball catcher's chest protector and face mask (which a puck could have easily passed through), a baseball glove, and 20 year old regular players' skates. Most importantly, he stuffed a plastic cup, which formerly held instant noodles, down the front of his pants. To round out the squad we picked up a German guy who was dating a female teacher on our staff. Dirk Diggler, we called him. Lord knows who he really was.

We rented a 13-seat van for the trip and filled it up with our plastic ball hockey sticks and several female friends—fans, we liked to think of them as. Sometime after midnight the night before, we had convinced an Aussie friend, David, to join us. He played a mixed role of general manager, mascot, off-ice goon, ambassador of all foreigners, and entertainment. Poor guy, his wife and kids were away and as a result he only thought to pack a can of sprite for the trip. He was grossly underdressed for the minus twenty degree temperature and to top it off, one of the lenses of his eye glasses popped out on the way up. He also had no clue about hockey and the Canadian obsession with it. He thought we were mad; we thought he was hilarious.

When we arrived, we were taken directly to the #10 Middle School. As our van crested a hill we glanced down and saw the most beautiful sight a Canadian in a far off land can see: No, it wasn't a Tim Horton's, it was an outdoor hockey rink.

The rink was flooded on the school's gravel soccer field and the boards were made of vertical 1x6 inch wooden planks. The red and blue lines were freshly painted, the only colours in an otherwise drab environment. Around the perimeter of the rink a speed skating track was prepared and beyond the skating track was a row of dreary brown, six story apartment blocks, typical of the older residential neighbourhoods.

A crowd of people and a television camera awaited us and we were immediately treated like celebrities; photos were taken and we were led to a teachers' prep room with a round table covered in fresh fruit and bottles of water for us. We were introduced to our hosts and several speeches were made. I was called upon to say a few words and stammered out something like this:

'Thank you very much. Canadians love hockey. Playing hockey with you will make us very happy and good friends. Thank you very much'.

That's about all I could say in Chinese. Since then I have given countless speeches at hockey banquets. They are now slightly longer and with a little more variety of vocabulary but are, in essence, the same simple speech.

The Chinese players all put on their hockey gear but we had none to put on. I wore jeans, a Team Canada jersey over a sweater, ski gloves, and a Cowichan knit toque. When we got outside we put on our skates and met all the players. Our team, in addition to the Canadians and Dirk Diggler, was Wang Jun, and four other Chinese friends of his from Dalian. Three of them I saw only rarely, if ever again. One of them, Yin Nanchang, is to this day one of my best Chinese friends. They were all dressed in pretty decent hockey gear and wore matching yellow and black jerseys.

The other team looked liked the biggest ragtag collection of players I had ever seen, not including ourselves of course. Actually the team was two teams that had joined together in great anticipation of playing the foreigners. Half of the team was the #10 Middle School teachers' team, captained by the Headmaster, a chubby man about 60 years old. A tireless hockey enthusiast, he was the driving force that kept hockey alive in Liaoyang.

It was really cool to be playing against Chinese teachers and we couldn't help but feel like kindred spirits. Many of these players had old, tattered, and even home-made equipment. The goaltender protected his head with a cage that was welded together and drilled onto a construction worker's hard hat. Even in a gentle, old-timer's recreational league in Canada you would feel vastly underdressed and vulnerable to injury wearing the equipment they had. Compared to us, they were well protected.

The second half of the team was a group from the nearby steel-producing town of Anshan. These guys were led by a tiny, but talented, player named Xiao Miao—Little Miao.

They were very concerned that we didn't have equipment and the referee—a 73 year old man who literally popped up in almost every city where I have played hockey in China—banned slap shots and raising the puck. Not a bad idea, not only for Jeff's safety but also because the rink did not have any glass or netting above the boards, and nearly a hundred local children and adults leaned over the boards to watch the play. We insisted that we would be fine playing without equipment and happily accepted a few wooden hockey sticks they passed over for us to use after seeing our plastic floor hockey blades.

I shoot right, but I received a lefty stick. My stick was uncut and I'm 5'8' so it wasn't really the best stick for me, but beggars can't be choosers. These sticks were produced in Harbin, a city of ten million people who live in a sub arctic climate; the Chinese version of Edmonton—in fact they are sister cities. The sticks were made of plywood and later after we had purchased some for fifty RMB each, Scott broke his in half, simply by leaning on it to gauge the flex.

We skated around in the customary fashion during warm up, checking out the opposition. They didn't look great, but we looked worse. We couldn't really skate and our passing was atrocious; we were too used to playing ball hockey with the orange plastic street hockey balls. Although the spirit of the game was friendly, we were anxious and excited. How would we do? We were Canadians, after all, and there was a certain pride on the line. This was supposed to be our game.

When the puck dropped, Eddy knocked it forward and I moved in from the right wing to pick it up. The game was on. It was half a second into the game and I had the puck on my stick heading for their blue line, hand painted the night before. At age 29, I still had some speed and with a gulp of the dry frozen air I took off, splitting the defence, and was in alone on the goalie. Holy crap, three seconds into the game and I was on a breakaway! Looking up, I saw only a figure wearing an orange jersey without a logo; if I had been less focussed I might have noticed the Mongolian barbeque restaurant and a row of shops up behind the goal. I didn't yet feel comfortable handling the puck, especially with the long lefty stick so I just pushed it forward and skated to catch up. If the goalie had only realized my predicament he surely could have predicted my only possible move: the back hand deke. Surging forward at my maximum speed towards the goal, I pulled left at the top of the crease and gently lifted the puck into the net, behind the goalie, about a foot off the ice. Arcing around behind the net I remember looking up, mostly to avoid smashing into the boards, and seeing the familiar faces of the friends who had accompanied us. They were cheering, and to this day, although I have scored a couple of shoot-out goals in tournaments the Dragons have won since then, this remains my most happy and glorious hockey memory. The thrill of that moment overwhelmed me in a crushing encapsulation: adventure, pioneering spirit, adversity, camaraderie, success, and Canadianness all wrapped up in a few seconds of experience on a frozen flooded patch of urban Manchuria.

Perhaps five seconds had passed; this was going to be a cakewalk. The next five seconds, no... make that sixty minutes, didn't go nearly as well. It seems that I had been a bit lucky on the first play and we were quickly outmatched by the ragtag Liaoyang-Anshan hockey team.

The first surprise in our introduction to Chinese hockey came when we skated to the bench to sub off. Our Chinese teammates weren't ready and told us to stay out longer. After the next stoppage of play we skated off, panting and insisting that they go on. We desperately wanted to sit on the bench, but there was no bench, just a speed skating oval with people skating by at various speeds.

There were fans, and I don't mean our several friends, but actual fans. We got swarmed by middle school kids with their notebooks out, asking for autographs. It was hilarious. Who knows if they thought we really were famous hockey players, it didn't matter to them. As a foreigner in China, unwanted staring and attention can get tedious at times, as I'm sure it does for genuine celebrities, but this was so innocent and wonderful that we more than happily obliged. Adults approached us too, wanting to find out who we were, and just to chat, forgetting that we were in the middle of a hockey game.

Much to our chagrin, our Chinese line was exhausted and completely out of position. They had looked decent in the warm up, skating beautifully, much better than I do, but they appeared to have no clue about positioning. In our zone the points were left open, in theirs, nobody would get in front of the net. And they stayed on for five-minute shifts! They looked confused when we started calling for them to sub off. Because there were only two lines we didn't have a chance to discuss this issue until the first period break. We explained to them the concept of, and rationale for, changing on the fly. They didn't like it; it messed with their five man unit that played together for a full five minutes. Frankly, we didn't like their five man unit because nobody seemed to play a position and they were always offside.

It turns out there was good reason for their strategic deficiencies. They had only ever played at the Blue Shell, the half-rink in Dalian, so named for its puffy blue roof. There they played 3 on 3, with no offsides, no subs, and no goalies. They could skate and stick-handle well but hadn't really ever played, or even seen, an organized hockey game.

For the record, the Canadian (and one German) five man unit wasn't looking much better. Although we had more hockey sense and better positional play, we simply couldn't skate. Darren was flopping all over the place and at one point crawling on the ice. Fifty percent of this was due to the fact that he had not skated much before, the other fifty percent from the old skates I had given him that were used on dusty ponds for two seasons and had not been sharpened in years (fighting against dull skates was to become a decade long battle for us). The other Canadians fared better on skates, but we were no pros. I was always a bent-ankle skater as a kid and to this day my skating is not that smooth.

We played our hearts out, our toques getting knocked off, and our knees and elbows smashed on the rock-hard ice. My elbow swelled up to twice its normal size and stayed that way for three months, but there were no regrets.

The game ended and we retired to the teachers' prep room for cheers and more speeches. I can't remember the exact score but 7 to 3 for the home team rings a bell. The score was inconsequential; we'd had the time of our lives playing hockey outdoors in a home-made rink in China. It was beautiful!

Once we had changed into warm, dry clothes, we were informed that we were being treated to dinner. Because our hosts were teachers, and therefore not well paid in China, it was certainly somebody else who hosted the supper. I can't picture a face but I think it was somebody from the local Labour Bureau who footed the bill. Generally, that's how it works in China; the person who invites a group for supper pays. If you need to take a group out for supper but don't have the funds to pay, you can use your *guanxi* to get someone else to pay. That person will start the evening off with a toast or will be honoured in a speech during the meal. This way, they are given face.

It was here, at this dinner, that I first realized that hockey trips in China were much more than just playing hockey. They were intense, hilarious, and amazing cultural experiences that involved bizarre customs and food—although the food was always of exceptional quality. Strong expressions of camaraderie, bordering on man-love, were the order of the day and heavy drinking was a key feature of these events. Teetotallers were looked down upon.

The dinners start typically with the food on the table but the Chinese don't dig in until the host, or his deputy, has given the signal, usually a short welcome speech, followed by an urging to 'eat, eat!' By this time the Canadians have already scoped out the grub and are curious about several dishes.

'What the hell do you think that is?'

'Looks like fat to me'.

'Could be jelly fish'.

'Might be a noodle of some kind. I heard the Chinese make noodles out of every possible kind of vegetable'.

Most of the guys will avoid those dishes until someone asks '*zhe shi shenme*?' What is this?

The nearest Chinese will proudly explain what it is, and how it's made. We may or may not understand what it actually is. Then a lengthy explanation of what it is good for follows. It's good for our skin...or our livers (Thank God, we joke, because the beer is already flowing fast). Eventually someone tucks in and declares it to be delicious or an acquired taste.

'Oh no, it's tendon'.

'I'll pass,' says half the crew.

I find ninety percent of the food to be incredible, but then again, I'll eat anything. I still remember a couple of the dishes from that weekend: Duck brain, plucked out of the head with your chopsticks, and prawns that were alive and squirming on a plate; we dropped them into a bubbling broth hot pot.

A short time into the meal, speeches are given by various people of importance: a government official, the school dean, the team captain. I am always called upon at this point. The liquid courage usually helps me spit out a few words but who knows if they make any sense.

The drinking starts immediately and if your glass gets empty the nearest Chinese fellow will top it up. Every couple of minutes someone at the table will hold up their glass and call out '*gan bei*'—dry glass. At this point we drain our glasses in one pull. The standard Chinese beer drinking glass is a short glass that holds about 200 ml of liquid. Any larger glasses and this style of drinking would be disastrous. Then various small groups of people will wander around the room giving a short speech and demanding a *ganbei* at each table. Some players from the opposition will target certain players on our team; myself for being captain, a skater who stood out, the goalie. Any excuse will do, even honouring a player for taking a stupid penalty. This is where we found out that the dinner and lunches are sometimes more competitive than the games. It seems that the *ganbei* orders are given out strategically. Generally speaking, the Chinese team has a designated 'drinker' who is unbeatable and he is sent around to challenge us.

Sooner than later, we are pissed as newts and then things really begin to get silly. The Chinese start singing songs and we are called on to do the same. Stompin' Tom's *The Hockey Song* is a favourite that goes over well. Once we were called upon to sing our host's favourite English song, a number he called 'ding ding dong'. After he gave us a sample, we figured out he was requesting Jingle Bells. We were more than happy to oblige, belting it out, all the while looking ridiculous, wearing plastic bibs given to patrons at BBQ restaurants.

Inevitably, there is a Chinese player or official who is bizarre beyond belief present at the meal. Once he gets drunk things get really weird. In Changchun, the Chief of Police, who happens to captain the hockey team, turns into a character off of Kids in the Hall after a few beers. He performs fellatio on beer bottles, rib bones, anything; it's pretty scary. In China, the concept of personal space is much different than ours and when combined with the tendency of Chinese men to touch each other in ways that North Americans would never do, this presents strange and uncomfortable moments. On our first dinner in Liaoyang, the Dean was definitely trying to get it on with our guys.

David, our Aussie mascot, had been drinking hard and we found out part way through the dinner that shockingly, one of our female colleagues, originally from Malaysia, was translating everything he said.

'Don't f—ing translate that,' he stammered, shortly before standing up and wandering off down a hallway.

A few moments later we heard a commotion. David was being led back to our banquet room and he was taking exception to being manhandled. He started pulling out his best Kung Fu moves and we had to intervene. The Chinese love this sort of tomfoolery and never get insulted by it. It helps that everyone is drunk.

Then without warning, someone stands up, gets everyone's attention, and declares the dinner over. There is a loud cheer and friendly handshakes and thank yous at the door. The Chinese head home to bed to sleep off the hangover. We head out to explore the nightlife in Liaoyang.

Go-go dancers, midgets or dwarfs (I can't remember which), a chubby guy piercing himself with a spike ... all this and more in a gigantic nightclub—but the nocturnal exploits of the Dalian Dragons best be left for another chapter in another book.

The next morning we were awoken from our uneasy drunken slumber in our rock hard hotel beds at 8 am and summoned for breakfast. Hotel breakfasts in China have never been my thing. I love Chinese food for dinner and lunch but I just can't get excited about a Chinese breakfast, because to me, frankly, it looks like lunch food. Fried rice, some steamed something or others, pickled vegetables; it's really not the stuff you want the morning after a couple too many *pijiu*, or beer. There's no coffee available but there usually is a pot of hot milk or sometimes *dou jiang*—soy milk—so if you have brought your own packet of instant coffee you can make do, because the one thing that is always available in China, whether in a hotel, in an airport, an office, or on a train, is boiling water to make tea.

I silently make my way past the tin bowls of food, hoping for something that seems edible at this early hour. A cookie, *mantou* and *youtiao*—steamed buns and fried breadsticks—, a boiled egg. That's about all I can handle. Aching for a coffee, head pounding, we head out into the freezing cold air and back to the rink for game two.

After a couple of laps of the rink in the dry, frigid air our headaches dissipate and we can then take in the scene. It seems the Anshan hockey players have mostly gone, and we are left with just the Liaoyang teachers' team. This game goes much better and a Dragons tradition is born; we always play terribly our first game because we haven't been on skates for aeons, but despite being hung over, we manage to play half decently the following day. We won game two about 10-7 and returned home high and triumphant, more because we had so much fun, and much less to do with scores. In any event, there would be many road trips to come where the Dragons would have been very pleased with a .500 record.

In the years following this great escapade, we organized our team more formally, created numerous logos and uniforms and toured over thirty times. The Dragons' road trips are always a wild and unpredictable adventure. In the ugliest incident we were involved in a bench-clearing brawl against a team of policemen in Changchun. As I attempted to patch up our relationship with our hosts as the brawl dwindled down I was forced to intervene and deliver a few punches when someone speared our goalie in the chest, narrowly missing his throat. That, in turn, resulted in a tomahawk to the head and a butt-end to the back of the neck for me. With a few nasty exceptions our games were friendly and with time we even managed to win a few games. Our greatest successes were coming sixth at the 2004 World Ice Hockey 5s, a tournament in Hong Kong on a mini rink that saw us come last in our division, where we played against very good players, including a former Vancouver Canuck, winning the Liaoning provincial Championships in a shootout in 2005, and winning the 2007 Bethune Cup, a tournament for expats, played in Beijing.

Playing hockey in China has been so much fun and added so much to my life here that I don't know if I could have lasted so long in Dalian without it.

The Dragons in Sweater Lady's cardigans, Imperial Palace, Shenyang.

10

The corner of Stalin road and democracy street, Jinzhou.

Stalin Road & Democracy Street

An impression of China and the Chinese surely can be gleaned from the previous and subsequent chapters. After all, this book is about China. But this chapter aims to do the impossible and, true to the word, I will fail miserably attempting to answer two questions: Who are these Chinese and what is China all about? I know I will fail because I am but one observer, and an ignorant one at that, not quite fluent in their language and illiterate to boot. My observations are, therefore, limited and biased too; but unless you have written a book on the Chinese yourself, given the aforementioned caveat, perhaps they are worth a read.

Most of this book pretty much wrote itself, but here I sit with fingers flaccid on the keyboard, not knowing how to go about describing these people and their country. I'd like to start at the beginning, with first impressions, but they have long ago morphed from experiences. I had to resort to asking newcomers to China about their impressions. Suddenly, it comes flooding back.

They say it is filthy here.

Plastic bags fly past with every gust of wind.

'Look, a bird' we joke to one another, but it's half joke, half reality; there are more bags than birds in the sky much of the time.

I recall a strike by the garbage collectors in Vancouver just before we left for China. Sara and I wandered about China Town and the stench of rotting refuse from the markets and restaurants that had been left for weeks in the summer heat was disarming. Extra sensitive during pregnancy, Sara asked if China smelled like this.

'Not at all,' I lied.

And now I recall the smell of China. Coal. Coal burning to keep the Chinese warm, burning in little metal tubs stuffed under tables in restaurants. Burning in giant boilers to fill radiators to warm schools, hospitals, and apartments. Piles of coal, filthy little mountains, found in nearly every neighbourhood.

Coal is not the only burning stink. Garbage is burned daily, on the side of the road, in the villages, at the neighbourhood dumps, located on street corners and behind markets, where donkeys and mules munch through the edible remains.

China smells raw and unrefined. It smells of dust and of wet cement. Urine and feces fill the air and as a friend described, it's like a ball-peen hammer blow to the nose.

China has long been known for its outrageously disgusting toilets. They have made strides improving these since my first days here in the early 1990's but there is still a long way to go. Even at my work, an 'international school,' when I brought two German friends out to visit, Robert took two steps inside the main teaching building and said—to be read aloud with your best Arnold Schwarzenegger accent—'smells like horses'. It doesn't help that the mops used to clean out the latrines are then used to mop the hallways, even the railings on the staircases and worse, the blackboards in the classrooms.

Some of us Westerners never quite get used to the stinking mess that is the Chinese toilet. The olfactory aspect is just one issue; the other is the squatting that's required. Some will tell you squatting is pleasant, more natural than the sit-down approach. In my back-packing days when I always stayed in places with communal squatty toilets I would cross town daily to visit the clean washrooms in the 5 star hotel lobbies. I simply couldn't deal with squatting in that squalor; the threat of toppling over into the filthy abyss was just too great.

The Chinese are adept at navigating these nasty waters. They are not deterred when the public toilet is a 3 metre long trench; they simply squat and do their business and perhaps read a newspaper, thereby creating a minor barrier between themselves and the plopping neighbour. I enter Chinese washrooms like a second- rate minesweeper in Afghanistan, treading carefully but always getting hit with a little shrapnel. The Chinese exit unscathed, their black leather shoes still shining. Somehow they maintain their dignity, whereas the Westerners succumb to whining or worse.

They say it is loud.

I wonder how many Chinese are deaf. Music blares from speakers everywhere: in front of clothing stores, department stores, grocers, and hairdressers. 85 decibels for a sustained period is the threshold beyond which hearing becomes impaired. I'm certain the average urban Chinese street corner experiences 100 decibels for most of the day. Horns are blaring and the bus and truck drivers can't resist the urge to blast their air horns. Firecrackers ignite in virtual perpetuity. Street-side infomercial men shriek into megaphones and the one *kuai* stores bellow to nobody about their cheap wares. At times it seems I can barely think with such noise. The Chinese don't seem to notice.

The Chinese scream at each other.

They scream at each other because they are happy and want to share their joy. They scream at each other to make a point, that something is absurd, or when something is funny. They scream at others in mock disapproval. Girls and young women put on pouty faces when they scream at their boyfriends, stamping their feet and turning away. The taxi drivers scream at you to get in, to ask where you are going. Restaurant hosts scream *'huanying guanglin!'*—welcome!—when you arrive and scream *'man zou!'*—go slowly!—and *'xia ci lai!'*—come again!—when you leave.

And sometimes they scream because they are angry.

They fight in the streets, in restaurants, shouting mostly. But if it does get violent, look out, because it will get really nasty. Rarely, if ever, do you see a fist fight in China. Usually there is a weapon produced when a fight breaks out. A brick or rock picked up to smash over someone's head, a meat cleaver swung clumsily, a hockey stick directed at my head.

No, the Chinese are not the demure and kowtowing folks you thought they were.

The Chinese are rude!

They push, shove, spit, and yell. In short, they have no manners. But manners are nothing more than a manifestation of a society's values, usually imposed upon the masses by those at the top of society. Manners may help to make up criteria for deciding who makes the cut into the upper echelons of society. It should be no surprise to anyone that members of a very different society located on the opposite end of the earth, with an extensive and unique history, forged by dynastics and religions foreign to ours, would not share our manners. So are the Chinese actually rude and 'uncivilized'? Absolutely, when measured up against the British evolved ideal that North American society has come to expect. We too, are seen as barbarian and ignorant of many age-old Chinese cultural norms, i.e. manners. And yet the Chinese are much more forgiving than we are. They have decided not to bother telling us we are rude and inconsiderate. They simply tolerate us in their country, and for that, I thank and applaud them.

But for every screaming match witnessed there are ten smiles aimed at the foreigner. Smiles of wonder from children, the bravest of whom call out 'hello' and 'what's your name?' Smiles of welcome from people who genuinely want the foreigners to enjoy their stay in China. Smiles that only appear after a look of bewilderment passes from their face.

The Chinese are so interested in foreigners, yet so ignorant of us. They lump the peoples of the world into several categories: The Chinese, their Asian neighbours, who are honoured enough to be referred to by name—the Japanese are *riben ren,* the Koreans *hanguo ren*—Caucasians, referred to as *waiguo ren*, while anyone with dark complexion is a *hei ren* —a black person. Thus, the Chinese-Canadian who speaks no Mandarin is considered some sort of fool and the Bangladeshi-Canadian is simply Black. Neither are Canadians in the Chinese mind. They believe that China is a multicultural society. They can't begin to comprehend the diversity that exists in the immigrant-riddled modern Western democracies.

Depending on where I happen to be I am usually assumed to be American or Russian, in which case the usual 'heller' becomes 'khorosho,' which I eventually determined means 'good' in Russian. Because of the lack of exposure to foreigners I have been able to pass myself off to various people as a Uyghur from Xinjiang and in one very bizarre case a country bumpkin thought we were a family of Japanese. Pretty amazing considering we are all fair and freckled with blue and green eyes.

Regarding the Japanese, the Chinese still hold negative feelings that spill over into downright hatred without much prompting, leftover ill tidings from WWII, perpetuated by the state-run media and textbooks. One of the saddest, and most worrisome, aspects of the Chinese psyche is the anti-Japanese sentiment that is a real threat to world peace in a future world when China becomes a true super-power. The Chinese seem to be all too eager to accept any manner of nonsensical rumours about the Japanese and other foreigners. Nothing is too absurd to be believed; the critical mind has not been nurtured and developed in China. I and other teachers work hard to make a difference but as one student said to a colleague of mine 'do you really think you can change our minds?'

Anti-Japanese demonstration outside of Japanese embassy, Beijing.

One of the more philosophical high school students that I taught once lamented that the Chinese don't criticize China until they go abroad. 'They are cowards,' he declared. I see his point, that they lack the courage to take personal risks to affect change in their society, but I believe they simply can't think critically until they have lived in a different environment and witnessed a society that values and practices critical thought. After all, it was only after I lived abroad that I could see Canada in the critical light that I now see it.

The Chinese are innocent, and this is at first sweet but it soon becomes maddening and perplexing. They don't see the irony at that street corner in Jinzhou, the corner of Stalin road and democracy street.

'This is unbelievable!' I called out when I first saw the street sign, rummaging around my bag for the camera. 'We *need* to get a photo of this'.

Communism lingers. Or does it? Perhaps it is more accurately thought of as totalitarianism that lingers.

Trust nobody and think everyone is out to cheat you, rob you, hurt you. Going to Harbin? Be careful, it's dangerous there. Travelling the Silk Road? *Xiao xin!*—Be careful! Those Uyghurs all carry knives and will stab you. Heading south? They'll cheat you down in Guangzhou, those sneaky little Cantonese. These are the feelings the Chinese hold about one another. And yet the local community is tight, in everyone else's businesses, mingling together, the men playing chess, the women line dancing, the children running free, looked after by nobody, by everyone.

Reflecting upon the Chinese a paradox emerges. They will rob you blind in the markets — that's just capitalism in practise, so says one friend of mine—but chase you for a hundred metres to return a five RMB note you dropped, or a fallen toque or mitten.

They are nosy and in your business but will not intervene if it means someone will lose face. The concept of face remains a mystery to me after all these years. It seems simple enough and your reputation is important, to be sure. But the Chinese conception of when and why one loses face is so different and perplexing to Westerners. We hear that showing anger is a loss of face, yet there seems to be people freaking out all around us. To my mind, face equals dignity. To many Chinese, dignity is a dream, a luxury, but not a reality. I guess the question is, does one have dignity or is it given by others' perception of you?

The Chinese are matter-of-fact people.

They tell it like it is. A friend who is married to a Canadian colleague, and therefore knows how Canadians feel about such things, was telling us a story of how when he was a child his uncle killed the family dog and they ate it. In his telling of the story there was no emotion expressed. The Canadian audience wants to hear how the poor child was devastated by the loss of his pet and how he couldn't stand the thought of being forced to eat it. But no, he recounted why the dog was killed — because government workers were scouring the neighbourhood catching and killing dogs without licenses— and without expressing any feeling, told us that they ate it. His Canadian friends were horrified, his wife just laughed. He went on to say that it was a dog and only a *dog*. They are not part of the family, they are animals with a purpose, to guard, and when they can no longer serve their purpose you eat them so as not to waste valuable meat. If they are behaving badly, you beat them. If they don't eat your scraps, you starve them, they'll eat next time. They are *dogs*.

The matter-of-factness comes across as another contradiction. How can the Chinese be concerned with saving and giving face and tell you, point blank, that you are fat. And don't pretend that fat is cool in China, it's not. It may have been a sign of prosperity at one point but it certainly isn't today. Tell a Chinese woman or girl she is fat and look at her face (her expression) and listen to what she says about herself. They don't want to be told they are fat, even if it is true, yet the Chinese will tell you that you are fat even if you are only a teeny bit softer around the middle than the last time they saw you.

Classism rules here and the hierarchy is evident. Abuse of power is prevalent and open for all to see. Bullying is subtle, such as when employees fear being dismissed without valid reason, and at times overt, like when the police chief walks out of the restaurant without paying, having just 'treated' a dozen friends. Or when the chief bites another man's ear and whispers something into it like some New York Mafia don.

The Communist Party rules, of this fact there is no debate. Yet communism is dead and gone here. The Chinese are much more entrepreneurial than Canadians, and see no contradiction. Ever since Deng Xiaoping declared 'it doesn't matter if the cat is black or white, as long as it catches the mouse' the Chinese have gone capitalist-crazy, investing in housing and stocks, starting and selling businesses, getting ahead. Yes, there is still state control over key industries, a socialism of sorts. But in new China corporate success is celebrated and the new heroes are CEOs of self-censoring enterprises. The new heroes are getting rich, but like Lei Feng and the heroes of yesterday they march forward to the same rhythm, the pace set by the band leaders in Beijing.

Fascism lurks in new China's potential.

'We love peace!' they exclaim, and recite the official line, that China opposes hegemony and does not interfere in others' business. I have spent a lot of time discussing this idea with my students. It soon comes out that they, like most people around the world, would be happy to throw their weight around, once they get hefty enough. Judging by their defence spending (fourth in the world in 2008) and growing economy that day could come soon.

When I arrived in China from India and Pakistan via the Karakorum highway I was immediately struck by something that changed the instant I crossed the border. It wasn't the colour of people's skin, the physical environment, the language, or the armed soldiers who stopped our bus. It was a sudden and complete drop in pressure. Not barometric pressure, but sexual tension.

In India, foreign women are harassed continuously. Elbows rub up against their breasts in the market, they are stared at in an almost menacing way on buses, and their crotches are snatched outrageously in train stations. In the hinterlands of Pakistan a foreign woman may be the only woman on the street, the only woman seen that day. To cross the border into China with a woman is to experience first hand the lifting of the veil, to cross from oppression into liberation. To don a skirt or shorts in the sweltering summer is a luxury not enjoyed in much of South Asia.

Uzbek girls selling stuffed flatbread on China's frontier with Pakistan.

The Chinese appeared to me to be asexual, and this was a relief for both me and my female travelling companion. I eventually found out how wrong I was, the Chinese are far from being asexual. China today has turned 180 degrees from the days of the anti-spiritual corruption campaign of the 1980s—when pornography possession and lewd behaviour resulted in harsh jail terms and even capital punishment—and reverted back to the seedier days of pre-communist Shanghai.

These days in China, sex is in your face. Dildos are on sale in pharmacies on the shelf above the blow-up doll, right next to the penicillin. I wonder if you need a prescription. Sex shops openly advertise and the duty free store has just four shelves: tobacco, booze, silk scarves, and pocket pussies. When the phone rings in the middle of the night in your hotel room, invariable it is a woman asking '*yao an mo ma?*'—do you want a massage? Once I was staying in hotel in Sanya, on tropical Hainan Island, with my whole family, when I was approached by a woman in the lobby in broad daylight.

'*Yao zuo ai ma?*'

'*Shenme? W*hat?' Did I hear her correctly?

'Do you want to make love?

Good God, we were the only foreigners in the hotel and surely she had seen me with my children, my wife, my father, even my mother-in-law!

The Chinese are not asexual, that's for sure. If you want it, it's there, but for women, a wonderful aspect of China is the relative safety from sexual predators. Women don't feel scared walking the streets, even at night. I have never worried about my wife out alone, nor has she ever worried. In fact, the Chinese men ignore foreign women to such a degree that many foreign women feel neglected and have a tough time in China. They simply don't get the attention some of them crave. I must say that these comments apply to foreign women in China, and the reality may be totally different for Chinese women. I admit full ignorance here.

The Chinese seem to have a love-hate relationship with the outside world, and indeed, with themselves. They are fiercely patriotic and proud of their economic miracles. But nobody who has the money to buy an imported car will stoop to buy a Chinese make. They extol the virtues of Chinese tea then pay $5 for a tiny cup of coffee imported from Japan, of all places. They love to tell foreigners about their 5,000 year history yet don't know what happened in Tiananmen Square in 1989, although they all know that something nasty went down, and they know why they are not to know.

Another fascinating aspect of the Chinese is their self image. Due to years of isolation, they have no concept of how China might be perceived or known by the outside world. They can't understand why foreigners would see China as a threat.

'China loves peace!' they proclaim, meanwhile they showcase their nukes in the largest ever military parade, televised for the world to see.

They are blown away, judging by their comments, when foreigners can use chopsticks. I'm from Vancouver so this seems absurd. Then we see what happens when Chinese encounter a knife and fork for the first time. It's not much prettier than the first time you tried chopsticks. On the topic of chopsticks, the Chinese are aware that there are great culinary traditions other than their local food. All of the great cuisines are, of course, from other regions of China. There is the sweet stuff down south, the sour stuff out west, the spicy stuff in the east and the salty stuff up north. As for Western food, well, they don't like it.

'Really? What Western food have you eaten?'

'McDonald's' they say, or perhaps, 'a sandwich'.

The sandwich probably was bought in a paper bag from a convenience store's shelf, where it sat unrefrigerated for God knows how long. I can't blame the Chinese for not liking Western food. It's next to impossible to find Western food in China that a) is edible and b) resembles Western food in taste. This, of course, is not true in the big cities. I'm talking about the China everywhere other than Beijing and Shanghai.

But more and more we meet the new Chinese. Take Yin, for example, one of my best Chinese friends. He loves hockey, making him fairly unusual in Dalian. After eating a home-cooked Western meal at our house he became obsessed with Western cooking. He proudly told us how strange he was, eating bread and drinking milk. His bar was always stocked with gin, rum, tequila, and whisky, never *baijiu*. At his annual parties, we would see more and more Western influences until he one day announced that his latest economic venture was not going to be the golf course or ice rink he previously planned, but a Western restaurant.

'Fantastic!' we thought, imagining ourselves frequenting his establishment. The problem was, he decided on a location that baffled us, way out by the airport, far from the city centre and even farther from the Development Zone where all his foreign friends lived. What was he thinking? Is this more mad Chinese economics?

Yin is no fool. His restaurant was practically across the street from a giant new government building. His market? The local government officials who will spend the people's money dining on hip Western grub. They probably won't even like it. Who cares, they are paying customers and Yin is getting ahead. He sold his honey business once he no longer had a monopoly in the city and bought stocks and apartments. Flipping those was profitable. His VW Santana turned into an Audi A6. He is one of the success stories and he's done it with his family by his side.

Many Chinese don't have this luxury, or don't make this choice. I can't begin to guess how many Chinese families live separately, with vast distances between them. I wouldn't be surprised if it was equal to half of all families in places like Dalian, where people have migrated to make it rich.

'We will sacrifice our life and our daughter's childhood for a better future' we heard as a mother justified sending her only child off to live with her grandparents in Shanghai. When half of the Chinese I meet tell me their significant other is working in a another city I can no longer take seriously their claims that the Chinese value family while we Westerners are individualistic. I understand there are financial reasons for these separations but ultimately the choices are based on values. Better explained, it's that the Chinese and Westerners express their common value differently. Both value family. One shows this by sacrificing for future family considerations, while the other sacrifices potential future security for present-day family integrity.

Racing ahead, steeped in tradition, abandoning all that they were, not forgetting who they are; they are perplexing, but good people, these Chinese.

Cosmo is entertained by a monk, Kumbum Monastery.

Dalai Clique

In the summer of 2000, Sara and the kids returned to Canada a couple of weeks before the end of the school year. Tony Primavera, a friend and fellow Social Studies teacher, was leaving China to live in Canada and suggested we make a trip somewhere out in the wild west of undeveloped China. Sara agreed to let me delay my return to Canada and the family by a week. It wasn't a long time but it was enough for a pretty good adventure for a couple of married guys.

Tony wasn't set on any place in particular but his interest in Western China had been piqued by a previous trip to Ningxia, a designated autonomous region of the Hui people, a nation of Muslims who are essentially hybrid from Chinese and ancient Persian traders along the Silk Road. I was able to easily convince Tony that Qinghai was a decent destination for an adventure.

I already knew that Qinghai was the northern portion of the Tibetan plateau. The Lonely Planet Guidebook on China contained only six pages for the entire province, despite the fact that it is China's largest Province, not including the autonomous regions of Tibet, Xinjiang, and Inner Mongolia. Most of those pages were devoted to the travellers who were passing through by bus on to Lhasa, in the days before the railway reached Lhasa, ending abruptly at Golmud (*Ge'er mu* in Chinese). Qinghai was untouched *terra incognito*; perfect for what we wanted!

An Internet search revealed the diversity of the north eastern section of the province. Xining, the capital, has a large Hui Muslim population that boasts a gorgeous 14th century mosque, the sight of which would convince you that you were in the Middle East or Central Asia, not China. Not far from Xining was one of the six great Tibetan Monasteries of the Yellow Hat sect, Kumbum, called *Ta er si* in Chinese.

I found a website run by a Christian Missionary group that provided facts about various ethnic groups in China. It was here that I first heard about the Tu people. Of them it was written:

# of Tu who have never heard the gospel: 90%

# of Tu who are believers: 0

The site detailed how unmarried women were distinguishable from married women by the type of braids in their hair. I read how upon entering or leaving a Tu village a visitor is presented with three shots of the local barley liquor. That sounded like fun!

Tony and I flew on the now defunct China Northern Airlines from Dalian to Xining in mid July. The flight was uneventful but we had gorgeous views of multiple ergs, desert seas of sand dunes. We are both geography teachers and were pretty excited to have aerial views of these landforms that are hard to find in Canada.

We settled into a simple hotel in Xining that cost no more than a couple of dollars a night. Xining is a smallish city with stunning arid vistas that reminded me somehow of the Thompson River near Kamloops, in the interior of British Columbia. There were no Big Macs or Slurpees here, but if you wanted a bowl of goat's head broth with a side order of flat bread, this was your town.

A local map revealed the name of a town, called Huzhu, designated a *zi zhi xian*, or autonomous county, of the Tu nation. Just outside the hotel a bus was heading for the town and we jumped on it. When we arrived we were very disappointed to find that it appeared nothing more than a regular Chinese town. Where were the untouched Tu people and their unique culture? None of the locals seemed to know. We trod, rather dejectedly, through the town's streets hoping to stumble upon an old or interesting neighbourhood. Maybe there was a Tu quarter.

Eventually, as we were walking towards the outskirts of town, we spotted an old woman walking with a girl of about nine or ten, both wearing brightly coloured outfits. We chased them down and indeed they belonged to the Tu nationality. They were returning to their village, several kilometres outside of the town and we were kindly invited to accompany them. At the intersection of the main rural road and a dirt track, two women wearing the same bright outfits stood by the side of the road. Apparently they were there to attract Chinese visitors to enter the village. Together with the excited ladies, who thrust beautifully embroidered satchels and wall hangings at us, pleading for a sale, we strolled into the village.

Our arrival caused a commotion and we were soon surrounded by some twenty women, all dressed in their vibrant garments. They wore royal blue tunics with arms of red, green, black, yellow and white horizontal bands. Their pants were light blue above the knee and pink below. Exquisite embroidered aprons hung on their front side, tied at the back of their waists with a large red knot. Curiously, their headdress resembled Mexican sombreros, black on top with a red, upturned brim. A man appeared from a mud-brick house, produced a menu, and announced that we were welcome to eat a 10 course meal in his house. At 60 RMB ($10) it seemed quite expensive, but he insisted we would be eating genuine Tu specialties.

We sat cross-legged on a Chinese bed-platform called a *kang* on which sat a short wooden table. The inner walls of the mud-brick house had originally been plastered white but now a monstrous multi-coloured patch of mould spread out like a pattern of a large tree. I suspect that the state of the room would have most Canadians' stomachs churning but Tony and I were elated to be there and ready to eat. The meal certainly was a treat and included tree moss, two types of unusual but savoury bread, and a salty, milky tea similar to that drunk by Mongolians, Tibetans, and Uyghurs. With the meal came a tray on which three small glasses of barley liquor were placed. We were instructed to shoot back the three glasses at once, to which there were cries of delight from the crowd of women who had followed us into the small room to watch us eat. The trays were endless and because they came in sets of three it was fairly easy to keep track of how much we had drank.

By the end of the meal Tony and I had knocked back eight trays each, 24 shots in total. When one last tray came out we declined, as we had for the previous several, and soon negotiated a compromise. We would share the tray with our host. We paid the bill, which turned out to be spectacular value considering the food and drink, I purchased a bag and wall hanging for Sara and Hanna and we stumbled out with more women following along.

Tony with Tu women, Qinghai.

In the centre of the village we were treated to an interesting dance/show that involved a pole and chains and men and women swinging around it acrobatically. When a car pulled up the dirt track full of Chinese, the Tu villagers swarmed them, and we made our escape up a terraced hillside and threw ourselves down on the golden earth. After a glassy-eyed glance over the beautiful valley, I had one of the most pleasant naps of my life.

That may have been the most memorable part of the trip if we had not had such an amazing experience as we did at the Kumbum monastery. Unlike Labrang Monastery (*La bu leng si* in Chinese) at Xiahe, in neighbouring Gansu province, Kumbum does not get many foreign visitors. We were the only visible foreigners at this particular time in the sleepy town, built below the monastery, and we got a double room with a view of the monastery and its green surroundings for a pricey 150 RMB (about 30 dollars).

The monastery and town was a mix of nearly 1000 monks, Tibetan and Mongolian pilgrims, and Chinese visitors. I don't recall how we met him but we became acquainted with a handsome young Tibetan monk named Norbu who invited us to his quarters for tea and *tsampa*. The tea was salty and greasy from the yak butter added to it, but I found it reasonably good.

Tsampa is prepared by taking a lump of yak butter, a handful of barley flour, a splash of tea, and mixing it up, kneading it by hand into a ball. You then munch on it raw, like you did when you stole a glob of cookie dough as a child. In Lhasa, the previous summer, we found that eight month old Hanna enjoyed a ball or two of *tsampa*.

Norbu shared a room, whose walls were covered in Chinese newsprint, with another young monk, and together the four of us conversed in broken Chinese. We could recognize their strong Tibetan accents and other older monks I encountered at Kumbum could not speak Chinese at all.

Talk soon got onto politics and, inevitably, the Dalai Lama's name came up. The two monks desperately wanted to know what we in the West knew of Tibet and its history, and Norbu asked me to send him English books about Tibet. There where no photos of the Dalai Lama anywhere at Kumbum, in stark contrast to what I had seen in Western Sichuan in 1994 and at Labrang in 1996. Obviously there had been a crackdown since then.

Tibetan prayers written on animal bones, Kumbum monastery.

His Holiness was public enemy number one in the eyes of the Chinese government, and indeed also for many, if not most Chinese, who see him as an evil 'splittist' in cahoots with foreigners and out to ruin China. As part of the campaign to discredit him, the Chinese government-controlled media refers to him as simply 'Dalai' and to the Tibetan government-in-exile as 'the Dalai Clique'.

I told the monks I had been to Dharmasala, India, where the Tibetan government-in-exile has settled, and to Sikkim, Darjeeling, and Kalimpong, in North East India where many Tibetan refugees and prominent former officials now live. I knew that the Dalai Lama was born in Qinghai (or *Amdo* to the Tibetans) and the monks told me that yes, his birthplace was not far.

'*Nimen qu guo le ma*? Have you been there,' I asked.

Everybody's eyes lit up as we concocted a plan simultaneously.

The monks, who live without money, would arrange a ride and we would pay for it. So for 400 RMB Tony and I and four young Tibetan monks in maroon robes squeezed into a tiny van, the kind the Chinese call a *mian bao che*—a loaf of bread, so named for its appearance—and set off into the countryside. It took several hours to get there. The scenery was fantastic and I was fascinated that each of the villages that we passed was Chinese in style, not at all Tibetan. The Dalai Lama was from virtually the northernmost extent of the Tibetan world, where pockets of Tibetans were ethnic islands dispersed among the Chinese and other groups such as Mongol, Kazakh, Salar, Tu, and Hui. The monks seemed very much like normal young men, singing along to Tibetan pop songs played on the tape deck by the Tibetan driver.

At one point, the view of blooming rapeseed fields was incredible and we stopped for a photo. I could never forget the sight; the sharp contrasts of the monks' maroon robes before the bright yellow of the rape fields, under a sky a deeper blue than ever seen in eastern China. The *chögu,* a sash the Tibetan monks wear over their shoulders, matched almost perfectly the yellow of the rapeseed.

Several hours into the ride we casually turned in to a village that had nothing indicating it was unusual. In fact, it didn't look Tibetan in any way. The simple farmhouses were all local Chinese style: flat-roofed mud-brick or plaster covered brick rectangular buildings of one or two stories. Perhaps two hundred villagers lived amongst sparse but tall trees—I can't recall their species. The village sat at the edge of a steep slope that was terraced and covered in green fields. I doubted that this was Taktser, the Dalai Lama's hometown. The *mian bao che* stopped and one of the monks walked hurriedly up to a house, enclosed in a simple undecorated wall, like virtually every other house in the area. The monk returned, and we all piled out of the *mian bao che* and were hustled up to the house. Although we were out in the open and plain to see, there was nobody around and I distinctly remember feeling that we were on a covert mission; we could be caught and charged with a crime at any moment.

Still, I was doubtful. First of all, how probable was it that the home of the Dalai Lama, a supposed enemy of the Chinese nation, was left undisturbed? I would have expected PSB officers to be lurking around or to have seen a policeman stationed outside. Instead, we were left alone as we entered through a large wooden door where we met a simply dressed woman in a pink shirt and plain dark slacks who, we were told, was a cousin of the Dalai Lama. The courtyard was made of plain, uneven bricks and still showed no sign of any particular significance. Coloured prayer flags fluttered on strings attached to a pole in the centre of the courtyard but otherwise the impression to a visitor was of a very ordinary local courtyard and home.

We were led into a living room of bare concrete that contained nothing more than simple wooden furniture. On the tables and walls were old black and white family photos. In the photos we could see the young child Tenzin Gyatso, who would be pronounced an incarnation of Buddha himself and become the God-King of the Tibetans: the Dalai Lama. It was bizarre to think that this was his living room, so simple and real, in sharp contrast to his later living quarters in the Potala palace in Lhasa.

The next room, we were told, was the room where His Holiness was actually born, and in the room a large prayer wheel, the size that one finds around the perimeter of large Tibetan monasteries, perhaps one metre in diameter, stood directly in the centre. The prayer wheel was draped in alternating yellow and white kata scarves. Several thankas, Buddhist paintings, hung on the filthy walls. The room contained nothing else. Silently, Tony and I followed protocol, passing clockwise around the wheel while turning it, awestruck. I was acutely aware that we were doing and seeing something so extraordinary that we would never, in our whole lives, meet anyone else who had shared this experience.

I was last in the queue and took the opportunity to snap a quick photo before I exited, being careful to not be seen by our Tibetan hosts. I wasn't sure if photos were acceptable but I made a split second decision to take one anyway. It is the only photo I have from the inside of the Dalai Lama's first home.

Prayer wheel that marks the birthplace of the Dalai Lama.

We were then led back through the courtyard to a staircase that went to the second floor. I'm not a religious person and can't even call myself spiritual. In the hundreds of churches, mosques, synagogues, pagodas, and temples that I have visited from all the major faiths I have never felt moved. Not in the Cathedrals of St. Peter or St. Paul, not in Istanbul's Blue Mosque or in St. Sophia's, not in the Golden Temple at Amritsar, nor at Angkor Wat or Bagan, and certainly not at the Potala in Lhasa. But as I ascended the steps, not knowing what I would see, I was moved to tears by an inner stirring. I fought the emotion, biting my lip and rationalizing in my agnostic way, but it was powerful and overwhelming. I still can't explain how or why I was so moved. There was no Hollywood soundtrack to cause tears to well up, and no words were spoken; as far as I can tell it was the pure and intense energy of the place that affected me.

At the top of the stairs we turned to see the four monks and our driver prostrating on the ground in front of a room set up as a shrine for the Dalai Lama, a photo of him at its centre. Not sure how to act, Tony and I instinctively stood back and tried not to intrude on what was clearly a most significant moment for the five men we had travelled with.

The whole time we had probably spent not more than ten minutes in the house, but it is a memory that I will take to my grave. I have read fairly extensively about Tibet, including numerous histories and travelogues. Never have I heard of anyone who had the experience of being in the Dalai Lama's childhood home. I still find it remarkable that the place exists as it does, unknown to China and the world, yet clearly known to a select group of Tibetans.

It seemed relatively easy for our monk friends to find it, yet they had never been before. Clearly, the house is kept as a holy shrine, yet it remains underground. How do they prevent pilgrims from flocking to the place from near and far as pious Tibetans do at so many other holy sites? I wouldn't blame anyone for questioning the credibility of this story. All

I can say is that it happened just as I have described, to which Tony and Norbu can attest.

The experience moved the Tibetans so profoundly that they didn't speak for some time after. We drove stealthily out of the village then suddenly stopped, the monks got out and Tony and I followed them up a dirt track that led to a hill top. On hill tops and passes Tibetans pile stones and erect prayer flags and yell something that sounds to me like 'woop a solo!' On this hill, just below the prayer flags and stones, we sat in silence and looked down upon the village of Taktser, whose Chinese name to this day I don't know. I never did know which direction we were travelling and couldn't find it on a map for the life of me.

Ceremoniously, Norbu presented Tony and I each with a yellow silk *kata* scarve and put them around our necks, and we all sat in a state of stillness for perhaps twenty minutes. The quiet contemplation continued for the remainder of the trip back to Kumbum. These were sombre monks, not at all the same lively boys we had travelled up with, just an hour earlier.

The monks look out over Takster in quiet contemplation.

Tony and I discussed the day with interest. I admitted the intense emotion I felt just before seeing the shrine to Tony but he, a former Mormon and then an avid reader of Nietzsche, had not felt anything near what I did. Regardless, I'm sure it remains a powerful and lasting memory for him too, being part of the 'Dalai Clique' for a day.

During our simple discussions of Tibet, Norbu asked me if I could send him some books on Tibetan history, written in English. He was no fool; it was clear that their history had been white-washed in the Chinese texts. I promised that I would, although I really had no idea how I could deliver the books. Kumbum, after all, may as well have been Timbuktu in terms of awkward locations. One doesn't find themselves just 'passing by' on route to somewhere else.

A year or so later I got a strange message at work. I had received a phone call from a *waiguoren*—a foreigner. The Chinese history teacher who shared our office explained that she had taken the call, and that the foreigner had called from Ningbo, a province in Western China. I was thoroughly confused. I didn't know anybody in Ningbo, let alone any foreigners. What was this person's name? She didn't know. The mystery *waiguoren* left a phone number but it didn't work when I tried to call. My Chinese colleague helped by calling the phone operator who explained that the area code was not from Ningbo, furthering the mystery.

Some months later, I received a letter from Norbu. Written in broken English, it revealed that it was he who had called me. Being a Tibetan educated in a monastery, rather than a school, meant that his Chinese sounded very much like a foreigner's accent to my Chinese colleague. His Chinese name, a transliteration from Tibetan, sounds very much like the province Ningbo. The confusion was further exacerbated by the manner in which the Chinese explain who is calling on the phone. If I was to call a company located in Beijing and I was dialling from Dalian I would say '*Ni hao, wo shi Dalian*'—'I *am* Dalian' rather than saying 'I am calling *from* Dalian'. From the letter I was able to put two and two together and figured out that my Chinese colleague had misunderstood Norbu telling his name to mean he was calling from Ningbo. The mystery was solved and Norbu reiterated in his letter that he would very much like me to bring him some English language books on Tibet and Tibetan history. Unfortunately, I had no plans to return to Qinghai.

Two years later I did return to Kumbum, this time traveling overland from Urumqi, via Turpan, Hami, Dunhuang, and Golmud, with Sara and our children, my father, my sister, and my mother-in-law. My dad and I walked the monastery from end to end, knocking on doors and asking for Norbu. It took a couple of hours but after a monk with a cell phone and a VW Santana (strangely yes, there was a car in the monastery!) helped out, we tracked down Norbu and I gave him the books I had promised him, purchased from the fantastic used book stores in Bangkok, Thailand.

The tour of Kumbum that he gave us was outstanding and we got backroom access to high ranking monks performing various Buddhist rites and rituals. Norbu explained that we were to meet him the next morning and that there was to be a big performance of some kind.

When we met him, we were simply instructed to sit on the empty stone steps on the edge of a courtyard about the size of a basketball court. We couldn't understand why we were sitting alone but the perimeter of the courtyard soon began to fill with pilgrims, until it was bursting at its seams. People were practically standing on each other to get a view. And what a view Norbu had secured for us! We had front and centre seats for a magical display of costumed dances by monks of all ages, children of six or so years to the elderly. The climax seemed to be a grizzly re-enactment or role play of a child being slaughtered. The whole time the dances were accompanied by monk musicians on the courtyard floor and the low haunting bellows of enormous horns blown on the surrounding rooftops.

When the head lama, believed to be an incarnation of Tsong Khapa—the monk who established the Yellow Hat sect of Tibetan Buddhism—appeared, pandemonium ensued. Pilgrims, who had travelled from the grasslands and barren plateau to the south, pushed their way through the throngs of people and tried to touch the lama, or prostrated in front of him. Several years later I read an account by a French doctor who passed through Kumbum in the 1930s who witnessed exactly the same thing. Norbu and Kumbum had delivered another magical experience.

I have been interested in Tibet since I read *Tintin in Tibet* as a boy. Although I am certainly not an expert on the subject, my reasonably extensive reading on Tibet, together with my travel experiences, allows me to make a fair commentary on the 'issue' of Tibet.

I have seen a considerable amount of greater Tibet. In 1994 my first backpacking trip to China took me to Zhongdian, now absurdly, and annoyingly, renamed *shang ge li la*—Shangrila—by the Chinese government. From there I travelled through a region that was then off limits to foreigners in China, although that's not to say others weren't doing it. There were a couple of foreigners who attempted the route from Western Yunnan to Sichuan through the Tibetan traditional province of Kham everyday, but many times they were prevented from getting on buses, detained, and sometimes fined by the *gong an*—the PSB, or Public Security Bureau. In any case, I, along with five others, travelled this route from Zhongdian to Xiancheng, to Litang, and finally down to Kangding. I was twenty-two at the time. It was incredible.

Litang is one of the highest towns in the world and even sleeping is difficult at that altitude. It happened to be Halloween and we decided to buy a pumpkin in the market. Using a Swiss Army Knife, we took turns, each of us designing and cutting one of the facial features of a Jack O' Lantern. We went for supper on the main road and set up the Jack O' Lantern with a candle in it at our table facing the street. Perplexed Khampas, tall nomadic warrior Tibetans with red wool braided into their long hair and gold teeth smiles, stopped to examine this bizarre creature. It was a riot. The altitude and our celebratory *pijiu* made for a terrible night's sleep and I was kept up by an asthmatic American traveller who gasped the whole night in a bed next to me. I couldn't complain, I was literally on top of the world, and my lumpy, string bed cost just five *renminbi*—less than one dollar.

The next morning half of our group set off together on another epic bus ride. The bone rattling bus rides were horrifyingly dangerous, but somehow awesome too. I slumped nearly horizontally in the back row of the bus, with just one other passenger, a monk, and fell asleep, my Halloween hangover in full force.

My nap ended abruptly when I was jolted awake by gunshots. Jerking up, I saw a Khampa with a rifle leaning across two people and firing out the window of the moving bus. Were we in a gunfight with Tibetan bandits? Had we stumbled upon an insurrection of some kind? As it turns out, a wolf had run across the road and was scampering off into the distance. Many of the Khampa nomads who flagged down the buses in the middle of nowhere carried their rifles on the bus and casually placed them up on the luggage rack, now a gun rack. This guy had seen a four legged version of a couple hundred *renminbi* and thought he had better give it a try. The funny thing is, nobody took much notice and the bus continued on at the same pace. In the markets in these towns there were always a few skins and furs hanging for sale from various animals, especially wild cats, undoubtedly some of these were the endangered snow leopard.

Those bus trips through Tibetan country were so memorable: valleys of yellowing larch forest reminiscent of British Columbia's Kootenays, then barren plateau, then back to familiar boreal forest, as we descended into Sichuan, home of spicy hot pot and giant pandas. Our descent was hampered by a rock fall, and all the men piled out to help clear a path through the rocks. No sooner had we done so, and the bus moved past the obstacle, a rumbling was heard above, and large boulders came barrelling down the cliff just ten metres or so behind me. That trip through Kham, or Eastern Tibet, fuelled a growing interest in Tibet and Tibetans.

In 1995 after a short stint teaching ESL in Japan, another Asian backpacking trip took me through the Tibetan refugee populations of Darjeeling, Kalimpong, and Sikkim. I should be clear that I'm not one who has romanticized Tibetan Buddhism. In Kham, I was astonished by the aggressive begging of some monks and at the Rumtek monastery, across the valley from Gangkok, Sikkim, it bothered me to see monks harshly kicking dogs. I was probably more disturbed by the Indian military presence in the region, however, even having armed soldiers in the monastery itself. In Sikkim, pages of your passport are taken up by ceaseless stamping at the ubiquitous police check points on all the roads. Compared to the Chinese, the Indians allowed foreigners more freedom to travel but were no less concerned about this sensitive region.

The next stop was Dharmasala, the seat of the Dalai Lama and the Tibetan government-in-exile. Swept up in the spirit of the place I bought a 'Free Tibet' T-Shirt. From there I passed through Indian Punjab into Pakistan and up and over the Karakoram pass, crossing into China at Tashkorgan, wearing my 'Free Tibet' T-shirt inside-out so it wouldn't be seen in my bag if it was searched. After crossing the Taklamakan and Gobi deserts of Xinjiang, I arrived back in the Tibetan world at Labrang Monastery in Xiahe, Gansu. There I spent a glorious afternoon sitting in the hillsides, chatting and miming with the pilgrims who were camped there.

In 1999, Sara and I, with eight month old baby Hanna, flew up to Lhasa from Chengdu. We loved every minute of our time in the Yarlung Valley, except the inevitable altitude sickness. Incidentally, the Chinese all thought us insane for taking a baby to Tibet, but Hanna seemed to fare the best of the lot of us. I was dizzy and had headaches, Sara the same, plus she was afflicted with a mysterious ailment she called 'sulphur burps,' while our friend Linda fainted in a filthy toilet stall, the poor thing.

These experiences, together with reading anything I could ever find on Tibet, give me a confidence to step up on my soap box and bellow to all about how it is and how it should be in Tibet.

Here goes...

What is Tibet? A simple question, but it is one that readers may wonder about. Many in the West may know of Tibet only from the Free Tibet rallies that pop up periodically in the streets of Canada, the US, or Europe, and from the celebrities who push the cause: Uma Thurman, Richard Gere, and the Beastie Boys, to name a few. Some may know of Tibet from religious and spiritual searching/learning that led them to the Dalai Lama, the current figurehead of Tibetan Buddhism—although in theory he is only the head of the Gelug-pa (AKA the Yellow Hat) sect—and the former paramount political leader of Tibet, currently the figurehead at the top of the Tibetan government-in-exile, located in India at Dharamsala.

As it stands today, Tibet is essentially a province of the People's Republic of China. On a Chinese map it reads 'Xi Zang Zi Zhi Qu,' meaning Tibet Autonomous Region, one of five provinces in China with 'autonomous' designation. The others are Xinjiang—home of the Uyghurs—, Inner Mongolia, Ningxia—set aside for the Hui Muslim minority—, and Guangxi—for the Zhuang nation.

Readers may wonder to what extent Tibet Autonomous Region is autonomous. From a Chinese perspective, Tibet and Tibetans enjoy many benefits. They are allowed two children because they have official minority status in China. This means that although the Han Chinese are migrating to Tibet in large numbers and may soon outnumber the Tibetans in Tibet, as they already have in the other autonomous regions, in due time the Tibetan population in China should grow at a faster rate than the Han Chinese. What effect this may have on their struggle to keep their culture and identity is as yet unknown.

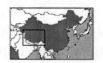

Ethnic and Cultural Tibet

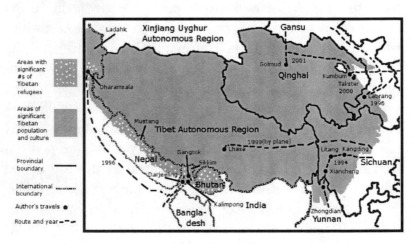

Tibetans also enjoy self government, that is, Tibetans have the right and power to govern themselves, according to the Chinese constitution. Like the other autonomous regions, the governor is to be from the designated ethnic nationality...but wait just a minute! Although the governor of Tibet—and this is true of governors of all Chinese provinces—is the *de jure* leader and policy maker, *de facto* power resides with the secretary of the provincial Communist party office. In this case, as in all the 'autonomous' regions, the party secretary is Han Chinese. This means that Tibet is run, at the highest level, by a Han Chinese rather than a Tibetan. Furthermore, the current paramount leader does not, by his own admission, speak any Tibetan and like the current President of the People's Republic of China, Hu Jintao, who was once a party boss in Tibet, gained a reputation for being a tough ass, declaring martial law in 2008 like Hu did in 1989, during the 30th anniversary of the 1959 uprising in Tibet.

The Chinese people don't see this as unusual, outrageous, or problematic; they see it as the way it is. Canadians couldn't imagine Quebec being run by non-Quebecers, never mind anyone other than a Francophone Quebecois. Indeed Canadians can't even elect a prime minister unless he or she can debate in French on national TV. It is no surprise then that Canadians and other Westerners would view the 'autonomy' in Tibet as a farce. The Chinese, on the other hand, see power held by the folks in Beijing as being the norm. This is the way it is in their province too, why would it be any different in Tibet?

Of course, democracy doesn't exist anywhere in China at the level of decision making that Westerners are accustomed to. So, while villagers may elect a village chief, the policies that affect the population as a whole are made by outsiders, men who are essentially illiterate in the local language, and therefore susceptible to the ignorant and condescending administrative style of an outsider who is unable to communicate with common people. True, many Tibetans now speak Mandarin, but these are only the educated, urban folk. The rural Tibetans remain a world apart.

And what of the purported genocide in Tibet? Again, perspective comes into play. Speaking from a legal perspective, genocide hasn't occurred because the Tibetan nation still exists, with a healthy population of millions, able and free to live in their homeland. And there is little evidence to suggest that the Chinese government or any significant number of Chinese people want to rid themselves of Tibet or Tibetans. In fact, the government and its propaganda apparatchik work overtime to convince 1.3 billion people that Tibetans are a valued and important part of their happy family of 56 nations. They even went as far as renaming the Chinese translation of Hergé's classic children's book Tintin in Tibet as *Ding Ding Zai Zhongguo Xizang*—Tintin in China's Tibet. That was upsetting. Don't mess with my Tintin!

When we hear the word genocide we naturally think of the NAZI holocaust of the Jews and their hideous anti-Jewish propaganda and gory means of killing mass numbers of Jews in concentration camps. This is, unequivocally, not the case in Tibet. In Canada, we have heard the word genocide thrown about when referring to the treatment of various First Nations peoples. The Indian Act, residential schools, a government propensity for policies of assimilation, and the undeniable racism from Euro- and other hyphenated Canadians towards aboriginal people, are the general, but considerable evidence to support such claims. Facts are facts: The First Nations in Canada are living in sub-standard conditions— Canadian standards that is—and yet they, and we, can not fall back on the excuse that 'at least they are happy and living the way they choose'. No, aboriginal people in Canada are lingering in a state of identity crisis; neither proud nations with intact languages and traditions, nor fully fledged Canadians, immersed and integrated into modern Canadian society. A visit to a few of the less fortunate reserves will convince anyone of that. Despite the sad state of affairs on the reserves of many Canadian First Nations, Canadians in general have rejected the claim that genocide has occurred, or was ever intended. We were mistaken but we were not ill-intentioned, or so goes the conventional wisdom in Canada.

Fathers and children, Lhasa, 1999.

Given the above point, I can no longer accept the harsh criticism of China by the West on the Tibet issue. Is what is happening in Tibet sad, when one considers the cultural loss, the modernization, the influx of the Chinese, the sinicization of Tibet? Yes, it is sad, but no sadder than what has happened in our own glorious lands. Perhaps we are too parochial to see that we Canadians could be viewed as a sad lot by other higher and mightier nations, concerned about the Americanization of Canada, the loss of our culture, the seemingly impending '51ˢᵗ state' status.

But I've been too audacious and I don't mean seriously to compare Canada and Tibet. After all Canada has, or had, sovereignty, and further, Canadians elect their leadership and can and do change it when they don't like the course they are taking.

The Tibetans, on the other hand, are very much an occupied people. The Chinese point to the great noble advances in Tibet since the 'peaceful liberation'; road building, education of the masses, breaking down the institutions of a feudal serfdom. Although nearly every Chinese I've met is fond of the expression 'everything has two sides' they can't see that these great roads that link Tibet with the outside, and modern, world, all lead to China, a rather insular place, even today. The roads don't go where the Tibetans decide they should go, which may or may not be primarily to China. India and Nepal, if the Tibetans were given a choice, may also prove today, as they were in the past, key partners in trade, cultural movement, and more.

I'm a teacher and I can't argue against education, but there is, again, the argument that the Tibetans could, or should, be the agents of decision making. What language should they be taught in? What choices do they have to learn or not learn particular languages? I am under the impression that many Tibetans send their children to the monasteries today because not only do they clothe and feed them, but they also educate them in a traditional Tibetan way. They learn Tibetan, and they learn to be Tibetan, through religious study. As an agnostic, I shouldn't rant too long about the benefits of religion, but the Chinese have been programmed to be anti-religious by sixty years of communist propaganda so it's not surprising that they don't get the appeal of Tibetan Buddhism.

The Chinese also can't see beyond the fact that Tibet was a feudal society and that they 'liberated' them from this hell. By all accounts, traditional Tibet was a nasty place for common folk, but so was China, wasn't it? They don't know that the Dalai Lama himself saw the plight of the commoner as an important issue and that he planned and hoped to implement democratic reforms. The problem is the Chinese we talk to today about Tibet are comparing the reality of today with a reality from a half century ago; apples and oranges. To top it off, they think anything the Dalai Lama says is a pack of lies. We Westerners, who might believe that his words are genuine, are gullible fools or the agents who have propped up the 'evil splittist,' and what can you say to that? I've given up arguing with Chinese about Tibet. I believe in the right to self-determination. They don't, unless you mean the PRC's right to self-determination—'non-interference in domestic affairs' is their modern mantra.

One area of agreement is that Tibet was, prior to the occupation/liberation, a feudal society in which, like in all feudal societies, the elites and the clergy prospered on the backs of the serfs, who were in essence slaves. The disagreement about the past arises when Tibet's historical claims to autonomy are questioned. The classic Chinese response to Tibetan independence claims is that Tibet is, and always was, Chinese, meaning that it was under Chinese control, a part of a sovereign China. The 'and always was' part is usually further articulated to mean going back to the Tang dynasty, some thousand years ago, when the Chinese Princess Wen Cheng was sent out to marry the Tibetan king, Songtsän Gampo. The Chinese see this marriage as the defining moment in the harmonious future that the two nations would subsequently share. The Chinese don't know, of course, that the Tibetan king quite enjoyed marrying ladies and supposedly married five women, including a Nepalese princess. This makes sense to me. If I were a Tibetan king and felt like marrying five women I think I too would take three Tibetans (but not locals, they should be from various Tibetan tribes of border regions to strengthen our position on the frontiers), a Chinese, and Nepalese, to expand the political and business interests of my people. I believe that Songtsän Gampo's marriages speak volumes about the reality of Tibet in the past; that it was, for a considerable time, independent of other's control, that China was important to Tibet for trade, and that Nepal and India were equally important. This was, and is, a geopolitical reality for Tibet.

What of Tibet's future? I was surprised to read recently that the renowned American Tibetologist, Robert Thurman (father of actress Uma) believes the Chinese leadership is coming around and will one day come to terms with the Dalai Lama's conciliatory revision of his goal for his nation. He has not called for Tibetan independence for decades now, instead preferring—or perhaps it is just a more practical change of approach—a greater semblance of autonomy for Tibet within the PRC. The Dalai Lama's compromise is not beyond the realm of possibility though. Hong Kong and Macau, since 1997 and 1999 respectively, have enjoyed Special Administrative Region (SAR) status. Why not something similar for Tibet? I don't want to appear too naïve and I understand that China had to give SAR status to Hong Kong and Macau otherwise they wouldn't have been 'handed over'. Remember the Falklands War? It was largely seen in the '80s as a warning to China that Britain wouldn't necessarily give up on old colonies. To bring them back to the motherland it was necessary to compromise.

Tibet, on the other hand, is already under China's firm grip, so there is no impending need to compromise. China doesn't want to appear soft, and the unity of the 56 nations is of paramount importance to the Communist Party—it's been part of their propaganda package for years. I don't share Robert Thurman's optimism.

First of all, the Chinese government simply is not savvy enough in terms of managing its international image. Time and time again we have witnessed their blunders on the international stage; the mishandling of, and lying about, the disease SARS in 2003 is a classic example and more recently, their inability to prevent tainted food products from killing their own people and from being exported to the West. In the lead-up to the 2008 Olympics, when the whole world was watching, they flopped again. Whether or not we should believe the government's line that the 2008 uprisings in Lhasa were orchestrated by foreign interests and designed to discredit and embarrass China is not important. The point is, Chinese leadership had a golden opportunity to solve the Tibet issue and change forever their blighted international image. Imagine the fanfare and celebration if the Dalai Lama had appeared in Beijing for the opening ceremony of the Olympics? They missed out, and ultimately I think they are simply going to wait until he passes away.

The 15th Dalai Lama will be so controversial—will he be found in China or in the exiled Tibetan population?—and besides, he will need another twenty years to develop into an adult who is able to negotiate on behalf of his people. Some supporters of the Tibetan cause have seen hope in the young Karmapa, the third from the top in Tibetan Buddhism circles.

From the Kagyu sect, AKA the Black Hats, he fled to India a few years ago at the age of 17. Following the Lhasa riots in 2008 the Chinese government dug up the Panchen Lama, a teenager who was the focus of a bizarre story in the mid 1990s.

The Panchen Lama, who traditionally resided in Shigatse, Tibet's second largest town, was number two in the Yellow Hat sect and, although the Panchen and Dalai Lamas were rivals in some political struggles in the past, they played a role in determining each other's rightful incarnation. The Communist Party, which claims to be not at all interested in religious happenings, all of a sudden decided it needed to be involved in determining just who exactly the rightful Panchen Lama was. As the story goes, the Dalai Lama had some inside info on who the new young fellow was and he gave his blessing and agreement publicly, much to the chagrin of the Chinese leadership. They then did an about face and decided the Panchen was actually another boy. The first boy disappeared—the authorities claim he is living peacefully in Lhasa but there is no known evidence of this—and the new boy was sent off to be raised properly, mostly in Beijing, some 3000 km from Shigatse.

Growing up in Beijing, under the tutelage of the central government authorities, it's not surprising that the teenage Panchen Lama is willing to add pro-China and pro-Communist Party nonsense to his public speeches, even when he is attending religious conferences. He no doubt is either told to say it or more likely is handed a pre-written speech. That's standard practice in China, to be handed something to read publicly. Neither the speakers nor the audience take any stock in what is being said, they are so accustomed to hearing propaganda, not just from government but from companies, schools, or other institutions. The poor Panchen, he's got no choice.

When I last passed through Tibetan areas, where the Dalai Lama's photos were banned, most shops had shrines with photos of the Panchen Lama, but it was not the current Panchen in most of the photos, rather it was the past Panchen. When asked where his photo was, people told me they didn't consider him the real deal.

In the end, I'm left feeling that the Tibetans will certainly not get their independence and I don't believe they will enjoy further autonomy, unless of course the entirety of China changes so radically. But this is not necessarily a tragedy. After visiting Tibet I feel that their identity is strong. Although the Chinese influence is pervasive, and in some cases offensive—like renaming the street in front of the Potala palace Beijing Road—there is no doubt in my mind that the Tibetan nation will survive and, in all likelihood, will retain more of its traditions than the Han nation does. The world is changing fast and all nations' cultures are increasingly affected by foreign influences. These influences prompt the nations' identities to evolve in particular ways. The Tibetans of tomorrow will not be the Tibetans of the past but nor too, will Canadians or Chinese of the future be those that we know now.

12

An evening at Shwedagon Pagoda, Myanmar.

God's Country

In 2001, a young fellow by the name of Chris Daniher showed up in Dalian and for the first few months—the honeymoon stage of culture shock—he could be heard exclaiming several times a day 'This is God's country!'

When Daniher popped open a 620 ml bottle of *Kailong Pijiu*—Keller Beer—and paid 1.8 RMB, it was God's country. When he found bottles of Qingdao whiskey for 12 RMB, it was definitely God's country. When he bought bags full of vegetables at the market and the *Chaoxian*—Korean-Chinese—grocer told him the price, which amounted to something payable with a single Canadian coin, it was God's country. When he and his wife Shawn taxied across our town for dinner and the fare was less than bus fare for one at home, it was God's country, and when they got the bill for the outstanding feast of spicy ribs, sizzling beef, broccoli and potatoes, sweet and sour pork with pineapple, bamboo rice, fried steamed buns drenched in condensed milk for desert, and all washed down with an endless supply of lager and the bill per person was 25 RMB, well, what else could it be but God's country?

You get the picture, God's country is cheap. There is no question that is one of the major reasons we have stayed in China for over a decade. When we vacation in Canada in the summers I just cringe every time I have to pay for anything. It seems outrageous to me that an unhealthy and bland lunch for the family in a greasy spoon in small town British Columbia costs me forty dollars with a tip. In contrast, we can feed our whole family at *Lao Ma Hundun*—Old Ma's Wontons—for three dollars. The other day we gathered in a fancy BBQ restaurant for a friend's birthday where we feasted on a variety of barbequed meat and had several good vegetable and tofu dishes, all of course with beer, and the bill came to 100 RMB each. People were outraged. How the heck did it get so expensive? Jeez, that's nearly fifteen dollars!

If something goes wrong with the car or motorcycle and the fix is simply replacing a hose or a small part, the bill might be as low as two dollars and you are left wondering how it could possibly be so cheap. I have had oil changes that include four litres of oil and it comes out cheaper than buying a single litre of oil in Canada.

There is no question that some things in China are simply not as convenient as in Canada, but in many cases the service and convenience is extraordinary. In our housing complex, a family originally from Inner Mongolia operated a small corner store similar to the classic 'Chinese corner store' in towns all over North America. Their location was conveniently located on the first floor of the building we lived in. If you felt too lazy to walk down six flights to fetch your groceries yourself, you could call them up on the phone and they would deliver whatever you wanted. There was no delivery charge or minimum order. Some folks I know even had the gall to call down for a single chocolate bar and a bottle of pop.

And then there are the numerous ways you can live the luxurious life of pleasure and leisure in China without having to stretch the pocket book. Massages quickly become part of an expat's weekly routine. A foot massage, depending on where you go, can cost as little as three dollars for an hour. In a fancier establishment, or a hotel, it might cost ten dollars for an hour. Sometimes excruciatingly painful, sometimes unbearably ticklish, but overall when it is done it is plain and simply the most relaxing experience you can have. The foot massage starts with your feet soaking in a hot broth of water, tea, and herbs. In one of our favourite local places while your feet are soaking the masseuses and masseurs loosen you up with a head, neck, arm and back massage. In our hectic life, juggling work and children and other commitments, Sara and I haven't taken nearly enough time out for such pleasures but whenever we do, we ask ourselves why we aren't doing it every week.

With very affordable hired help, *Ayi*, becomes part of every expat's family. Readers from North America or Europe might find it shocking, and Sara certainly took a long time to get used to the idea of someone cleaning in her home. But the reality is, life is tough in China. Everyday things can be very stressful. Ayi makes it easier to deal with the steady inflow of dust, blowing through the windows from the deserts—this is called *deflation*, I tell my students—and the construction. She helps with the laundry, which is perpetually needing to be hung up to dry and then ironed and folded—there are no dryers to be found here. And when you need to get out for some socializing, Ayi is there to baby-sit. She's one of the family. We were lucky enough to find such a wonderful woman and we have stuck with each other for a decade; our children have grown up with a Chinese grandmother.

On the beach, Ngapali, Myanmar.

For me, one of the most incredible and valuable benefits of living and working in China, especially as a teacher, is the tremendous opportunities for travel. In addition to the far flung places within China we have had the chance to visit, we have made eleven tropical vacations in the past 12 years, having returned to Canada just once during a winter break. Just as northern China gets miserably cold we take a five-week holiday for Chinese New Year. What in the past we may have considered 'once in a lifetime' has become routine: finding Nemo in a coral reef; cruising a mangrove in Borneo on the lookout for giant Monitor Lizards and proboscis monkeys; climbing the ruins at Angkor Wat; dining on lobster and avocados at Myanmar's unknown beaches; island hopping in the Philippines; gazing across the Mekong River at Laos; getting married in Vietnam; riding elephants; even popping 'down under' to visit friends and family in Australia.

It probably sounds like I'm bragging but this *is* the life a humble teacher in China can lead, with a wife and two children in tow!

Winning 100 pesos betting on a cock fight, Samar, Philippines.

The author's fiancée enjoying a beer in a *menggu bao*, Dalai Lake.

Familymoon

Some would say we did it backwards; I think we did it right. Courtship, marriage, career, kids, in that order, that is how it is supposed to go, but life doesn't quite always work out the way Hollywood says it should. We certainly didn't follow an orthodox route, but in the modern world anything goes, right?

Sara and I both had lived with partners before we met. Things didn't work out with those people. And then we found ourselves preparing to be parents before we had careers in place. Plus, we'd only known each other a couple of months and hadn't lived together. When we set off for a life together in China I had no intentions of getting married. My parents were divorced and had remarried, thus marriage didn't seem necessary to me. Besides, after our daughter was born, it was official in my mind that we were a family, and Sara was my wife. I didn't need a legal piece of paper or a ceremony to tell me that. Hanna's birth was, in essence, that ceremony as far as I was concerned.

At 29, I had two kids and a wife threatening to get pregnant again. I felt our family was perfect as it was, although I am sure that if more children appeared I would love them just as much. A large family didn't seem to fit our lifestyle because travelling and working overseas gets more expensive with each child. Sara began telling me I should get a vasectomy if I didn't want any more kids. Apparently she was only joking—I took her seriously.

One afternoon while we were vacationing in Thailand, we all settled down for an afternoon nap in our hotel room in Phuket Town, on Thailand's famous and beautiful Phuket Island. I couldn't sleep, and kept hearing in my head Sara's warning about the inevitability of more children. It dawned on me that I could probably get a vasectomy in Phuket so I quietly slipped out of bed and got dressed without waking the family.

In the lobby, I asked the concierge to write the address of the nearest hospital for me in Thai script. Outside, I flagged down a motorcycle taxi and jumped on. In a few minutes I arrived at a small, local hospital. I know now that Phuket boasts an international clinic with an excellent reputation, similar to the famed Bumrumgrad hospital in Bangkok that lures medical tourists from around the world, but I didn't know that then, so in I went, rather optimistically, thinking that the place didn't look too bad.

It was simple and clean, especially compared to the hospitals in China, which are full of smoking people—I've actually been examined by a doctor with a cigarette hanging out of his mouth—and piles of ill-placed vomit that don't get cleaned up for hours. At the front desk, I asked in English to see a doctor about a vasectomy. I was seated in a waiting room for no more than a few minutes before a doctor invited me in for a consultation.

The doctor seemed surprised by my request and inquired about my reasons for wanting the procedure. I was 29 and already had two kids, I replied as a matter of fact. That seemed to satisfy him and he set up an appointment for 8 am the next morning. Back at the front desk, I asked how much it would cost. I didn't have insurance to cover an elective surgery like this. It was going to cost 1,500 Baht, or about $50. I am a noted cheapskate, how could I resist?

Instead of returning to the hotel, where the kids and Sara were still napping, I took the chance to visit an Internet bar and do some research on vasectomies. I had never actually considered one before that day and knew nothing about them. It is probably considered backwards by most people to make the appointment and then do the research, but anyway, that's what I did. In the net bar, I pulled up photos of the procedure. Thailand is well known as a safe haven for all manner of perverts and sexual deviants and I couldn't help but feel nervous and insecure about viewing graphic photos of male genitalia on my computer screen in a public Internet bar. I kept looking over my shoulder to see if anyone was watching. At least it was adult genitalia I was viewing. There was probably much worse to be seen on nearby computer screens, and no doubt elsewhere in the neighbourhood; more than one person warned us to take extra care of our children in Phuket Town, so prevalent are pedophiles.

I should interject and add here that I am an avid fan of hockey, and at this point hadn't seen a professional hockey

227

game played on TV for several years, since I had left Canada. Many times I was fooled by a channel found in Asia called Star Sports. They advertise NHL hockey games, but whenever I tune in the game is replaced by Formula One, tennis, or sailing. After researching vasectomies and coming to terms with the fact that I was to undergo this procedure the following morning, I met up with my good friend Darren Brown, a fellow teacher in Dalian. He and I excitedly discussed the fact that the local TV guide clearly showed that an NHL game was to be played at 8 am the following day, precisely the time I was to be under the knife. I told Brownie I would meet him in the hotel bar for the second period. I wasn't going to miss a hockey game, and the doctor assured me the vasectomy would only take 45 minutes or so.

So there I lay, at 8 am, on a hospital bed with a cloth placed over my face so I couldn't see what was happening. What I could hear and feel happening was five Thai doctors and nurses huddled around my nether regions, speaking the clickety-clack sounds of Thai. Anyone familiar with Thailand knows that every sentence seems to contain the sounds *Kaa* and *Kaap*! 'Holy Crap' was the sound I was hearing in my head. One of the lucky five got the job of shaving me in an area I normally wouldn't dare take a razor—evidently other people seem comfortable enough with this though, and I later learned that in China I became what is known as a q*ing long*, a clear dragon! Then I was given a couple of needles to the testicles, and let me tell you, that's not fun. On the bright side, it meant I could feel without pain, the slicing, chopping, tying, and sewing that happened next.

When it was done, I was sent off with a receipt and a 'enjoy your day' type of attitude. I didn't get any warnings about pain I might feel or what I should or shouldn't do. Out on the street in front of the hospital, I was in a surreal state of mind. I hadn't previously given the vasectomy much thought, but I was now aware that somehow I was no longer the same man. All of this was second thought to my immediate concern, which was getting back to the hotel to catch the second period of the hockey game. I felt a bit weak, a normal state of being after surgery, and I actually had no idea where I was, so walking was out of the question. I looked around for a taxi but didn't see one, which is unusual in most of Asia. So I returned by the same means of transport I had used to arrive, by motorcycle.

Numb Nuts, a term I have used in the past to refer to someone, shall we say, less than average in intellect, was a fair description for me for more than one reason that morning. Maybe the doctor's poor English was the reason he didn't tell me not to bounce my wounded testicles across town, on the back of a motorbike driven by the maddest of all elements in Asian society, the taxi driver. Or maybe I should have known better. Regardless, I arrived back at the hotel in one piece— although technically missing a piece or two—to find Brownie, Sara, and the kids waiting in the lobby. Brownie still tells the story of how I hobbled in, looking like a faint John Wayne, with a worried expression on my face.

'What are you doing here? Isn't the game on?' I demanded.

Once again, the game was pre-empted by a TV program deemed much more important by people who cared much less and most likely had their genitalia intact. It was precisely at that moment that the anaesthetic began to wear off.

Although Sara had been telling me to get a vasectomy, she claimed later she was just kidding, and her maternal instincts returned before long. Pretty soon there was talk of adopting a Chinese baby.

China is a major source of babies for adoptive parents from the West. Americans alone adopt up to 8,000 Chinese babies a year. We have seen the American adoptive parents *en masse* in Guangzhou's Shamian island district, a funky old colonial neighbourhood that is quiet and mostly pedestrian, located on the Pearl River. The American consulate is found there and so is Guangzhou's famous White Swan Hotel. Back in 1997, I was teaching ESL in Guangzhou and my company's main office was down on Shamian, and I began to notice quite a few foreign parents with baby strollers. It is unusual to see foreigners with babies in China and it struck me as odd. On closer inspection I saw that the babies were Chinese. Over the years, we passed through Guangzhou many times on our way in and out of China at Chinese New Year. We always stay in Shamian and have witnessed the thriving industries based on adopting Chinese babies. One of our favourite old restaurants on the river's edge—photos of Pierre Trudeau and Henry Kissinger indicate that others like Lucy's too—now has what surely is the world's largest pile of baby high-chairs and the menu now features food that caters to American kids, because many of the adopting parents bring their other kids with them. The touristy shops around the area now sell t-shirts with Chinese characters that say *ma ma, ba ba, lao lao, ye ye, di di, mei mei*—mother, father, grandma, grandpa, little brother, little sister—and so on. It's a pretty interesting sight to see, all of the excited new parents with their babies.

I can only imagine that there are similar groups located around each consulate or embassy from all the Western nations. In 2001, when we were down in Nanchang looking for the Chiang Jiang motorcycle factory, we happened across a group of thirty Belgians all adopting babies there.

Sara's adoption talk got more and more serious so I began looking into it. The cost, I found out, is astronomical, up to US $20,000 for a single child. I began to see the whole thing as a racket, human trafficking. After all, the costs that are in theory to be reimbursed to the hospitals and orphanages, for caring for the babies in their early days are minimal. I know how cheap a birth is in China, and staying in a government-run orphanage can't cost that much.

So who is getting all the cash? First, adopting parents are required to go through a recognized adoption agency in their home country. That means you are paying Western salaries to Americans or other nationalities to act as an unnecessary go-between. Then there is the adoption agency in China that handles all adoptions, the China Centre for Adoption Affairs. All levels of government in China are prone to corruption and, without a doubt, a lot of cash finds its way into officials' hands. Add to that legal fees on both sides and you are looking at an exorbitant amount of cash to buy a baby. I was, and still am, strongly opposed to supporting this kind of racket. My take is that if there are orphans that really do need homes and if I can help out, then fine, but I will not line people's pockets to 'buy' a human life. If I could not conceive my own child, perhaps I would feel differently, and I do not mean to condemn the people who adopt Chinese babies; I'm sure their intentions are good.

We heard that as legal residents of China the process should be cheaper, because we could deal directly with the China Centre for Adoption Affairs. Seeing how important this idea was for Sara, I began to take it seriously. One of the requirements is that adopting parents must be either single or married, but cannot be in a common law marriage, as we were. It was the prospect of adoption that first led me to plan to propose marriage to Sara.

If I was going to get legally married, I may as well try to pull off something decent and romantic, I thought. My work provided flights back home to Canada each summer but on a few occasions we took short summer trips in China before visiting Canada. That year, in the middle of the hysteria surrounding SARS—Severe Acute Respiratory Syndrome—, we planned a trip up to Inner Mongolia and the Russian border. My plan was to carry out a romantic proposal in a yurt or on the grasslands, but first I needed a ring.

I'm not a diamond ring kind of guy. To me, giving a diamond engagement ring is a horribly clichéd act in North American society, akin to giving a dozen red roses on Valentines Day, only much more expensive. I also don't see the sense in going into debt for a ring. Diamond or not, I had to find a ring, and in China finding something of decent quality is always a challenge.

When Hanna was first born I had a mother's ring custom made for Sara. It was platinum with three topaz—the birth stone for November—stones set around the Chinese character 家, pronounced *jia*, meaning family. It didn't turn out exactly like I had hoped, but it is a unique ring and Sara has worn it ever since. I wanted to find a ring that wasn't too glitzy—after all, I wasn't actually trying to impress her into marriage, we were already married in a sense—and Sara isn't a huge diamond type of girl. I hoped that Sara would appreciate a ring that somehow captured our life experiences that we had shared together. Our life together had primarily been in China, so something Chinese would be nice, but finding 'nice' in China is not always easy. Jewellery for sale in China tends to be gaudy, even tacky, and ostentatious. I knew I would have to wade through a lot of junk to find something I was happy with. Every market and mall in China has a jewellery section and there is no shortage of rings to choose from. Most are a similar style, and the gold is very yellow, which turned me off. There is plenty of white gold to choose from and I started to see a few rings I liked. I was particularly enamoured by rings with green jade stones.

Jade, more than any other precious stone or element reflects China. Pearl S. Buck said 'jade is the most sumptuous jewel against a woman's flesh'. That settled it; the ring was to be jade.

The Chinese love their jade, and they wear it in so many ways, shapes, and colours. I am not a big fan of all-jade rings, what I was looking at was a white gold ring with a jade stone. Green jade is my favourite and Sara has very stunning green eyes—I fell in love with those eyes—and I thought that the jade would compliment them. There were a few rings around that had a jade stone surrounded by several small diamonds. Hmm, the small diamonds might give the ring legitimacy as an engagement ring, all the while keeping it unique and reflecting our life in China.

But where to buy it? I really didn't trust the vendors in the markets and malls and I would never know if the stones or metal were fake or not. Finally, it dawned on me to try the Friendship Store, the state-owned department store found in every city in China. On my first trip to China, the Friendship Store was the only place in town to find anything of decent quality and the only source of imported goods. Times have changed and I don't know anyone who shops there nowadays, the Friendship Stores have faded into insignificance in

China's modern consumer driven retail landscape. I thought, though, that the Friendship Store would be the one place I could get a ring with a guarantee of its integrity.

I found a ring there I liked. It was in the several hundred dollars range, so I didn't feel too cheap, yet didn't spend too much. I asked our friend Suzanne to drop by and check it out and she gave it the thumbs up. It was all set, I just had to hide it for a couple of weeks.

In the summer of 2003 the SARS pandemic had whipped China into frenzy. People were encouraged not to travel, and anyone getting on a train or plane was scrutinized, forced to fill out medical health declarations, and had to pass through high-tech temperature sensors. God-forbid you might feel a little warm. We passed successfully through the sensors at Dalian Station and boarded train 2083 for Hailar. The train was empty due to the SARS-related travel restrictions.

We usually travel in hard-sleeper, which is second class in Communist, post-liberation lingo. Hard-sleeper cars have ten compartments that are open, each containing two facing rows of three bunks each. This is where the middle class mingle. Not as crowded and filthy as hard-seat, hard sleeper allows the traveller to experience the Chinese—gnawing on pig knuckles and chicken feet, playing cards, refilling their tea cups from thermoses of boiled water, piles of sunflower seeds heaped on the floor—while still getting the chance for a half decent night's sleep, horizontal on a bed. I find that it is necessary to drink a few beers to help me sleep through the screeching and lurching of the train; too many beers though, is a mistake, it means getting up to visit the repulsive toilets in the dark.

Because this trip was long, 27 hours, Sara requested soft-sleeper. Soft-sleeper is first class, with four beds in a closed compartment. It is quiet and cleaner, but otherwise similar to hard-sleeper. The one drawback to soft-sleeper is that you may get stuck with room-mates that you don't jive with. Sometimes you are not in the mood for the chatty fellow with a million questions about Canada or the bouffant-haired woman who is molesting the children, or worse, the *baijiu* drinking official who feels it is his right to smoke in the comfort of his own compartment.

We could have bought four tickets and had the whole compartment to ourselves but that would have cost double the price, and the kids were technically not required to have a ticket, still being under 1.1 metres in height. We arrived in our compartment to find ourselves the sole occupants and crossed our fingers that nobody would join us. We got lucky, thanks to SARS, and enjoyed the long ride in peace, with a bed for each of us.

The kids really enjoy the train. For them, as for us, it is an adventure. They are not so much intrigued by the social aspects of Chinese train culture, rather more excited about the new environment, and being able to climb up and down ladders and play on the top bunk. After a supper of sandwiches brought from home—train meals are nasty rice and slop affairs or instant noodles—we settled down for the night.

When we awoke the landscape had changed. I saw, for the first time in years, valleys in China without human inhabitants. Everyone arrives in China with an existing expectation of throngs of people, but for most of us, who have come from urban environments in the West, the density doesn't seem that shocking. It is only when one travels outside of the cities that China's dense population appears. As the city makes way to rural landscapes the first thing the Canadian traveller notices is that although the cars and concrete structures have disappeared, the people have not. There is always somebody in sight: an old man in a field with a hoe, a girl on a bicycle, a family on a mule cart, a fellow crouched on the side of the road having a semi-public poo.

Where I am from, you can drive for 20 minutes to the top of the nearest mountain and look out at an endless expanse of peaks and valleys with nobody there, save a logger or two. It took 20 hours by train from the Yellow Sea to get way up here, where there was actual uninhabited land. When you haven't seen it for a while it sure looks beautiful. When we did see people and villages they looked different too. The flat roofed farm houses of Southern Manchuria had changed to exposed red brick long houses with sloped roofs, surrounded by primitive looking stick fences.

This was the Great Khingan Mountain range that separated Manchuria from the Mongolian grasslands. The short, green mountains and valleys soon gave way to the flat grasslands of Hulunbeier. In early July the grass was just coming up and many areas were still holding on to their winter brown. From the train we could make out herds of sheep and the occasional *ger*—the traditional Mongolian tent the Chinese call a *menggu bao* and we call a yurt—in the distance. Compared to the Canadian prairies this was a barren and undeveloped place, pastoral rather than agricultural. Evidence of desertification was easily seen. Cowherds led their flocks to eat even among the small but growing sand dunes.

A lonely *menggu bao* in the distance on the grasslands, Hulunbeier.

When we arrived in Hailar we found a typical Chinese city, complete with wide roads and white-tiled buildings, some with blue tinted windows, the kind that sprung up all over China in the 1990s. Initial thoughts were of disappointment. Where were the Mongolians? Mongolians, it appears, are still very much people of the grasslands, the towns and cities are left to the Han Chinese to develop. When we did see Mongolians, walking in groups, they brought a wild-west flavour to the city. They reminded me of Tibetans, with wind-worn faces and gold earrings, colourful clothing, and striking hats. We stayed in Hailar only a night, just long enough to find the bus station and buy tickets to Manzhouli.

Manzhouli is the border town with Russia, where the Trans-Manchurian Railway trains stop to change their bogies, or chassis, before they continue on the wider gauge of the Soviet-era railways, meeting up with the Trans-Siberian Railway. I had passed through here on the train in 1994, but didn't see anything other than the platform and the immigration counter. Manzhouli today is a bustling border town, reminiscent of American border towns like Blaine, Washington, where Canadians flock for cheap gas, electronics, booze, and cheese. Manzhouli, in its current conception, seems to exist solely to outfit Russians with all their consumer needs.

The Russians have special cross-border rights, allowing them to drive across into China and load up their cars with goods. Their vehicle of choice for cross-border shopping is a heavy duty van made by GAZ, the short form of *Gorkovsky Avtomobilny Zavod*, or Gorky Auto Plant. Imagine a Volkswagen Van, circa 1972, crossed with an armoured vehicle and you've got a picture of what these vans look like. Now imagine sliding open the side door and seeing it packed to the roof full of anything and everything made of plastic: brooms, kitchen ware, slippers, toys, coat racks. You name it, the Russians bought it in Manzhouli. We walked the town and marvelled at the shopping. In every store front we were addressed in Russian.

'*Nyet Rusky*' I responded and usually had to follow it up with some Chinese: *Women bu shi Elousi ren*—We are not Russians.

A Russian GAZ van parked in Manzhouli.

The hotel we stayed in was full of Caucasians, all but us were Russian. The hotel, and indeed the Russians, had a particular and peculiar smell. One element was definitely smoke, but the others were not so clear. It wasn't a clean smell, that's for sure; perhaps best described as musty and stale. We sat in our room and watched Russian satellite TV. It was odd, yet familiar. American documentaries were dubbed in Russian, but since you crave anything from home when you have been away for a while, we sat mesmerized, in front of the TV set for hours. Although there has been a schism between Russia and the West for centuries, after watching their TV we couldn't help but feel a cultural closeness.

The biggest treat for us in Manzhouli was the food. As Canadians, we've been exposed to the foods of the Eastern Bloc from various waves of immigrants. We dined on familiar cabbage rolls and fried potatoes and borsht. Best of all, the restaurants served this amazing Russian food at Chinese prices. Normally in China you expect to pay handsomely for a Western meal, however mediocre. This was fantastic fare, and the breakfasts of blintzes—Russian crepes rolled with cottage cheese and sugar—were out of this world. The coffee wasn't the best, it was instant Russian-style, but overall we were tickled pink by the food.

A few of the waitresses in the Restaurants were mixed blood and one looked pure Caucasian. I asked her if she was Russian and she told me in clear Mandarin that she was Chinese, born in Harbin, but her grandparents had come from Russia. I recall once seeing a chart of China's official minorities and it included about 600 ethnic White Russians who had settled in China, fleeing the Communists following the October Revolution. Meeting a member of a population of 600 scattered throughout a country of 1.3 billion, that's like bumping into a white rhinoceros or some other endangered and rare species. China doesn't seem exotic to me after all these years, but experiences like this in China's hinterland do bring back the excitement of my early travels.

From Manzhouli we travelled by car to Dalai Lake. 'Dalai' means ocean in Mongolian. It was a Mongolian who named the Dalai Lama and in that context it implies a ocean of wisdom. Dalai Lake was indeed large like an ocean, the largest fresh water lake in Northern China. When we arrived I had hoped we would find a Mongolian yurt to stay in but the taxi dropped us off in an area of concentrated tourism. Actually there were only two hotels and a parking lot but compared to the vast openness seen in all directions it seemed crowded and overdeveloped. I tried to convince the driver to take us somewhere less built up but he insisted this was the only place. Sara and kids were tired and there was little chance to venture off to find anything better. We would have to make do for now.

Cosmo at the Russian frontier.

The first hotel was overpriced and grungy. The second was expensive but well kept. We opted for the expensive digs. That evening after supper I went for a walk along the lake with Cosmo. I soon found that virtually anywhere else on the lake would have been better, more peaceful, and more Mongolian. I could see several yurts in the distance and wondered if they were places to stay or simply family dwellings. Within a few minutes Cosmo and I came across a group of five men sitting around a fire. They had fishing rods propped up in the lake and they were cooking a leg of lamb over the fire.

The men invited us to sit with them and they offered me a drink. I took a chug of their *naijiu*—milk liquor—and it burned as it went down, similar to *baijiu*, the rocket fuel preferred by Chinese drinkers. They happily shared their lamb and fish and as I sat there around the crackling fire, under a sky full of stars, with the sound of lake waves lapping up on shore, I couldn't help but feel like I was sharing a Canadian moment with these five men in Inner Mongolia. We were kindred spirits for the hour, while Cosmo slept on my lap. I didn't stay long; Sara would be wondering what had happened to us.

Armed with this new knowledge of the surroundings, we set off the next morning for a quieter day on the lake. Bizarrely, we came across an abandoned playground, a relic from an earlier attempt at tourist development. Grass grew knee-high throughout rusted teeter-totters and merry-go-rounds. The chipped paint and squeaky parts didn't bother the kids, ecstatic to find themselves in a playground, and Sara and I were moved by the fresh air and the stillness of the grassland. It was a perfect moment, the one I had been waiting for.

I dropped the ring, in its box, into a little boat that lay partly decomposing in the playground and called the kids over to see it. Hanna found the box, opened it, and exclaimed that she had found a beautiful ring. I told her to show her mum and that was how we came to be engaged. We celebrated with a lunch in a nearby yurt and found that our kids loved *nai cha*—salty milk tea. Even more than the tea itself they loved saying '*nai cha!*' and we laughed and laughed over the kids yelling out 'milk tea, milk tea!' It was a beautiful day, a beautiful moment as a family. A photo of Sara enjoying a beer, sitting at the door of the yurt remains to this day one of my all time favourite photos of her.

I've always said I would like to return to Dalai Lake with our car and go camping, but so far it hasn't happened. I read something quite disturbing recently, that the lake's water level has fallen three metres and its area shrunk by 500 km² since our visit, one more sad example of the mismanagement of a precious resource.

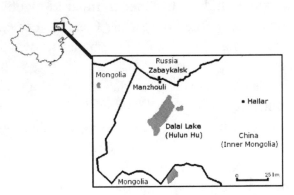

The grassland region of Hulunbeier.

We discussed on a couple of occasions the options for where we might get married. If we did it in Dalian, there would be a lot of people, many of whom are good friends, but not our old friends from home. If we got married in Canada we would have difficult decisions about where exactly to do it. My family and many of our friends were in Vancouver, but Sara's family was in Kelowna, in the interior of British Columbia. In Canada, we would also have to deal with issues like whether or not to have a church wedding. Plus there was the expense to consider. After having lived together for years with two children it seemed pointless to spend money on a wedding. I suggested to Sara that we get married on our next winter holiday and that we do it in Vietnam, at a beach we loved when we visited it the year earlier, in 2002. I also suggested we set the date for Valentines Day, it was right in the middle of our holiday and had significance because it was the anniversary of the night we conceived our daughter Hanna. Sara loved the idea and we set about planning it.

From China there wasn't really a lot we could plan. Our friend Rowena drew cute invitations, with dancing pigs (we were both pigs according to the Chinese zodiac) which we sent out to friends and family in Canada and I contacted the small bungalow guesthouse that we stayed at and loved on our previous trip. Other than Sara's dress, which was made in Dalian from elegant white silk, most of the planning took place after we arrived in Vietnam.

To get to Vietnam we cashed in some of our frequent flyer points and flew via Bangkok, Thailand. The trip down went smoothly until we arrived in Ho Chi Minh City. Sara and the kids passed through immigration without incident, but I was stopped. The immigration officer told me my passport was damaged and that I wouldn't be admitted into the country! With Sara and the kids already behind the counter they were technically in Vietnam, while I was not. Suddenly our wedding trip looked poised for disaster.

My passport had accidentally gone through the washing machine several months earlier. Indeed, it looked as if it had been tampered with. In my infinite wisdom I had tested the usability of the passport by flying to Beijing with it and applying for a Vietnamese visa there. I surmised that if I was able to fly, and if the Vietnamese authorities issued me a visa in that very passport, which they did, then it had passed the test and wouldn't be a problem. Leaving China and entering and exiting both Hong Kong and Thailand went without incident. Once or twice immigration officers inquired why my passport looked in such rough shape but they accepted my answer as valid and non problematic. A quick review of Murphy's law, of course, would have predicted that the Vietnamese immigration officials would be less forgiving.

The officer told me I would have to return to Bangkok on the same flight I arrived on. Obviously, I kicked up a fuss, but more officials arrived and confirmed the verdict. I was illegal and had to return to Thailand.

I had heard numerous stories about Vietnamese border officials scamming travellers by finding fault in their visas and then denying them entry, only to eventually offer a solution, if some US cash dollars appeared. I was determined to enter Vietnam, but without paying a dime.

Sara demanded that she and the kids be allowed to pass back through immigration to sit with me, which the officials allowed. There we sat on plastic chairs in a waiting game. It dawned on us that they probably wouldn't actually want to separate a family and also that Thai Airways wouldn't want to pay for four tickets back to Thailand. Eventually, after an hour or so of waiting and debating with various officials, I was given an offer to pay to solve the problem.

'I don't have any US dollars,' I lied quite easily. I had lied about this years earlier when entering Myanmar too. The officials there required that foreign travellers exchange $300 worth of hard currency (but they only accepted US dollars, UK pounds, Deutschmarks, and Japanese Yen) at the airport at an exorbitant official rate that was ten times less than the black market rate. In Myanmar I told them I only had traveller's cheques and that I was going to use my credit card at the only bank in the country that accepted one. It worked in Myanmar, it might work in Vietnam.

I knew there was an ATM in Saigon and told them I planned to use it to get all my money for our visit. Somehow this seemed plausible to the authorities, and eventually the waiting game was won. I was too stubborn to pay and they needed to get back to their posts. They were losing valuable opportunities to scam money from other suckers. Of course, it was only a minor victory when I consider that my actions caused my fiancée great stress just prior to her wedding. 'I told you so' was tossed my way a few times, but ever the stubborn fool, I was remorseless.

We had hoped that our family would come and we were pretty certain that at least our parents would make it. I thought that there was a chance for a couple of friends to make it out as well. In the end we had only 11 guests: our mothers, my father and step-mother, our good friend from Dalian, Suzanne, Sara's old friend John, who was teaching in Taiwan at the time, and a couple and their children who worked with us and were also vacationing in Vietnam. The visiting couple also had a friend with them who just happened to be a professional wedding videographer, so we got free video footage. The local photographer we hired turned out to be a flop. All his film was somehow destroyed. Not a single photo turned out. We do have amateur photos of our wedding though, taken by our family and friends.

Initially Sara expressed some disappointment about the lack of people and friends, but over time she has come to look back on the day as I do. I felt, and still feel, that it was perfect. We had the people there who mean the most to us, our children and our parents. Having several friends present was a bonus too. Suzanne was Sara's best friend for years in Dalian and she made a wonderful bridesmaid, helping out in so many ways. John, an old friend of Sara's from high school, showed up to play the role of priest.

We met my dad and step-mum in Ho Chi Min City—Saigon —and then drove up to Mui Ne, the beach area where our wedding was to be held. We spent a week there getting things sorted. The bungalows were booked for $11/night, $15 for the ones right on the beach. Hiep Hoa Resort was a steal, simple but amazing, right on the sand. It was run by two young brothers, Hiep and Hoa, who kept it low key. They served breakfast but no other meals. For lunch we wandered a hundred metres up and across the road and dined on lemon grass fish or squid for a dollar fifty. Flowers were ordered from the nearest town, Phan Thiet, and although I had wanted Vietnamese food originally, Sara convinced me that we should hire Fernando, who ran an Italian restaurant bizarrely named Good Morning Vietnam a few kilometres down the road, to cater. That turned out to be a fantastic idea.

With the basics booked, we headed north to Hoi An, a gorgeous town, situated on a river just a few kilometres upstream from the Pacific Ocean. Hoi An was at various times a Chinese trading post, a centre of French colonial power, and a Japanese occupied town. The influences of the foreign delegations are stunning and well preserved hence Hoi An has been designated an UNESCO heritage site. The town is very touristy, but retains a romantic feel.

Two industries that have thrived in Hoi An since the arrival of tourists are tailoring and painting. Artists and their studios line nearly every street and lane. We had found a gentleman we liked on our first trip and bought two oil paintings, which he pulled off the canvas and rolled up for us to frame once we got them home. We bought two more on this trip. They are all Vietnamese scenes of women, dressed in their traditional *ao dai*, in the fields, walking through town, all in vivid colours.

Hoi An's tailors are cheap and work incredibly fast. They will size you up and have your suit or dress ready the following day. Hanna had a Chinese dress made, while Cosmo and I had cream coloured linen pants and a black shirt with an Asian collar and the Chinese wedding character 囍—meaning double happiness—embroidered on the front.

Sara's mum arrived by plane at nearby Danang, and we all returned to Mui Ne for the wedding. I made a quick trip back to Saigon to pick up my mum, who arrived the day before the wedding.

John, an overtly gay friend who travelled from Taiwan to join us, performed the duties of minister and made witty jokes about clergy and homosexuality. Our simple ceremony on the sand, under a palm tree in between the bungalows consisted of a few poems and an exchange of vows. I hardly kept my composure, choking back my tears, surprised by how emotional I was at a ceremony I hadn't previously thought important. I'm glad we did it the way we did, with our children, our parents, and a few friends in a faraway land.

Wedding day, Mui Ne, Vietnam.

Dinner was fantastic. My Dad graciously offered to pay but he got off quite easy, it was no more than $200 for us all. We danced for a few hours outdoors and then I, after taking a swig of cobra snake liquor for honeymoon vigour, rode off into the night with my bride on the front of a *cyclo*, the Vietnamese version of a bicycle-rickshaw. Romantic? Yes, but stressful too. The road was pitch black and lit only by a mini-flashlight that Sara shone ahead, both to illuminate the way and warn the occasional car of our matrimonial suicide carriage.

The next morning we awoke in our fancy hotel room already missing our kids, sleeping several hundred metres down the beach with their grandmas. We hurried back and began preparing for the familymoon. While most couples take a honeymoon, we were lucky enough to have taken a familymoon, and survived. Two mothers, a step-mother, a father, a gay male friend, a female friend, two young children, and the groom and bride all packed into a van, and off we ventured into the highlands of Vietnam. We visited Kham ruins, the lovely French hill station Dalat, rode elephants, saw monkeys, and yelled at our driver in French to slow down. The erratic driving drove some members of the familymoon to drink a tad earlier in the day than normal, and this lead to further humorous moments.

Photo © JCR

On the *cyclo*, February 14, 2004.

One curious incident occurred during the familymoon that we didn't hear about for more than a year. Outside of the Vietnamese town of Dalat we visited the beautiful Dambri waterfalls and took several photos. The following year Smirls was holidaying in Vietnam with his family and came across a poster in a travel agent in Saigon that looked strangely familiar. On closer inspection he saw that the poster, an advertisement encouraging people to travel up to Dalat on a tour, was actually a photo of Hanna and Cosmo in front of the waterfall. He was sure that we hadn't sold the photo or given permission to the business to use it and inquired where they got the photo but did not receive an adequate answer. My best guess is that I must have left copies of our holiday photos on the desktop of a computer in an Internet café in Saigon when I burned several copies of a photo CD for my mum and the others. I'm sure Hanna and Cosmo would be happy to hear of their potential modelling career in Vietnam.

The stolen photo of Hanna and Cosmo from Vietnam.

The miracle of the familymoon was that everyone, ex-spouses included, kept their cool, even when people got violently ill, as does happen when travelling in less developed places. I feel privileged and honoured to have celebrated my marriage with such decent family and friends in such wonderful places. Some families can't even be civil to each other over the course of an afternoon barbeque, never mind a month-long familymoon.

Portrait of the author on a motorized Red Flag bicycle.

Tour de Dandong

If it wasn't clear from an earlier chapter, Smirls loves old-style stuff and he loves projects. He had got pretty excited about my *Chiang Jiang* and set his mind on getting himself one. They cost a few thousand dollars though and his wife wasn't exactly sold on the idea. A more easily attainable goal became getting a motorized classic Chinese bicycle.

Think of China and you may very well conjure up images of the masses all peddling away on their simple, black, one speed bikes. China's roads are now choked with cars and today all sorts of fancy modern design bikes are to be found, including an impressive array of electric bikes, but the old classics are still everywhere. There are three famous brands of vintage Chinese bike, all virtually identical and all modelled on a 1932 English Raleigh Roadster. Best known perhaps is the *Fei Ge*—Flying Pigeon—produced in Tianjin. *Yong Jiu* and *Feng Huang*—Forever and Phoenix respectively—both from Shanghai, round out the Big Three. The bikes have a certain old-school charm and one day Smirls came home with one.

He could have gone down to pretty much any bike store and bought a brand new one with shiny chrome parts, but that would have been too easy. Instead, in classic Smirler style, he approached a man selling skewers of candied crab apples attached like a flower arrangement to the front of an old Flying Pigeon and started bargaining, not for the crab apples, but for the bike.

Incidentally, these bikes not only make for a decent vehicle from which one can vend candied crab apples, they also can be fitted with a cotton candy spinner that sits on the rat trap. Somehow, by pedalling the bike while the kick stand is engaged, the pot spins...and *voila*, you've got cotton candy. One such cotton candy vendor just down the road turned out to be a trusty bike mechanic himself.

But Smirls wasn't quite satisfied with his bike. He began talking to me about finding a motorized version of a Flying Pigeon. We'd see these guys buzzing through traffic powered by a two stroke engine mounted on the inside of the bike frame with a gas tank hanging from the frame's horizontal bar. It was quite frustrating because whenever we asked about the bikes we couldn't make any progress on our quest to locate and buy one. All the bike shops simply told us they were not for sale in Kaifaqu, and besides, they were junk. With most Chinese that we encounter just recently leaving a life of poverty behind, they can not fathom why we would want to buy these relics, symbols of a more desperate era.

When we pressed them further, insisting that they must be for sale somewhere (after all, we could see people riding them so logic told us they must have bought them somewhere) we were told that they were available in Jinzhou, the nearby city where we had bought our furniture when we first arrived in Dalian. Eventually, we learned that part of the problem in finding these bikes for sale was that they didn't come motorized. People bought a motor kit in a box and assembled the engine to the bike frame themselves. By the spring of 2008, Smirls had found the shop in Jinzhou that sold these engines. And then it came to him and he began plotting the most reckless of all his projects: a race on motorized classic bikes from Dalian to North Korea, some 400 km up the coast.

'Brilliant, this is pure genius Smirls,' I recall saying to him the day he described his plan. I got totally caught up in his dream, convinced that this was a terrific idea.

The more he learned about the Chinese bikes the more refined his plan became. The race was to be organized around teams of four riders, each on one of the classic brands: Flying Pigeon, Phoenix, and Forever. Before we knew it, the number of interested participants grew beyond three teams. After moving to Manjiatan, I noticed many of the locals riding brand new bikes that were painted green rather than the usual black with the characters *You Dian*, implying they were postal delivery bikes, painted on the back fender. Their brand name was *Hong Qi*—Red Flag—a name with great Communist era association. I got on the Internet and started searching and soon found out that the Red Flags were made at Tianjin #2 Bicycle Factory. Eventually I determined that they were made by the same company as the Flying Pigeons. I knew when I saw the *Hong Qi* that it was the bike that I was going to ride.

Initially, I had bought a *Yong Jiu* and had a local fellow mount the engine that Smirls picked up for me, a six horsepower two stroke that came in a small box complete with chain, muffler and gas tank. After I had bought my *Hong Qi*—Red Flag—I dropped by the bike shop in Jinzhou one day with Massoud, a friend and captain of Team Phoenix. I noticed a motor in the shop, and told the guy I wanted to buy two of them.

'*Bu dui, nei ge shi jiu ma li de*' he said, perplexing me somewhat. Why didn't he want to sell it to me? I didn't understand what he meant by '*jiu ma li*'. I quizzed him some more and suddenly I got it...he was saying that it was a nine horsepower motor.

'What engine does Lin Hai Gang have?' I asked, referring to Smirls' Chinese name.

'Six,' the shop owner answer with a smile.

Beautiful! I was able to one-up Smirls before the race even began. That afternoon I attended a child's birthday party and informed Smirls that the six horsepower engines that his team had all purchased just weren't going to cut it. *Hong Qi* was going to be riding with more horsepower than that. He was devastated and called me a few nasty names before he disappeared from the party, consulted with his team, and made plans to buy the more powerful engines. All the work that he and his teammates had put into breaking in their engines was for naught; the engines required about three hundred kilometres or so before they ran well and now they had to start all over with the larger engines. Shortly thereafter we agreed to a nine horsepower maximum, to make sure our competitiveness didn't get out of control.

Following this *coup* I began assembling my team, the Red Flag Faction. First to sign up was our office mate, neighbour, good friend and my centre on the Dalian Ice Dragons, Blake Defieux. Next came two fellows named Darren and pretty much simultaneously Cam Secret. Oops, we now had five members. With interest in the Tour growing daily Smirls soon decided that teams should have five members rather than four. As it turned out only Blake and Cam remained on the actual Hong Qi team that set out for Dandong—one Darren had a family visiting and the other suffered a devastating double fracture to his leg while playing roller hockey.

I was having so much fun riding around on my *Hong Qi* when it dawned on me that my brothers, both back in Canada, would absolutely love these bikes. I hadn't been around for ten years and hadn't sent them any Christmas or birthday presents so I decided to get two of these bikes home during the summer holiday. Both my brothers were motorcycle enthusiasts and a little bit quirky, the type of guys who would really appreciate these bikes.

The problem is you can't just put two motorized bikes on an airplane as checked in luggage. Or can you? I carried a scale down to the carport that we had rented, picked up a bike and stood on a scale. It was about 30 kg. Perfect! Up until 2009 JAL allowed 32 kg per checked bag. Each passenger is entitled to two bags. Because we are a family of four we can take eight bags each time we fly. I confirmed with Sara that we only had six bags and planned to get these babies on the plane. I contemplated removing the engines but I had run out of time, and after I weighed them I figured everything would be okay. Two years earlier, I had brought back a *Yong Jiu*, *sans* motor for my sister and it was no problem. So I bought two used bike boxes from the Giant store in Kaifaqu, asked the local bike guy to drain the gas tanks and take off the front tires and I stuffed them in the boxes and wrapped them up with a bit of padding and packing tape.

We arrived at the airport two and a half hours early and were near the front of the line, but somehow—and this can only be understood if you have queued up in China—we ended up the very last ones to check in. By the time we got to the counter it was a mere ten minutes before the plane was scheduled to take off.

The attendant took one look at the boxes and said '*bu keyi, tai da le*'. Nope, too big.

'What? Why?'

'*Shi guiding*'. It's the regulation.

'Nonsense, I've taken a bike before on a JAL flight. It's very common to take bikes on airplanes. It's big but it's not heavy. It's less than 32 kg,' I half pleaded, half demanded. Sara was not too impressed at this point and started muttering about how pissed she would be if we missed our flight because of these stupid bikes.

I demanded to speak to the manager and a Japanese woman appeared. She very politely, as is the Japanese way, told me there were, in fact, regulations and that I could find them on JAL's website. I repeated my spiel about how I took a bike the same size the previous year and nobody told us then about the regulations. What were we to do with these bikes now?

The manager came up with a compromise: she allowed us to take the bikes on the plane this time, to not inconvenience us and would double check the regulations and if she was wrong she would email me an apology. So we hoisted the bike boxes up onto the scale...oh crap, they weighed 35 kg! Normally that would be it; there was no way you could get your boxes on the plane without paying an exorbitant fee, but because of the further delay arguing about the bike boxes we were in a desperate rush to get onto the plane and they just let us go. Up around 30,000 feet Sara looked at me sternly and asked if I had drained the gas tanks. With my straightest face I said yes, although I suddenly felt sick, realizing that I hadn't actually checked. The job had been left up a man of dubious integrity; a character so inimitable I felt it necessary to give him a name: The Blob.

The Blob is middle aged, overweight, not quite totally deaf, with a mouth disfiguration that combines with his deafness to make him next to impossible to understand. He has a case of perpetual plumber's butt and he has yet to have ever worn pants without a gaping crotch and it seems he may be to some extent mentally challenged. The Blob is usually found sleeping in The Blob's Nest, a blue tin shack that kind of resembles a 30 year-old Boler camper, pressed up against the side wall of the Manjiatan market just down from the one-armed locksmith and the cobbler with few teeth. He is often asleep when you need his services and waking him up is an issue because he is deaf, so I found myself on many occasions banging furiously on the Blob's Nest making a huge racket. Luckily making a uproar doesn't bother the Chinese one bit—in fact they seem to enjoy a good hullabaloo—but makes us foreigners feel self conscious nonetheless. If he is already up you will most likely find him sitting on the ground breathing like Darth Vader, covered in grease, totally immersed in his work fixing bikes.

The Blob shares his nest with a small white puppy that he seems to care about considerably. At any rate, he cares more about the puppy than either himself, or keeping his nest organized. It's chaos in there; tools and bikes parts, nuts and bolts scattered everywhere. At one end is a metal frame bed on which sits a five-inch black and white TV that he cranks up so loud in order to hear that it's a wonder his nest doesn't collapse from the sound waves. The Blob has two modes: asleep and awake; and two temperaments: giddy or grumpy beyond reason. The Blob is one of those characters that can't really be described. You need to meet him and you will be at once enamoured, shocked, perplexed and frustrated.

I named him The Blob because he seems like a comic book character. I'm just not sure if he is a hero or villain. The Blob seemed a bit nicer than some of the other names that were thrown around and as for his real name, it would be virtually impossible to understand, given that he growls rather than speaks. It doesn't help that he calls me *ge er*—brother —which really does come out as 'grrrrrrr'. One day we were in the local hardware shop trying to dig up another Hong Qi for our newest team member, Mike Hovanes, and The Blob was about to make a call to a bike supplier when the shop owner reprimanded him.

'What are you going to say? "Rah, rah, grrrr, grrr," nobody will understand you. Give me the phone!'

Photo © JCR

The author and The Blob, in front of the Blob's nest.

The whole shop exploded with laughter, five men stopping their card game to howl on their little wooden stools. I chuckled too but then felt a little bad for The Blob. He just stood there quietly growling and grinning like an idiot.

One day I had gone out riding with the fifth team, the *Jin Lu*—the Golden Deer—a team made up of newly arrived teachers and captained by Mike Bishop, a very handy fellow who was pretty much always able to fix whatever went wrong with their bikes. During the ride my throttle cable broke and Bishop was able to patch it together so I could get home, but I dropped my bike off with The Blob for a proper cable replacement. The next day I stopped off after work at The Blob's Nest, and curiously, my bike wasn't there. The Blob muttered something but I couldn't understand any more than that it was broken somewhere and tomorrow it would be back. When I returned the next day my bike was there but something was amiss. I had painted my gas tank quite distinctively, and clearly it was my gas tank, but the chrome parts on the suspension, and many of the nuts and the front handle bars were rusted, although they had all been shiny and new when I dropped the bike off.

'What's going on here?' I demanded.

'Grrrrr...*shenme*? Grrrr,' growled The Blob in a question.

'Is this my bike?'

'Grrr...it's your bike!

I knew something was up, but I couldn't really understand what had happened. Why on earth would The Blob have replaced just some of my bike parts with old rusty parts? Anyway, I was pleased he had fixed the throttle and I jumped on it to give it a try.

I got not more than two metres and the pedal chain fell off. The Blob put it back on and made some adjustments. I jumped back on, pedalled up to speed, popped the clutch and, just as the bike fired up, the drive chain came off its sprocket and the bike came to a screeching halt. I hadn't even made it out of the parking lot. The Blob, as if he expected as much, said nothing and got right to work fixing the chain, breathing like Darth Vader, but adding a light whistle to the 'Huuuu prrrrrr, huuuuu prrrrrrr'.

With the chain back on I raced up the main street, away from Manjiatan's market. Passing the mechanic, the car wash, Master Lin's Ping Pong shop, and Big Fish restaurant, I turned left and rode up behind Jin Hai Ren Jia and then north, up past the graves on the hill towards the reservoir when the bike suddenly lost power and died. I turned it around and started coasting downhill towards the market when I noticed the distinctive smell of gasoline. Stopping, I got off the bike and examined it. I immediately noticed gas pouring out of the carburetor, which had disengaged from the engine, and spilling all over the road. I pushed the carburetor back on and pedalled back to The Blob's Nest.

When I got there I was greeted not by The Blob, but by another fellow who took it upon himself to solve the problem. He seemed to be playing charades with me and only after a few minutes did I realize that he was dumb, in the literal sense. The perfect sidekick to The Blob, Grunt—I couldn't resist this nickname—decided that my fuel filter was frivolous and yanked it off and, despite my objection just grunted and did what he wanted. After a bit of tightening he jumped on to start the bike only to find that all the gas had drained out when the carburetor had fallen off. Grunt didn't wait for The Blob's lead, instead he headed straight for the nearest motorcycle parked beside the market, pulled off the fuel line and helped himself, filling a discarded bottle of ice tea with free gas. They were quite a pair, The Blob and his sidekick, growling and grunting at one another. The Blob then turned to me with the cheeky smile of a child and told me that actually my bike had been run over by a truck while in his care and that's why he had replaced the parts and also, I surmised, why the chains and carburetor were not tightly in place. You can't really get mad at The Blob and I just shook my head and drove off. Two days later I stopped in again and he asked me in all seriousness how I knew it wasn't my bike. What a guy!

As the race got nearer it became clear to nearly everyone that only two of the teams were in any way prepared for a ride of this gruelling magnitude on such poorly made and finicky bikes. Team Jin Lu and Team Yong Jiu—The Golden Deer and Team Forever—had all worked their bikes in well over the course of at least a half year. These teams, with the exception of Smirler, were made up mostly of single guys who didn't have kids at home and had plenty of time to get together for long, weekend rides. They all experienced so many problems with their bikes and were able to work out the bugs themselves or with the help of local mechanics. Even with their preparations all our Chinese friends predicted that we wouldn't make it even half way to North Korea.

That didn't bode well, for the remaining three teams, mine included, were hopelessly ill prepared for the race. One of the reasons the Red Flag Faction was in such poor shape was that I had been counting on my brothers to come out for the race. Both of my brothers are really mechanical types and one of them is a motorcycle mechanic by trade. Because I had sent them bikes the previous summer I figured we would be way ahead of the other teams in terms of preparedness and mechanical ability to keep the bikes running. As luck would have it neither of them were able to make it out which meant that three of our team members got bikes just weeks before the race and were able to only go for a handful of rides to test them out.

In fact, one of our guys had only ridden once or twice and we had never actually met him. He was an American who worked for Intel, the computer chip giant who was building the world's largest chip plant in Dalian. Without ever meeting him, I set out to get his bike ready. The problem was, the supply of ubiquitous green Hong Qi bikes had dried up in Manjiatan. Suddenly, there were only black ones available. With time running out, I found a solution that illustrates another charm of living in China.

I had noticed for a couple of days a green Hong Qi bike in near-new condition, parked on the grass next to a garbage pile near Manjiatan's main intersection. I asked around and found out that it belonged to a street sweeper/garbage collector who kept the main street clean day after day, or at least attempted to keep it clean. I approached him and told him my story; that I and four friends were a team in a race to Dandong and that a team should look similar, but we couldn't find any more green bikes. Would he consider trading his green bike for a brand new black one? He agreed at once and I bolted up the road, bought a new black bike and we exchanged them right then and there on the street. I try to imagine the same situation in Canada. If a strange Chinese man approached you with a ridiculous story in broken English about racing to Alaska and asked you to trade your bike would you even entertain the idea?

I sent Jeremy his bike, delivered on a truck to Kaifaqu. To this day, I haven't met him because the day of the race he called to say he couldn't make it because he had a cold. So the Red Flag Faction set out with just four members: Blake Defieux, Mike Hovanes, Cam Secret, and yours truly.

I had envisioned and planned getting uniforms made but life is hectic and the race snuck up on us. The other teams all had uniforms so the day before the race Blake and I popped into the market to see what we could find. It just so happened that it started absolutely pouring rain that day and was unseasonably cool. Although we had originally conceived a postal delivery theme, the rain prompted us to decide on large green military overcoats as our uniform. We would stay warm and they matched the green bikes and the green saddle bags that Jimmy the Leather Man—our name for the cobbler two shacks down from The Blob—had stitched up for us. In February I had the foresight to buy five pairs of old-school goggles while in Bangkok, figuring they would make a good look for the Tour de Dandong. To complete the look, I commissioned five red scarves from a seamstress in the market. At five *renminbi* a piece they were a steal and although some other teams' members told us we looked like Christmas trees, I think we looked like real classics, part vintage flying aces, part stalwart Manchurian communists.

When I stopped by Mike's office to drop off his uniform he wasn't there. The Chinese lab technician who shared his office, Julia, got really excited when she saw the old green PLA jacket.

'These are symbols...,' she said, struggling for the English word for era. 'My husband always wore this kind of jacket on our university campus. When I see it I feel so, so...'.

'Nostalgic' I interjected, helping her find the right English word.

Julia asked if she could put on the jacket, then added the goggles and red scarf. Another office mate took our photo together, both of us wearing the uniforms. Our uniforms had passed the test and made a good impression. This incident made me feel great about the uniforms because Blake especially had been concerned that they would either make us look like imbeciles, be insulting to the Chinese, or perhaps both.

I had driven my bike to work that day and it got drenched in the rain. On my way home, it started backfiring and running rough, so I pulled into a mechanic's shop. They looked it over, replaced a spark plug and told me the engine was wet and that this was problematic. I went home and hoped for the best; that my bike would be fine the next day. It wasn't, and I stopped in at another motorcycle shop. They assured me that it would dry out as I drove and that getting to Dandong would be no problem. Still, I worried this would cause me significant problems in the race.

The author and Julia in PLA overcoats.

Race day was a Saturday, but the majority of the teams' members were all required to work until 3:40 pm that day. We planned to leave at 4 pm from Jinshitan Beach. With some trepidation about the potential for stormy weather and the fact that we had to travel 90 km but only had three hours of daylight, we gathered for goodbyes and photos at a statue of a giant bull on the shores of the Yellow Sea.

Our colleague Hubert Wong was there as official photographer as was Marshall Bradbury, our marshal who would ride

along on his 250cc motorbike. Darren Brown, originally
slated to be a member of Team Hong Qi, drew the starting
order and then rode along with the mechanics and the film
crew, hired from a local TV station.

With a burst of firecrackers the race began. Some riders
struggled to get their engines started and one rider fell off his
bike. Wives and girlfriends cheered and waved with nervous
faces — they thought we were reckless, crazy fools. Few
believed we would make it. In fact only the local old men
believed in us. It seems they had a soft spot for vintage bikes
and in nearly all cases showed support and enthusiasm for
our race.

We drew third spot, but soon caught and passed Yong Jiu,
who had a broken chain just 3 km from the start. Amazingly,
it was to be their only breakdown of the whole race. At the
third corner, about 10 km into the race, we were neck and
neck with Team Jin Lu. Although we all were given a directions package and were required to follow the same route,
some confusion occurred because the TV crew car driver
insisted we should turn right while our directions indicated a
left turn. Technically, the driver was right but because I had
spoken to Smirls about his directions I knew that this 'long
way round' was in fact a short way to the main road to
Dandong, the 201 highway.

Armed with this knowledge, Hong Qi pulled into an early
lead for the first hour of the race. The 201 was a typical
second tier highway in China, complete with all manner of
traffic such as was described in an earlier chapter of this book.
We drove around cyclists and ox carts, battled with tractors,
and were made insignificant by luxurious cars and nearly
knocked over by large trucks.

The scenery was decent, although in late April the rural landscape was still about ten days from really blooming. Its beauty was tempered by a glazing of dull brown colours.

When we pulled into the little town of Hua Jia, at about 6 o'clock in the evening, we were a little cold but a feeling of exhilaration predominated. The gas station we rolled into was closed and we were just discussing our progress, congratulating ourselves on a good start, when I spotted a policeman eyeing us up from across the street.

We had no idea if this trip would fly with the authorities. We had no permits, no official permission and were travelling through areas that were not necessarily open to foreigners. Not to mention we were travelling on motorized vehicles that were surely illegal and I was the only one on our team with a driver's license.

The policeman sauntered up to us looking rather serious and determined to find answers. Where had we come from today? And what country were we from? Where were we going? To Dandong, on those bikes?! The ice was broken quickly and soon we were snapping photos and promising to send him copies. He left us with well-wishes for the rest of our journey.

Within a few minutes of the policeman leaving us, the Jin Lu boys arrived and we crossed the road for refreshments. Dinner was pretty much beer and chocolate bars or other Chinese junk foods sold in the little shop. We chatted with the other teams as they arrived one by one, with Phoenix in the rear, as they would be for much of the trip.

It was clear that darkness was soon to fall upon us and many of the guys turned on their lamps or headlights and started pulling out reflective vests. Sandy bought us reflective vests, which might have saved our lives, considering we drove in the dark, although none of us had even considered wearing anything for safety. Unable to get mine over my coat and backpack, I strapped it to my bag.

And off we went into the evening, heading in a North-east direction, hoping to arrive in a town called Chengzitan, where a bathhouse would be our lodgings for the night.

It got dark quickly, and it got cold! The wind was worst of all. It howled down from the north, a taste of the real Manchuria, originating even beyond the border, in Siberia. The wind threatened to blow us off the road and to counter it we leaned into it, our bikes angled some seventy degrees from the pavement. Gale-force gusts blew us to the edge of the shoulder and then let up, and we careened dangerously back onto the road. We drove in packs, some riders were without lights and they stuck close to others. Cars and trucks passed dangerously close. Bikes and pedestrians appeared at the last second out of the darkness. We mostly drove along the shoulder, but every kilometre or so a bridge appeared a metre narrower than the road and we swerved just in time. Several times I barely missed smashing into the bridge post, which would have meant either splaying out on the road and being crushed by traffic, or bailing into a stream, perhaps to drown in darkness.

After an hour of driving like this we all convened in a gas station to fill up and to check over the bikes. When it was time to pull out I pedalled around the pumps three or four times but my engine wouldn't turn over. The other teams had all pulled out except for Phoenix, who were huddled in a back room at the gas station warming up and waiting for one of their guys who had already had several flat tires. I was exhausted, pedalling frantically trying to get enough speed for the engine to turn over. After a frustrating ten minutes it started, but it didn't quite feel right. I seemed be stuck at about 75 % of the usual engine capacity.

I limped along at full throttle, desperately trying to keep up with the team. The other teams had sped ahead but we eventually arrived in Chengzitan, about an hour after the others. It was a miracle no one got hurt or killed that night.

When we pulled into the parking lot of the bathhouse, the mechanics were outside looking over the bikes. I told them about my sluggish engine and they began working on it. I climbed the steps to the bathhouse certain that tomorrow would be an easier ride.

Inside the bathhouse we were greeted by the gang of three teams who had arrived earlier, some of them looking very relaxed, wearing the pyjamas supplied by the bathhouse. If you haven't spent any time in China you just can't imagine how funny it looks to see grown men parading around in pyjamas in public. The Chinese will stroll down the street leisurely on a Sunday morning walking their dog in their pyjamas. If they are off to the bathhouse for their weekly soak, they will often not bother to dress in street clothes, instead sauntering down the sidewalk with a basket of toiletries and wearing silk. This is equally true of men and women, young and old.

Seeing our friends dressed like this was a riot. Beer in hands, the laughter and camaraderie continued well into the night. This was a very simple bathhouse but like all bath-houses in China it had a common room with reclining soft chairs to lounge in where we all gathered for dinner. There were a couple of girls and several fellows who gave foot massages and we put a classic hockey game—the 1976 Montreal Canadiens vs. the USSR—that we had brought on DVD up on the big screen TV. There we sat, reliving the ride, swearing up and down that we wouldn't ride at night again, generally having a grand ol' time, when we were told that we would have to vacate the common room and return to our rooms upstairs. We were totally bewildered; there was no one else staying at the bathhouse except for us and, without a doubt, they had never made so much money in a single night.

This was a grotty little place; the nicer places in town had all refused our requests to stay. Likely they didn't have a license to accept foreign guests. We fought and argued but to no avail. Eventually, we learned from Leon, a Chinese rider on our trip who had set up the accommodations that we were kicked out because a local government official was consorting with a prostitute in a room just beside the common room. Our boisterous behaviour was upsetting his ride! 'Dirty Chinese business,' Leon called it. We were to hear him use this term a few more times before the trip was over.

In the morning, we all rose with pounding headaches, the kind brought about by copious amounts of *pijiu*. Nevertheless, we were in good spirits. The weather looked good, and the daytime temperature was probably near 20°C. It was, however, a bit disconcerting to see the mechanics still working on my bike. They had worked on it for a couple of hours the night before, what could possibly be the problem? The other teams were all ready to hit the road, meanwhile the Hong Qi boys patiently waited for me.

Just then a commotion distracted me from my frustration with my bike. Two riders just realized they had been robbed in the bathhouse; it was more dirty Chinese business! The theft had without a doubt been done by staff at the bathhouse but the owners were uncompromising, even going so far as to threaten us by claiming our guys had been up to 'dirty Chinese business' of our own in the bathhouse, which was certainly not the case. The police arrived and mediated a settlement, as they usually are able to do in China. Rony and Trevor got some compensation for their stolen camera and MP3 player, no doubt less than they were worth but better than nothing. With that dirty business done, the teams hit the road, leaving only Hong Qi and expecting us to be right behind them momentarily.

Portrait of the author and his Hong Qi in Chengzitan.

'*Hao le! Deng liang fen zhong*'—It will be done in two minutes, the mechanic told me at about 11 am. At noon the bike still would barely start and wouldn't push itself uphill at all. By pedalling, I could travel about 20 km/hour on a flat and perhaps 30 km/hour when downhill. Finally, the mechanics gave up, shaking their heads.

'*Bu zhi dao*. I don't know'. They had tried everything and still had no clue what was wrong.

I was pretty frustrated at this point and I felt like I was letting my team down. It didn't seem right for my bike to be having all the problems because I had worked my bike in better than the other guys on my team. In fact, I had arranged all the bikes for the team. Why me? Karma wasn't working as it should. I had also been under the impression that the mechanics were going to bring a couple of extra engines along. They didn't. I asked them if I could buy one in Chengzitan.

'*Mei you*,' they said.

It's very common for Chinese to tell you things are un-available when, in fact, they are available. I think it is prefer-able for them to give you an answer than to admit that they don't know where to find something. I didn't believe them and set off to find an engine or a mechanic who could fix the bike.

An hour and half later, I returned to the team, who were still waiting patiently. Indeed, there were no two-stroke bike engines in Chengzitan. The mechanics told me there would be no engines until Dandong. We decided as a team to give it a try anyway. Worst case scenario, we thought, someone could tow me. Mike had a rope, he said.

Off we went, the team driving slowly ahead while I strug-gled behind, pedalling like mad just to keep the motor running. This went on for an hour or so. Ultimately, I simply couldn't keep it up. It was frustrating, and a shame, because the road we were now on was one of the most beautiful I had ever driven on in China, but I was in no mood to enjoy the scenery. I came to a stop in a village to find Blake surrounded by perhaps eight villagers. A woman in a headscarf and a white powdered face was chatting excitedly with him. She welcomed us warmly and immediately let on that she was a practitioner of Falun Gong, the banned spiritual movement.

I was shocked that she would admit being a believer so publicly. I asked her if there were many Falun Gong believers in the village, imaging that we had stumbled upon a remote hotspot of spiritual dissidents, but she claimed to be the only one. She babbled on about the merits of Falun Gong for her health and gave us a DVD and a card, which I assumed was underground info about the embattled faithful.

Years earlier, when Falun Gong was first banned as an 'evil cult' in China, we found a CD posted on our door. Outside our building, tens of CDs were thrown in the trash. I put the CD in my computer and watched footage of Falun Gong followers being arrested, beaten, and imprisoned. I couldn't under-stand most of what was said, but I caught the gist. I assumed the woman in the village had given us a similar CD, but when I returned home and popped it in my computer I was per-plexed: it was nothing more than coverage of a Chinese New Year's performance.

The village had a small shop and we bought bottles of ice tea and bags of dried fruit. What we really needed was a rope. Mike's rope was in the mechanics' truck—Lord knows where that was! The shop didn't have a rope but when we told Miss Falun Gong that was what we needed she was more than happy to help. A moment later, when an old man arrived on the scene pushing a bicycle with a large tree stump tied to the rat trap, she simply told him to give his rope to us. Feeling a little guilty, we handed over a bungee cord in exchange, said *xie xie* and set about tying the rope to Mike's seat post, and off we went, Mike towing me behind.

We were able to make pretty good progress, although it felt a little bit dodgy, and on a couple of occasions I let go of the rope, frightened I was going to crash. The mechanics had told us back in Chengzitan that there was no way I could buy a new engine on route but I called Marshall, who was somewhere up ahead on his 250 cc motorcycle, and asked him if he could try to find one in the next city, Zhuanghe. Luckily, Marshall was able to find an engine for about 500 RMB, and when I arrived, at about 6 pm, having been towed by Mike for 40 km, we caught up with the mechanics who were working on a bike that had its frame break in two—being China, they were able to find someone to weld it very easily.

We had a decent supper of fried squid, vegetables, pork, and rice while the mechanics put on my new engine. When dinner was done my bike was almost ready. The mechanic jumped on to start it up and set off up the street when he ran right into a street sweeper, knocking her down. This was a minor side show for the crowd of forty-some people who had gathered around us and soon we were back on the road.

Despite our assurances to ourselves the previous night that we wouldn't be riding in darkness again, we set out at dusk with at least a 60 km ride ahead of us. Fortunately, the wind wasn't blowing like the previous night and we had all purchased extra flashlights and taped them to our handlebars, giving extra illumination of the road.

The ride was reasonably smooth for team Hong Qi. Hours behind the others, we were pleased to catch up to Harry and Trevor from the Flying Pigeons—Trevor had suffered a broken frame on the dark road and had to put his bike on the mechanics' truck when they found him.

Our destination for night two was a farm house in a village about 10 km off the main road, the 201. We found the turnoff without too much trouble, but nearly crashed a couple of times on the pitch black country back road when we encountered a stretch of road strewn with boulders that had fallen off a truck.

Arriving in the village, we found that everyone had already eaten, but there was still plenty of food left for us. The Village Head was a tiny little man dressed in army fatigues with a smile that stretched ear to ear. Leon and Smirls had arranged for his extended family and neighbours to put us all up for the night. This was, for most of the riders, the first and only time they had stayed and eaten in a traditional country home in Northern China. The meal was delicious. It was an assortment of meat, seafood, tofu, and vegetables, all steamed or fried in a large wok that was heated by a fire made of corn stalks and twigs.

The overpopulated Chinese have made an ingenious invention known as the *kang*. The *kang* is an elevated bed as wide as the living room that sleeps the whole family. It is heated by a pipe that runs underneath it and is connected to the fire that also fuels the wok in the kitchen. After supper and a few more beers and laughs, each team retired to their own farmhouse and *kang*. It was quite funny to curl up for the night, all four of us, plus Darren, on a single bed. After a few farts and a couple of jokes, we five men slept like babies. The only complaint was that the *kang* was too hot. We woke up in our clothes and heavy PLA jackets sweating, but well rested.

Given the frustrating delays the previous day we decided to take off early and left the village even before some riders had gotten out of bed. As we rode out of the village we marvelled at the gorgeous scenery. We had missed it on our arrival because of darkness. Mountains and fields of corn and rice mingled under a clear blue sky. We were pretty excited about being on the road in first place on a beautiful day on the last leg of the race—North Korea here we come!

Back on the 201, we fuelled up at a gas station and found that team Phoenix, who had struggled on day one with flat tires, and on day two suffered a broken frame, had caught up to us. While they were fuelling up we took off but had to stop just 500 metres down the road when Blake had a broken chain. Cam and I helped Blake, but Mike was still back at the gas station. We were not sure what was taking him so long but soon found out; he had gotten his jeans stuck in the chain and on his way out of the gas station had crashed. He had sprained his ankle quite badly and his jeans were torn up to his shin, but as always, Mike wore a smile like a Cheshire cat. He seemed to be having the time of his life. I didn't know Mike well before the race, but moments like this led me to respect and appreciate him. He's a terrific guy and was the perfect team mate for a trip like this.

With Blake's bike fixed, we took to the road again, this time with Phoenix just a few hundred metres ahead of us. They soon broke down and we sped off in first place on the last day!

Our route took us over the Da Yang River, but as we got to the large bridge we were stopped by a barricade. The bridge was under construction—we would have to turn around. Damn!

We were told that we could find a detour route about five km back down the main road. If we could get there before the next team they would all continue down the road the wrong way and get stopped at the bridge too. We raced back the way we came but just before we got to the detour route Phoenix and Yongjiu caught up to us. We had lost our lead. Our efforts to set out early and get ten km ahead were all in vain.

Flustered, we rode alongside Yong Jiu for a few km and then got stopped by another breakdown. This time Cam's pedal was broken. Shortly after, we had another minor breakdown. While we were on the side of the road a group of Chinese seniors on a bike tour approached us from the opposite direction. They were all wearing matching biking uniforms, and their bikes were good quality European racing bikes. They were riding from Dandong to Yingkou, a port city on the Bo Hai Sea. It was ironic to think that a group of elderly Chinese were riding expensive road bikes imported from the West, while we were a group of young Westerners riding crappy old Chinese bikes. It was also ironic that the seniors were pedalling and we youngsters were motoring.

Just then team Jin Lu caught up to us and took off ahead. We were now in third place. A storm threatened from the distance to the north and temperature dropped by ten degrees. At Da Dong Gou, there was some confusion about how we were to get on the route that followed the Yalu River. Our language abilities helped out and we made good time through the small city and caught up to Jin Lu, who had stopped to take photos just as we approached the river. When they saw us they jumped back on their bikes and we rode along together, following the North Korean border.

The border separating China and North Korea is normally the Yalu River, but here, at the mouth of the river, the North Koreans occupy several of the estuarine islands. Our road ran right along the border. Canadians are accustomed to unmarked and undefended borders but this border was marked by a ten foot-high concrete wall with an electrific fence on top. I hadn't seen anything like this since 1990 when I camped beside the Berlin Wall. But by then the wall was a remnant of a previous era, having been torn down, in the figurative sense, some eight months before I saw it. This wall, separating the world's most populous nation from the world's most reclusive and enigmatic country, was brand new; the white plaster hadn't yet cracked and peeled off. Electric wire was strung along the top of the wall. It might have seemed a sinister symbol had I not grown accustomed to such things living in China for so long. Nevertheless, we were exhilarated riding alongside it.

There was no traffic to speak of on this road and the first vehicle we came across was a military car stopped at the curb. A soldier stood on the road and pulled us over. He demanded to know who we were and what we were doing. We all had to show our passports. He looked over our bikes and seemed impressed by our ride from Dalian. He let us pass but told us not to stop on route. This was a sensitive area.

By now we could see Dandong's skyline, totally changed since I had last been there four years earlier. Skyscrapers dotted the formerly sleepy, low-rise city. Blake had started complaining about engine trouble and when Mike stopped without warning he sped on ahead of us. Cam and I stopped with Mike and we were there no more than thirty seconds when a military vehicle stopped and special ops soldiers jumped out and interrogated us again. I have seen thousands of soldiers in China and they are always very poorly dressed and equipped. Rarely do you even see a soldier with combat boots; normally they are in baggy uniforms and soft Kung Fu shoes. These guys were decked out in smart black uniforms, and armed with guns and all sorts of gadgets. They were very anxious for us to move along. We could see North Korean buildings and boats no more than forty metres away. The soldiers told us the North Koreans might shoot at us if we lingered there. The situation was made worse because we were all dressed foolishly in semi-military gear. Yong Jiu were dressed as China security forces, Jin Lu in pseudo-military uniform, the Flying Pigeons were actually wearing military fatigues with North Korean and Chinese flags on their shoulders. We looked like whackos, but to the suspicious North Koreans, who knows how we might be perceived.

The problem was, Mike's motor had unbolted from the frame and threatened to shake completely loose. We didn't have the tools to fix it and the soldiers demanded we move on quickly. So Cam drove off on the soldiers' orders while Mike and I hooked up our rope again, this time with me returning the favour. I would tow Mike the final fifteen km to Dandong.

The towing went well; we only had to stop once more. Once again, the special border patrol pulled up in their armoured vehicle within a minute of us stopping. I was shocked at the military and police presence. When we returned back to Dalian we read that 100,000 troops had been sent to the border regions, but we never did find out why. Obviously, something had caused the Chinese and North Koreans to have a rift of some kind.

Things got a little dodgy as we entered the city. The riverside road was a one-way street—the same road that I had hit the cyclist in The Hulk four years earlier. I knew we would have to pull into the city but the whole time I was paranoid that a car would attempt to turn in between Mike and me, smashing through the rope and knocking us down. Other than the night driving, this was the most dangerous part of the trip.

When we finally made it to the broken bridge that marked the finish line, we did a victory lap in front of the Yong Jiu and Jin Lu teams and the crowd of nearly a hundred people who had gathered to stare at the foreigners and their bikes. Because I was still towing Mike, the rope went slack during our tight turn and we almost crashed in front of the crowd.

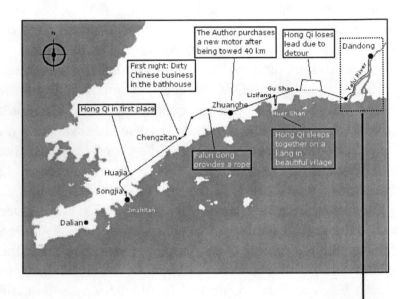

Route of the
Tour de Dandong:
March 2009

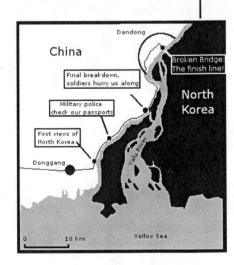

We were handed a beer and celebratory congratulations were the order of the hour. What a great feeling it was to have completed the ride. The breakdowns, the towing, and the military check posts made it all the sweeter. We were not far into our celebration when the Flying Pigeons arrived. Time for another beer and more congratulations! About an hour later team Phoenix finally arrived. Apparently they had stopped for a meal at the broken bridge (stopping for meals all the time helped give them the nickname The Hobbits) and eventually they convinced someone to let them pass across the bridge. They had managed to avoid the extra 30 km detour that the rest of the teams made and yet still came in last by an hour. There was plenty of ammunition for a year's worth of joking at their expense.

Each team took a turn posing for a photo with the bikes in front of the broken bridge (blown up by American bombers during the Korean War) and then all 25 riders lined up together for a photo op. With the TV cameras rolling, we took off all together down the street, looking more like an environmental disaster than anything else, clouds of blue smoke puffing out behind us. Down the street we went, stopping a few hundred metres on at a Korean BBQ restaurant. We feasted on spicy Korean meats and pickled vegetables and drank toast after toast to ourselves and the ride. There was just one sombre moment when we gave a toast to Massoud, our fallen comrade, who had passed away unexpectedly a month before the race.

After supper, we piled our bikes onto a long truck for shipping back to Dalian, and except for a few guys who stayed on in Dandong, we jumped on a bus and arrived home tired at about 2 am.

Foad, from team Phoenix, who has lived in China for twenty years, said that he saw more of China in those three days than he had his whole stay in China. No doubt an exaggeration, it nonetheless says something of the awesome experience that the Tour de Dandong was. Jack, another rider from Phoenix, said to me after we had been back for a week 'I can't believe it. That was one of the most incredible experiences of my life'.

Red Flag Faction celebrates with a *pijiu* across the river from N. Korea.

Like many of the things we have done over here, the magnitude of the awesomeness doesn't sink in until the moment has passed.

15

Cosmo and Hanna under house arrest, Guanglu Island.

Freedom

It is well known, or believed I should say, in the West that China is a country run by a brutal and cruel government that oppresses its people. They are locked up for dissenting political opinions, lack religious freedom, and can't even choose how many children to have. Who would want to live there?

Paradoxically, many expats in China feel exceptionally free, sometimes to the point where they consider there are no boundaries whatsoever to their behaviour, acting in outrageous fashion, doing things they wouldn't dare do at home. Before I sputter on about all the ridiculous freedoms I have enjoyed in China I should recount several cases in which I was severely restricted.

Coincidentally, China and Canada share 1982 as the year their modern constitutions were written, or rewritten. In Canada's constitution, The Charter of Rights and Freedoms spells out clearly that Canadians shall enjoy the right to unrestricted movement. The Chinese constitution, while it does spell out various freedoms for Chinese citizens that are enforced to varying degrees, does certainly not guarantee freedom of movement. This became clear to me when I travelled to China the first time in 1994. My goal had been to head westward from Guangzhou, travelling overland to Tibet via Yunnan or Sichuan provinces. It seemed simple enough from looking at a map. There were roads, so there must be buses on those roads, I surmised. It is these very roads that the Chinese use as evidence of the kind-hearted, helpful nature of the 'liberation' of Tibet in 1950.

'We built them roads! Where would they be without our help?'

There, in western Yunnan, I found out that foreigners couldn't just go or stay anywhere they liked. There were only certain hotels that were licensed to accept foreigners and, of course, these tended to be the pricier ones. Many towns were off limits to foreigners too. When we tried to board buses heading into Tibet we were sent off by *gong an* officers and some travellers were fined.

When we arrived in Dalian in 1998 we were excited to visit historic Lushun, formerly known as Port Arthur, just south of Dalian at the tip of the Liaodong peninsula. This was the southern terminus of the Russian-built Manchurian railway, site of major battles between the Russians and Japanese, and more recently a Chinese naval base. There is a well known look-out spot that is popular with locals, especially during the cherry blossom season. Unfortunately, there is a restriction on foreigners and the unsuspecting tourists are turned back, much to the embarrassment of their Chinese friends and hosts who are usually unaware of the rules.

October 1st, 1999 marked the 50th anniversary of the Chinese Revolution and the founding of the People's Republic of China. There was to be a monumental celebration in Beijing at Tiananmen Square. I felt it was an opportunity of a lifetime to see this kind of Communist propaganda party, not to mention the awesome display of military hardware that would be paraded down Chang An Jie, the ironically named Avenue of Eternal Peace.

I bought plane tickets and booked a hotel, just a stone's throw from Tiananmen Square; I was really looking forward to this. But my dreams were squashed just several days prior to the big event when the phone rang at work. It was the hotel in Beijing calling to tell us that we needed to arrive by 12 noon on Friday. The police had announced that they would seal off the city at the third ring road; nobody was allowed to enter or exit without proof of residency. Friends from Beijing then called to say that they had been warned to stay off the streets, to remain indoors, and to keep the curtains closed. No foreigners were allowed to even see the parade. This came as a shock but also a disappointment. I couldn't understand what the government was afraid of. What harm could foreigners possibly do to their anniversary celebration? Surely they couldn't be worried about us seeing their military technology because the whole thing was going to be televised. First I was denied my dream of travelling to Tibet and then this. There was one more travel restriction we were soon to experience, this time closer to our home.

Sometime around 2001 or 2002 we were invited by Ayi to visit her cousin on a nearby island. We jumped at the chance to visit what sounded like it would be a remote fishing community. We set out early one morning in May, crammed into a *mian bao che* with Ayi, her daughter, and a brother. Sara and I also had with us a reluctant visitor.

James was the 18 year old brother of a friend of ours. He had come with his dad to visit and travel with his sister and her husband and children. Because they couldn't all fit in a single taxi, James rode down to the train station with some other friends. Their taxi was delayed, and like a scene from a movie, James arrived on the platform just in time to see his family on the train, pulling away. Left alone in downtown Dalian with very little money, no phone, and absolutely no Chinese language, he was for good reason distraught. Our friends called us to ask us to keep an eye out for him, but the reality was he would be virtually impossible to spot. He was ethnically Korean, so he would simply blend into the crowd. A couple of hours later, with a knock at our door, James appeared. Luckily, he had one of his brother-in-law's business cards in his pocket and he showed this to a taxi driver who took him to the development zone. From there he walked, recognizing the way, to our apartment. So for the May holiday week we had James with us as a guest, and rather than spend the day alone he decided to accompany us to the island.

The island, called Guang Lu Dao, was about an hour ride by ferry from the port at Shang Miao Cun. We were not disappointed by the scenery and it reminded me of a Chinese version of the Gulf Islands, on Canada's west coast. There was no industry other than fishing and farming and I guessed there were several thousand inhabitants. Ayi's cousin met us at the ferry terminal in a pick up truck and took us to his home a short drive away. The fishing families lived in semi-detached houses that sat in rows like the plastic hotels on a monopoly board. Each family had a small courtyard with pigs and chickens and an outhouse for a lavatory. Behind the house was a littered assortment of green glass fishing floats, resembling overgrown mutant peeled grapes, and other necessities of the fishing industry, which eventually made way to cultivated fields.

When I visited the outhouse I was surprised to find a western-style toilet rather than the usual hole-in-the-ground 'squatty' that are common in rural China. Normally I am pleased to see a western toilet but this one was a repugnant mess. Although it was free of human waste and probably seemed clean to our hosts, the sight of the rust coloured stains and layers of scum on the seat prevented me from using it in the way it was intended. I am no stranger to filthy, revolting toilets—after all China is famous for those—but this one struck me as odd. Why bother installing a sit-down toilet if it is kept so filthy it can't be sat on? In a moment of impulsiveness I pulled out our new digital camera and snapped a photo. Why exactly I did so I can't say for sure. Later that day when our host asked to see the photos on my camera—he was impressed by the new technology—I forgot about the nasty toilet shot. When he scrolled through the photos and stopped at the toilet photo I felt embarrassed. He laughed when he saw it but I'm sure he must have felt a 'loss of face'. What a maroon I am!

The inside of *biao ge's* house was much like other Chinese rural homes, very simply furnished with low wooden stools and a table in the dining area. The food was cooked in a large wok that sat over a stove fuelled by twigs, corn husks, or dried grass. From the stove, pipes transported heat to a raised platform bed, a *kang,* on which the whole family slept.

The walls were typically bare save a calendar with images of churches and a picture of Jesus. Was it possible that Ayi's family were Christians? They were indeed Christian, they said. There was no church on the island and it appeared that they worshipped in private. How they came to be Christian we were not able to discern but likely their parents had been converted by missionaries prior to the Communist Revolution in 1949.

Ayi stokes the fire for the wok and *kang*, Guanglu Island.

Ayi's family had prepared a huge seafood feast for us that belied the image of the abject poverty of their living conditions. Clams, mussels, prawns, seaweed, jellyfish, and scallops; it would have cost a fortune anywhere else in the world, but here, Ayi's cousin had harvested it all himself. The meal was helped down with beer and *baijiu* which inexplicably was poured from a four litre plastic jug that resembled a Jerry Can. Given that *baijiu* has been likened to rocket fuel by many foreigners perhaps it was fitting. I later learned that *baijiu* is sold bulk, by weight, in the markets.

Just after lunch the woman of the house implored us to stay for several days. We thanked them but insisted that we had to return home in the evening. The surprise on their faces was easy to see and seemed to indicate more than disappointment, it was worry. They explained that there was only one ferry leaving the island for the mainland that day, and it was about to leave any minute. In a great panic we insisted that we had to leave immediately, for we had brought only one diaper for little Cosmo and had no changes of clothes because we were under the assumption that this was a three hour cruise. It turned out to be more like a Chinese Gilligan's Island.

After racing back to the port, we saw the ferry just pulling away, the second time in several days poor James had seen such a sight. A little bit perturbed, we nevertheless returned to the house and got mentally prepared to sleep all together with the family on the *kang*. Cosmo wasn't feeling well and we just hoped for the best, that he wouldn't get diarrhoea or vomit on his only pair of clothes and use his only diaper. Sara wasn't too happy about the situation but what could we do? We just had to make the best of it.

We had been back at the house for not more than an hour when a young man appeared at the door, wearing a white track suit, looking fit but casual. He introduced himself and explained that he was from the *gong an*, the Public Security Bureau. He asked to see our passports, and luckily Sara had brought them along. After examining them for a minute or so he informed us that we were not permitted to be on the island and would have to leave immediately.

Our hosts were furious, but the policeman was adamant; there were no foreigners allowed on the island, it was the law. We explained that actually we had intended to leave but the ferry had already gone and there was nothing we could do until morning. Not completely satisfied with this, the policeman insisted that we go with him to the port and charter a boat to take us home. We refused, citing a lack of money, which was true. Alternatively, we could stay, under house arrest, in a hotel at the port until morning. Fury was turning to embarrassment for our hosts and they pleaded with the officer to be lenient. They had invited their foreign friends and wanted to show them the temple, the pride of the island, and to eat homemade *jiaozi* together for dinner. In case they hadn't lost enough face from my toilet photo they were losing a lot of face from this incident.

A *jiaozi* dinner with family and friends is the ultimate expression of Chinese warmth and happiness and after some negotiations the policeman agreed to allow us to stay until dinner. We were not to leave the house under any circumstances and he would be waiting for our arrival at the hotel after dinner.

We contemplated why we were not allowed on the island and surmised that it must be due to military or naval operations nearby. We also wondered how the police had caught wind of our presence so quickly and how they found the house we were staying in. Obviously we stood out from the locals, but had someone actually reported us? Curiously, James, who was wearing a Roots Canada fleece jacket, went undetected by the *gong an*. He sat quietly the whole time, scared to say a word because his passport and his entire ID were with his family in Beijing. We joked that he would make a great spy in China but he would have to learn some Chinese.

Ayi's cousin, a proud host, insisted that we defy the order and took us out the back way to his boat, and Hanna and I set to sea for a very pleasant ride while Sara and Cosmo remained at the house. Dinner was wonderful and, true to his word, the officer was waiting in the lobby of the hotel for us to arrive. Perhaps it was a twist of fate because with two young kids and Western expectations it could have been a miserable night on the *kang* with Ayi and her whole family.

We returned to Dalian the next morning with quite the story of being under house arrest on the forbidden Guang Lu Dao. Shortly after this incident I searched the Internet to find out more about exactly where we, as foreigners, could and could not go in China. Interestingly, I found a Chinese government run website that detailed the names of each place in China that foreigners could legally visit. All other places were therefore off limits. In popular, well travelled provinces like Yunnan there were fifty or so places we could visit but in our Liaoning province, incredibly, there were only eleven places we were technically allowed to go. I was blown away by this, but in reality, other than Lushun and Guang Lu Dao, I have never been prevented from travelling in our province, or anywhere in North East China.

It is not just foreigners who have their mobility limited in China. The citizens themselves are subject to a system of household registration known as *hukou*. In the *hukou* system, each citizen is tied to their place of residency and is deemed to be either urban or rural. Clearly there is an advantage to having a city *hukou* and some people have called it China's apartheid, although obviously it isn't based on race or ethnicity. The *hukou* system has been relaxed in the past few years but I have witnessed its power and effect on several friends.

In one horrible case, the sister of a friend, who ran a small clothing stall in a local mall, was questioned by police and asked to show her ID. Her *hukou* was from a smaller town several hours north of Dalian. According to her sister, she was beaten and detained for several days in police custody. In the end, she got free, probably by paying somebody off. In another case of seemingly unlawful confinement, Pengyou was arrested and thrown in the slammer for no apparent reason and wasn't ever given a reason: No *habeas corpus* in China. On his second day in custody he happened to see a policeman he recognized. He convinced the policeman he was innocent and was let go. In neither case was there any trial or hearing.

The *hukou* also gets in the way when people want to get married or have a baby. Alice, a good friend of ours and a Chinese citizen, was able to register herself as living with a family in Dalian city. Whenever she needed to do anything, like apply for a passport, have a baby, or get married, she would have to go down and visit these friends and take their paperwork to whichever public office required it. In reality, she was married to, and living with, a Canadian man and living some 30 km away from her fake *hukou*. Without it she couldn't do anything and could be subject to imprisonment or deportation to Heilongjiang province where she was originally from. For another couple I know, a Canadian woman and Chinese man, getting married meant having to take a train way up to Qiqihar, his hometown near the Russian border because his *hukou* was there. They couldn't get legally married in Dalian, despite the fact that they were both living and working there.

Restrictions on mobility exist not only on Chinese soil but in Chinese cyberspace too. Websites that I use regularly that are currently or have been blocked in China include: Wikipedia, Hotmail, Yahoo!, Google, Facebook, YouTube, and even my beloved CBC. The Great Firewall of China, as some like to call it, can be broken down by use of proxy servers but it is a nuisance. Sometimes I simply don't have the energy to fight like the Mongol hordes just to get through the wall.

'Why?' the foreigners ask, knowing full well that the answer is obvious: the Chinese government is scared of free flowing information.

'But it's so futile!' we scream to each other a couple of times a week.

We can get information from other sources so mostly it is an irritation—or *ma fan* as the Chinese say—and nothing more. It certainly is frustrating for teachers in China who rely on the Internet as a source of teaching materials that are scarce in hard copy.

It is frustrating for the Chinese too. Many of my students think their government is ridiculous for such extreme censorship, but others are less deprecating, calling the demands of the pro free-flow groups 'information imperialism'. They point out, quite rightly, that most of what is written about China in Western media sources, including the Internet, is biased and anti-Chinese. The direction of information flow is also seen as unbalanced, favouring English language, US-dominated media. When was the last time Canadians were heavily influenced by anything or anyone Chinese? Bruce Lee maybe?

People in the West can't seem to fathom that the Chinese could ever support censorship. When the Canadian Broadcasting Corporation's website cbc.ca was blocked in 2008 the comments posted by readers told the story.

From a reader with a Chinese surname:

> 'That sounds right thing to do. CBC is biased on any issues related to China. Chinese people won't get true stories from it anyway'.

And a response from (presumably) a 'Canadian':

> Communist sympathizers on here? Nope. They are paid shills using pseudonyms operating out of or orders of the PRC consulate.... doing exactly what their masters in Beijing would never allow their own citizens to do. The PRC has lots of trolls surfing the net posting pro PRC propaganda on sites just like this one.

And this is where the Canadians and other Westerners miss the boat. Yes, the Chinese government does have 'trolls surfing the net' and perhaps they do post propaganda as part of their job. But that is nothing compared to the real number of regular Chinese citizens who are so bursting with patriotism for China that they will post propaganda for free, because they want to and because they believe it. I see an irony here in that Canadians who cherish so dearly our freedom of expression have become so cynical while our poor oppressed Chinese friends remain optimistic about their future. Ultimately, which do we prefer, optimism or cynicism?

Having described some of the ways people are limited in China, I now can turn to a discussion of the freedoms that I've enjoyed living here.

It seems that while the Chinese miss out on the large issue freedoms there is more freedom to do things as you wish day to day than there is in Canada. When I want to cross the road in China, I cross it, regardless of whether or not I'm near a marked crosswalk. If I want to ride my bike, I don't worry about finding a helmet, scared that I might be stopped and ticketed by the police for doing something we grew up doing. I don't even need to wear a helmet to ride a motorcycle.

It has long been a pet peeve of mine that the opportunity for responsible decision making has been taken away from the individual in North American society. Americans can complete a tour of duty in the Gulf or Afghanistan, kill or be killed for their country, and on their return they are deemed not yet responsible enough for a can of Coors Lite. In Canada, the consumption of a bottle of beer requires one to be an adult of nineteen in most provinces and to make your way down to a government-run liquor store. God forbid you want to buy a drink after regular business hours, or on Sunday.

In China, if you are thirsty and need a drink, you go to the nearest store. They will fix you up. Coke, almond juice, goat's milk in a bag, and yes, even booze. All these choices are side by side on the shelves, presented with the assumption that the consumer is free to choose and to act responsibly. The bars in China close when there are no more patrons. They don't get too uptight about drunks in the street waking people up, but then again, with all the firecrackers going off and horns honking you would hardly notice a few drunks yelling at one another.

Another irony that you notice after living in China a while is that although there are police everywhere, nobody really fears them. Yet, in Canada, I don't know anybody whose heart doesn't beat a little bit faster when they are driving and see a police car nearby.

Other freedoms enjoyed in China include the freedom to get things done, and in a timely manner. The shops are open for business and so are the artisans and workers. There is a general willingness in Chinese society to make things happen. Need a bus to take 24 people on a day trip and want to leave in two hours? 'No problem sir, do you need a driver?'

Although there are undeniable merits to North America's safety conscious modern manner, the freedom from legal action in China is a huge plus too. It means that if you are a teacher, you can still take kids on a field trip without everybody signing forms and giving six month's notice. It means you can open a gym and not be responsible when your friend breaks his leg playing roller hockey in it.

Of course, we also get to the play the white card. Got a big nose, blue eyes, and 'yellow hair'? Well, you'll be forgiven for a lot of things, and in exchange for this latitude that you are given you will have to let a lot of strangers take photos with you and have people call out 'heller' as a greeting about thirty times a day.

With freedom comes responsibility, and to be fair, many foreigners in China—myself included—have crossed the line. Most often irresponsible and rude behaviour can be attributed to culture shock and ignorance of local norms. The things I have heard foreigners say about and to Chinese people are shocking; they would never even dream of saying such words back in Canada to anyone, anytime. It's a reaction to the helplessness that we feel when we can't communicate and when we perceive the locals' behaviour to be irrational.

When the subway train pulls into the station and you want to disembark you find yourself being stampeded, it's like the running of the bulls in Pamplona but going the wrong direction. The crowd of people that forces their way on the train doesn't seem to care if you get off or not. Is there a right way to deal with this situation? I'm not sure, but deliberately knocking people over 'to prove a point' is definitely not appropriate. Telling people to 'f— off' in English isn't appropriate either but nearly everyone I know has done it at some point in their stay in China. Looking back, I feel embarrassed about the hissy fits I have thrown over the years here but I have come to see them as 'understandable wrongs' that luckily tapered off with time.

Other examples of over-the-top behaviour that I have witnessed and been a part of have occurred during stag parties.

Grown men + cheap beer + sense of freedom=idiotic fun. One night as twenty or so adult males walked from a sushi restaurant to a bar, two fellows started a friendly wrestling match. The spirit was contagious and before we knew it there was an all out brawl amongst the twenty friends and colleagues in the middle of the city's oldest and most central public space, *Zhongshan* Square. In Canada the police would have been called but in China we were simply ignored by everyone and allowed to act like fools. Later, a Chinese wife told one of the wrestlers her friend had witnessed a gang of Russians fighting in the streets that night. She was terrified by the sight. If she only knew they weren't Russian gangsters but Canadian teachers!

On another occasion—a double stag party—I came up with a game to occupy the guys on our walk between venues. Each fiancé had a team of men that he had to transport on a 'chariot'. The chariots were bicycle carts borrowed from the local Korean grocer and the relay races were run through large gates on the main street in 'Korean Town'. It was ridiculously fun but irresponsible; the chariots fell over and banged into cars, all on the main street in the dark. Crowds of people stopped to stare and wondered what on earth we were doing. When we explained that the chariot drivers were soon to be married they nodded their heads in understanding; stag parties were okay! On that particular occasion the police did drive by but didn't even bother to stop. Instead they slowed down and called out over their loudspeakers 'go home'. We decided to interpret that as 'go somewhere else' and moved on. I was horrified to see the chariots badly damaged when I returned them to the grocer and tried to pay several hundred *renminbi* compensation, saying '*duibuqi*' and '*baoqian*'. No need to be sorry, the grocer replied, threw the carts on their side and jumped up and down on them until they resumed their original form, sort of. With a laugh and a wave he sent us on our way.

I could go on and on. I'm sure going to miss the freedom of living in China.

16

Photo © Sara Lang

The author drinking a medicinal tonic sold on the street in Macau.

Mongolian Doctors

An apple a day keeps the doctor away. If only it were that simple. Our health is of paramount importance but in China health care might be better termed health scare. Every expat in China has horror stories from local hospital experiences. This chapter tells just a few that come to mind.

The Chinese have an ancient tradition of interest and research into medicine that is world renowned and many

Chinese are very proud of TCM—Traditional Chinese Medicine. Perhaps as a result of this pride every Chinese has a portfolio of home remedies. One of the funniest home remedy stories went like this:

A small group of Canadians were playing hockey in Liaoyang with several of our Chinese friends on an outdoor rink. The weather was unseasonably warm and the ice was in poor condition. My good friend Yin had the misfortune to get his skate stuck in a deep crevasse in the ice and he twisted his ankle quite badly. Back in his hotel room after the game the team gathered around to have a look and give advice. The Canadians felt it ironic that the Chinese didn't know about RICE—Rest, Ice, Compression, Elevation. Instead we were told that Lao Fu, our eldest Chinese team member, would perform a traditional Chinese treatment.

We had only just met Lao Fu the day before. He was in his mid-forties but looked much older. Dressed in a long green People's Liberation Army overcoat he sat quietly on the bus and periodically pulled a seemingly endless supply of small *baijiu* bottles from his pockets. As it turns out *baijiu* was not only a vice for Lao Fu, it was also a solution to nearly any problem he encountered.

'Step back, step back' we were ordered, as Lao Fu, like a magician, pulled out yet another bottle of *baijiu* from his pocket. This one was an ornately painted white ceramic bottle with a feminine hourglass shape. It looked like the good stuff. We watched in amazement as Lao Fu poured the foul smelling rocket fuel into an ash tray, pulled out a cigarette lighter, and lit the spirit on fire.

'What the hell is he doing?' demanded the Canadians. 'No, no,' we pleaded, 'he needs to *ice* it'.

'*Hao, hao, mei wenti*'—It's good, no problem—our Chinese

friends insisted. They assured us that Lao Fu knew what he was doing. He was in the Chinese military, after all, and this was Chinese tradition. Who were we to argue?

We watched in amazement and horror as Lao Fu dipped his fingers into the flaming alcohol and spread the boiling spirit over the patient's ankle. How Lao Fu didn't burn his own hands I can't say; it was like watching a fire walker. Meanwhile the patient, Yin, moaned in pain.

After the treatment our Chinese friends declared the procedure a success and insisted that Yin would be better in the morning. The patient himself stated emphatically that he would skate the next morning in the game. The vigorous assurances from our Chinese friends nearly fooled us but when we awoke we found Yin's ankle had swelled up to the size of a grapefruit and had all the colours of a New York Rangers hockey jersey. He didn't play hockey again for a year.

'What happened to the Chinese medicine?' we jeered at our Chinese friends in the playful manner of hockey teammates. 'You said Lao Fu was a Chinese doctor'.

'He's a *menggu daifu!*' one of them said.

'Menggu daifu, menggu daifu' we repeated to ourselves trying to ascertain the meaning. Finally we got it: A *menggu daifu* is a Mongolian doctor, and when said in this context means a quack.

It seems that *menggu daifu* are not only masquerading as Chinese hockey players but have infiltrated the hospitals in China as well. Misdiagnosis is so common I am tempted to call it the norm. I catch pneumonia or bronchitis about every other year, ever since I first came down with it when I was eight years old. I can diagnose it myself but usually go to the doctor for confirmation and to get a prescription for antibiotics. When I did so in China a couple of years ago the doctor insisted that I run through a battery of tests. The doctors and hospitals make money this way and they especially take advantage of foreigners who have medical insurance plans. Rather than fighting them I submitted to their tests. Blood tests and a blood pressure exam I expected, but I was rather surprised by the need for a CT scan. Once it was all said and done the diagnosis came in: I had heart disease!

I was only 36 years old and given what I knew about Chinese hospitals I was tempted to ignore it. Considering that my father had just undergone a triple by-pass surgery and both my maternal grandparents had heart disease, combined with my penchant for eating copious amounts of bacon and eggs and prompted by some urging from Sara, I thought I should at least look into it the next time I was near a hospital I trusted. That opportunity comes once a year when we pass through Bangkok, Thailand on our winter holiday. The doctors at the amazing Bumrungrad hospital all speak English and have been trained overseas. They ran me through a series of exhaustive tests in which I was hooked up to expensive machines and then was declared totally, one hundred per cent healthy. The Thai doctor just shook his head in wonder when I told him that I had been diagnosed with heart disease in China.

The following year while getting a massage from a traditional medicine doctor as treatment for a sore back I was diagnosed with kidney failure and instructed to avoid eating black fungus. That's easier said than done in China. I re-

peated the process in Bangkok and was told 'Chinese traditional doctors have a tendency to blame nearly everything on
the kidneys'. Again I got a clean bill of health.

In a case of mistaken identity Sara was told she had Hepati-
tis B after a blood test was taken in order for her to work at
the local kindergarten our children attended. After insisting
that she had received immunizations for Hep A and B and
further arguing the unlikelihood of her contracting a disease
that required body fluid exchange, the Kindergarten nurse
returned to the hospital and *voila*, her real test results
appeared. Sara was deemed fit enough to work at the kindergarten after all.

Misdiagnosis isn't funny, but that's because you haven't
heard this story yet. When 'foreign experts' first arrive in
China they are required to pass a medical check before
residence visas will be authorized. The medical check is fairly
standard but one year an extra keen doctor decided he
needed to see all the male teachers' genitalia. I suppose he
was looking for signs of STDs. In any event, one fellow I know,
who shall go unnamed, was deemed by the doctor to have
testicles that were too large. The doctor informed the patient
that his bulbous sac was so hefty that he would be unable to
have children. Naturally his wife was quite concerned about
this diagnosis, but the Ol' Bull has since fathered two children.

The diagnoses are not the only problem in Chinese health
care, the medicine itself is a worry. It is well known in the
West that traditional Chinese medicine relies on natural
ingredients and that harvesting such ingredients causes
environmental degradation in some cases and poaching and
inhumane treatment of animals in other cases. Those issues,
although valid and important, are not the primary concern

for people in China. Foreigners are especially concerned about the inclination of Chinese doctors to prescribe mass quantities of medicine and the locals' proclivity to consuming said quantities. It may be fine and dandy to eat copious amounts of herbs, or even Tiger penis, if you think it will help but these days it is pharmaceutical products that are being pushed on the public. In China nothing is spared from being copied and medicine is no exception. Fake or poor quality medicine has become a huge problem. In the campaign to become self sufficient and profit making, hospitals look for cheaper sources of medicine. One Chinese friend was engaged in a business that basically involved driving around and selling medicine out of the trunk of his car. Lord only knows where they got the stuff from.

One day my good friend Darren Brown contracted a case of Pink Eye. It didn't seem to be clearing up on its own so he popped down to the local private health clinic a few hundred metres down the road from our apartment complex. They put him on an intravenous drip. Within minutes he felt that something was seriously wrong and got the nurse's attention. He told me later her face told him his situation was grave. He barely had the strength to call his wife who was rendered helpless while on an overnight train returning from her hometown in Heilongjiang province. She did, however call a friend to check on him. This friend called me the instant she saw Darren.

I rushed over to the clinic to find a disturbing sight. Brownie was a twisting, moaning mess. Blood had erupted out of his eye socket and drenched his pillow. Leaving the room so he couldn't hear my conversation, I called another friend and together we scraped up as much cash as we could find and called an ambulance. We took him to the main hospital in the city centre and with strong demands from our Chinese friend, Sophia, managed to insist that the *menggu daifu* from the clinic accompany us to the real hospital. She would be needed to explain how things went so terribly wrong from a simple intravenous drip. Within a few days Brownie had recovered but it was a close call. Around the same time the father of one of our students actually died as a result of fake medicine administered by a doctor in a hospital. Brownie was lucky.

It seems a bit inappropriate to call Brownie lucky, considering I've taken him to hospital on several occasions. One afternoon while we were playing roller hockey he collided with another friend, Bill, and cut his head open. We decided he needed a stitch or two and emptying our pockets our group of friends came up with about two hundred *yuan*, more than enough for a few stitches. At the hospital the doctor started prepping Darren for stitches and told me to go and pay the cashier before she would begin stitching. When I asked '*duo shao qian?*' she replied outrageously '*si bai kuai*' —four hundred *yuan*.

'What! My son was born in a room just around the corner and it only cost 900, how can three stitches cost 400?' I demanded.

'The thread comes from Austria,' the doctor replied.

'Bollocks!' we both said and Brownie got up and we walked out.

It was clearly an example of the hospital deliberately trying to scam us, and we assumed this was because we were foreigners. I had assured Brownie that the two hundred *yuan* in my pocket would be more than enough to cover the job because I myself had required stitches from a hockey game a couple of years earlier.

In that incident I was playing ice hockey without any equipment because I hadn't yet brought any from Canada and after charging the net it fell on me and cut me just above the eye. My Chinese friend Yin drove me to a nearby hospital in downtown Dalian. After purchasing a small blue booklet for three *yuan* I visited a doctor who agreed that I did need stitches but after a search through various drawers and cupboards declared that the hospital didn't have any thread so they couldn't sew me up. I was completely bewildered. How could a hospital, located in the heart of a city with a population of six million inhabitants, not have any thread? Yin didn't seem to find it that odd, shrugged, and simply said 'let's go to another hospital'. The next hospital did have thread and although I don't recall the actual cost, I know it wasn't the golden Austrian thread and amounted to only a few dollars. I do recollect that getting the stitches removed, at the clinic that poisoned Brownie, cost only six *yuan*, or $1.

Children get sick. That's an unavoidable reality in any country. Chickenpox and measles we expected but they didn't turn up. Instead our kids came down with diseases with scary names like Scarlet Fever and Hand, Foot, and Mouth Disease, names that invoke images of nineteenth century death. In actuality they too are relatively innocuous diseases but require medical attention nonetheless. Without fail the doctors in China will prescribe an intravenous drip. For whatever reason the IV drip is the method of choice, but who wants to sit around in a cold Chinese hospital for three hours with a needle in your arm hooked up to a bottle? And that's the best case scenario. Sometimes they stick the needle directly into your forehead, as they did to Cosmo when he was just a year old. A toddler had better be really sick, basically listless, to sit still for an hour with a needle in his forehead. There certainly isn't any 'child friendly' medicine in China either. Nothing that tastes like grape or bubble gum and Cosmo simply refused to swallow pills. We tried crushing the pills into a powder and putting them in juice for him to drink but that didn't work either. So when he had Scarlet Fever I took him to hospital every night and hooked him up to the IV drip and read him Tintin books.

The propensity for intravenous injections is bizarre and I have one lasting image that I will never ever forget. It occurred in the first few years we were in China when the main road in the town of Manjiatan was just a pot-holed track lined with dirt sidewalks. A middle-aged Canadian woman I worked with had come down with some sort of ailment and was hospitalized in the local hospital, which was at that time still government-run. She had been put on a drip and told to stay the night. Everyday at five o'clock in the evening a bus took us home from work, a twenty five kilometre trip. Not wanting to spend the night in the hospital, the woman, with the aid of her husband, decided to make a run for it. As our bus rounded the corner about to drive off and leave her for the night we saw a desperate scene: battling through a dust storm, dirt clouds and garbage swirling around her in disgusting tornados, Marilyn pathetically struggled down the road towards the bus, frantically waving at us to stop for her, all the while still attached to the drip, while her husband scurried beside her with a fraught look on his face balancing the desire to bolt onto the bus and escape the madness with his responsibility to hold the apparatus that held the drip bag. It was sad, yet so absurd that we couldn't help but laugh.

It is perhaps unfair to write a chapter on Chinese health care without noting at least a few positive points. One friend who broke his collar bone had several pins put in during surgery and claims that the care he received was excellent and that his shoulder has never felt better. Others I know underwent knee surgery with favourable outcomes.

One nice advantage we experienced in China was getting preferential treatment in the hospitals. As foreigners we were often pushed to the front of the line. And because we either paid cash for our treatment or were covered by medical insurance, treatment occurred then and there, as opposed to the months or even years people in Canada have to wait for some procedures.

Although as a foreigner you could cut the queue and that was appreciated, should you be a woman visiting the gynae-cologist, once you arrived at the front of the line you would have to spread your legs and get examined not only by the doctor but by the entire line of impatient patients. I guess it was payback for queue jumping. At least it was a good opportunity to find out if foreigners look different in the nether regions.

Some readers may be thinking 'how awful' to use our status as foreigners to get preferential treatment. The reality in Chinese hospitals is that doctors are underpaid and are 'on the take' so really our only advantage is that we didn't have to pay to get an advantage. Others simply paid off the doctors to get to the head of the line. In one case I know, a Canadian friend's Chinese mother-in-law paid the doctors to ensure that her granddaughter was the first baby to be bathed in the communal baby bath water. We didn't bribe any doctors and that might explain why Hanna came home from the hospital still covered in amniotic fluid!

Another funny hospital moment came after Brownie broke his leg playing roller hockey in late June. We felt sorry for him missing our annual Canada Day beach party in Jinshitan so we decided to take the party to him. Twenty five Canadians crammed into his VIP hospital room with a keg of beer. The nurses didn't look pleased—neither did Brownie actually; he was in pain—but they didn't really say anything and left us alone to celebrate.

There is no shortage of irony in China and the medical situation highlights it. While there is growing interest in Chinese medicine in the West, and the Chinese continue to take pride in their medical traditions, for many foreigners living in China an unhappy experience with a *menggu daifu* is the last straw that sends them packing for home.

Part three:

CLOSING CEREMONY

Distinguished readers,
Ladies and gentlemen,
Dear friends,

Dragons, Donkeys, and Dust is coming to a conclusion. The curtain is about to fall on...*yawn*...the previous pages have witnessed...*yawn*...a grand celebration of life in China...

...*yawn, yawn*... if I have to sit through one more ceremony I will scream. Or perhaps just fall asleep in my chair. Don't worry, I won't be the only one asleep and we will surely be awakened by the firecrackers.

17

Troops stationed outside the Japanese embassy, Beijing, April 2005.

Da Wenti

I teach history. It's funny how I can remember the dates of events that occurred long before I was born but recent events are mixed up in an indiscernible mash of memory. Perhaps it is because the events that we experience and witness don't seem like history. No matter how much passion an event draws out from us, we can't fathom how it may be looked upon in the future. It's bizarre to even consider that today will be recorded as history tomorrow. When I reflect upon what I have witnessed in twelve years in China I am astonished at just how much is *history* in the sense of being noteworthy and significant. I've seen, heard, and felt, a lot of major events and *da wenti* —big issues or problems.

1989, Tiananmen Square. You can play it up or play it down, call it a massacre or merely an incident, either way, it was, and is, a *da wenti*. On June 4th, 1989, I was just finishing up high school in Vancouver, but I remember seeing on TV the tanks roll down Chang An Jie—the Avenue of Eternal Peace. The lasting image, of course, is the famous photo of 'The Tank Man,' that brave soul who stood up to a convoy of tanks, and stopped them. The massacre by the PLA on June 4-5th was the culmination of a span of several months of students, workers, and ordinary Chinese who were standing up for their rights, for their new conception of a future China. And they weren't radical fools. There was support within the upper echelons of the Chinese government. Zhao Zi Yang, in particular, the former Premier of China and then the General Secretary of the Communist Party, was actively working to reform China, including fighting corruption, a major concern of the Tiananmen demonstrators. He appealed to the students to end their hunger strike and go home and admitted the students' right to criticize the government and party, about which he famously said 'we are already old, it doesn't matter to us any more'.

Martial law was declared in Beijing the day following Zhao's appeal to the students and he was purged from the party. He lived the rest of his days essentially under house arrest until his death from pneumonia in 2005. His death was largely ignored, his funeral was not televised and he received neither a eulogy nor a burial plot with the other revolutionary leaders.

Jiang Zemin took his place while Deng Xiaoping remained China's paramount leader, although technically without a position in either government or the party. Although I wasn't in China for this event, the China I first saw in 1994 was very much just emerging from the shadow of the Tiananmen massacre. Even today under-cover police still lurk all around Tiananmen Square. The last time I was there was about 3 am, taking a team photo with a trophy our hockey team had lost in a tournament and then had stolen from the banquet. As we set up the Bethune Cup under Mao's portrait, a plain-clothed PSB officer paced back and forth nearby, pretending to be making a call on his cell phone. It was an absurd display, and we called him on it.

'Hey, who are you calling? Your wife?' we chided in our simple Mandarin, a tad braver than usual, encouraged by *pijiu* consumption.

He scampered away.

The Dragons, Tiananmen Square, 3 am.

Internationally, Tiananmen may have tarnished the otherwise unblemished and heroic rise of Deng Xiaoping, a revolutionary who was twice purged and then returned to power to kick start the reforms that led to China's opening and modernization. In China, Deng is, and I presume always will be, viewed as a magnificent visionary leader. By coincidence I arrived in Guangzhou in February 1997 on the day of his funeral.

I was put into a windowless room in the Guangdong Victory Hotel. Exhausted from jet lag I didn't have the energy to go outside but couldn't sleep from the excitement of being back in China. I hadn't brought a book and I didn't keep a diary. That left watching TV. Every channel was showing the same footage of Deng's funeral procession and a retrospective of Comrade Deng Xiaoping. I didn't realize at the time that it was truly the end of an era. Although China's government can still be seen to be authoritarian, no more would it be run by a dictator with an indefinite term in office. Ironically, it was Deng who changed China, yet he needed to pass on in order for much of his New China to really take shape.

My job in Guangzhou was teaching ESL to primary school students at Wen De Road School for a company called Open Sesame. I was required to use teaching materials made by Sesame Street and I soon found myself a little uncomfortable with the indoctrination of American popular culture. After finishing the food unit in Big Bird's Yellow Book we were instructed to take our students to McDonalds, were they could practice saying 'I like hamburgers!' and other insidious phrases I was forced to teach them. This didn't sit well with me. I also had some unfinished personal business in Canada and had received a letter of acceptance to UBC's Bachelor of Education program, so I packed it in after only three months and headed home.

On my way home I had one last weekend in Hong Kong with a friend I was teaching with. The atmosphere in Hong

Kong is always exciting but in May 1997 it was electric. The Handover, the return of administrative control to Mainland China was just weeks away. The tension was palpable and it was the only thing on people's minds. Hundreds of thousands of Hong Kongers had emigrated to Canada, the US, Australia and elsewhere in the few years preceding the Handover, in anticipation of a nasty regression, or at least to watch from a distance.

Little has changed, in real, measurable terms, since the return. The comrades in Beijing were smart enough to leave them largely alone and the Hong Kong administration has done a decent job of balancing the rights of their citizens with the expectations from Beijing. In other words, they know when to censor and shut down and when to let business carry on as usual, which is most of time. It was perhaps the greatest non-event to have been speculated about for so long and it ended happily for most people involved.

We can't begin to comprehend the pride felt by the mainland Chinese when Hong Kong returned. Their pride quadrupled the anxiety and trepidation felt by the Hong Kongers. The 'One Country, Two Systems' policy was the first test of a modern and increasingly strong China to see if it could regain and assert its sovereignty and integrity. There would be more tests to come.

As you have read already I returned to China in August 1998 with Sara and a foetus that would soon be known as Hanna. There was plenty of excitement and uncertainty in our first year in China. Apartment break-ins and job insecurity created some. An international incident brought some more.

In the spring of 1999 NATO began bombing Yugoslavia under the pretext of helping the Kosovars, ethnic Albanians who had claimed independence from the former great federation of nations that had diminished by then to essentially one nation, Serbia, and a sprinkling of minorities. Those were the pre-911 days, when it was okay to help out Muslims, they were freedom fighters back then and not the terrorists we know and fear today.

The Chinese were adamantly against this war. They spewed their usual spiel about non-interference in others' domestic affairs. Their policy is bunk; they've made it up to justify demanding others to keep their noses out of the Taiwan issue, the Tibet issue and the question of Uyghur separatism. And worse, they are hypocrites; they themselves do in fact 'interfere'. But this time I happened to agree with them.

Belgrade, 1999. The Chinese embassy was rebroadcasting, according to some sources, Yugoslavian army communications. Apparently the Americans believed Yugoslavian president Slobodan Milosevic happened to be in the Chinese embassy and the CIA planned an attack to kill him. Sound implausible? Remember that previous American president Bush Sr. regretted not killing Saddam Hussein when he had the chance. Luckily, Junior got the chance. When the bombs fell on the Chinese embassy in Belgrade, three Chinese journalists were killed. The Chinese media made a huge deal of it and the masses were outraged. Who can blame them?

The American embassy in Beijing was swarmed and pelted with rocks and bricks. Luckily for us, the state-run media insisted on referring to the offenders as 'US-led NATO'. This meant that Canadians were off the radar of the common irate

Chinese. There were a few studious fellows out there who bothered to look up NATO and realized that the Canadian embassy was a decent target too. Canadian officials decided to shut down the embassy. We were registered at the embassy in case of emergencies like this. They forgot to call.

There was a brief moment of uncertainty and a lot of our expat friends—British, American, and German—discussed our predicament. Would the locals who have been so friendly and open towards us turn on us now? Some of our friends lived in an apartment complex a few hundred metres down the road from our place. They received a notice on thin beige paper posted on their door:

> Dear foreign guests,
>
> The Chinese people are incensed and are swarming. Stay off the streets for your safety. If you need anything we can help you.
>
> Main office, Huaying Mansions

We survived this crisis unscathed. The worst of it was a minor incident on the street where Sara, with baby Hanna in her arms, was accosted by a young man who demanded to know if she knew of N-A-T-O. The Chinese spell out each letter instead of using the acronym. Sara played dumb and walked away.

Shortly thereafter the Chinese government began their official crack-down on the Falun Gong spiritual movement. So powerful is the government propaganda that even today, a decade later, high school students are adamant that Falun Gong is evil and will result in your death. Every year this comes up in my classes and every year the same response.

'Why?' I ask.

'Because [Falun Gong founder] Li Hong Zhi tells the people to not take medicine or see a doctor when they are ill, so many people have died'.

Then I have to tell them that all over the world people refuse medicine and medical treatment for all sorts of reasons, some of which are religious.

'Many people killed themselves because of Falun Gong' a student will explain.

'Yes, they burnt themselves in Tiananmen square, even a child!' calls out another.

Then I go into my usual routine.

'How many Muslims do you think committed suicide this year, around the world?'

'Many...thousands!' they exclaim based on their impressions of Muslim suicide bombers.

'How many Christians do you think killed themselves this year?

'Maybe thousands'.

'Buddhists?'

'None!' says a student before another interjects 'also thousands, even in China, because the pressure is so great on us'.

If this discussion has come up while teaching about the Canadian constitution and the Charter of Rights and Freedoms I will also be teaching basic law concepts and procedures so I'll finish this up with 'your Honour, I rest my case'.

But faith is faith and it can't be suppressed. CDs began to appear on our door, full of Falun Gong denouncements of the government's treatment of them. Posters were slapped up on walls and doors, even on our school's gate, propaganda to counter propaganda. One prominent Chinese teacher at our school 'disappeared'. The official line at the school was that he was sick, but an email from friends said they got a phone call from his mother: he was imprisoned in Beijing for his Falun Gong beliefs. He returned to work some months later but was promptly let go.

In the far-flung villages of Manchuria, 'heaven is high and the emperor is far away'. One woman I met declared without fear that she was a Falun Gong practitioner. The meditation and exercises kept her young and healthy, she claimed. She wasn't scared of her neighbours or the authorities in the slightest. I am scared of them though, and steer well clear of the Falun Gong protesters who camp out at the Chinese consulate in Vancouver. I'm not interested in Chinese Hare Krishnas ruining my chance for a visa.

In the last days of that year Macau was returned to China after more than a century of Portuguese rule. The 'One Country, Two Systems' model got another boost and so did Chinese nationalism. There was a huge celebration among the Chinese.

While the Chinese were celebrating the return of Macau to the motherland the rest of the world was alternating between excitement and anxiety. We were all excited about the greatest New Year's Eve party ever, December 31st, 1999. For my generation, we'd been anticipating this night for 17 years, ever since Prince sang 'tonight we're gonna party like it's 1999!' But much of the world was anxious. Remember the Y2K scare? It seems a bit ridiculous now but many folks were seriously worried. I recall how several friends emailed to ask how we were coping. They had read that China was one of the least prepared countries and the consequences would be devastating. People worried that key infrastructure would shut down and stockpiling of food and other supplies was commonplace. My quick assessment was this: The donkeys will continue to bring vegetables to the market. 'We're better off in China than anywhere else,' I told Sara.

As it turned out the millennium scare was rubbish. With Sara and two visiting friends from Canada sick and in bed, my midnight millennium celebration involved smoking a lonely cigar, washed down with a beer, outside on the street. Across the road, after the fireworks had died down, I watched two men fight over the empty cardboard fireworks box, presumably for the value of the cardboard. Hmmm, business as usual.

The next day we stopped in at the apartment of German friends who had satellite TV and we watched the midnight celebrations around the world. There were no terrorist attacks, as predicted, just the usual singing of Auld Lang Syne. The Millennium was a precursor to the rest of the year; the whole darn thing was uneventful.

2001 was action packed though. On April 1st an American surveillance (spy) plane was flying over disputed airspace near China's Hainan Island in the South China Sea. The Chinese sent up an interceptor jet which collided with the American plane. The Chinese jet crashed and its pilot was killed. The Americans managed, after an inverted roll, to safely land their plane. Unfortunately for them they did this behind enemy lines, on Hainan Island, the very place they were likely spying on.

The Chinese were enraged, and I'm with them on this one. The airspace in question is disputed largely because the US has not signed The United Nations Convention on the Law of the Sea and therefore does not accept what virtually every other country does, that a country controls the seas surrounding its coast and the air above those seas. This time the government carefully controlled the demonstrations and they didn't get out of hand like after the Belgrade embassy bombing. Thankfully this wasn't a NATO mission and being Canadian in China in 2001 was as good as it usually is.

The world's biggest event in 2001, indeed in the 21st century to date, was the terrorist attacks on the Twin Towers in New York. I remember clearly hearing about it first thing in the morning at work and watching the replays on TV in the teachers' cafeteria. Everyone, Chinese and Canadians alike, was mesmerised by the footage. But following the initial shock our views differed greatly. When I told my class what had happened, there were cheers and celebrations. I had to point out that, besides being a horrible thing to be happy about, New York was a multicultural city and without a doubt there were Chinese nationals in the wreckage.

Anyone from North America who wondered 'why us?' and 'what did we ever do to them?' would have learned a thing or

325

two about the perception of America in other countries from being in China in September 2001. Without taking an official poll, I recall that I estimated seventy percent of the Chinese that I talked to thought America got a just punishment for their hegemony, as they like to call it, and interference in other countries. With four Chinese killed by American military action in the preceding two years it is not that surprising really.

Sara and the kids had stayed back in Canada for a few extra weeks to extend their summer holiday. Sara called me that night in a panic. The news in Canada originally reported that China was a suspect country and Sara's mum had scared her by reminding her how her grandfather got stuck with his mother back in Romania at the outbreak of WWI and didn't see his father for nine years. It was an awful thought, but I was able to talk sense into her.

Just days after September 11th China attained an economic milestone it had been looking to achieve for some time: membership in the World Trade Organization. The WTO had seemed out of reach for China. It had been 15 years since China applied to join the WTO predecessor, GATT. Tiananmen didn't help their case. Neither did the anti-American demonstrations following the embassy bombing. But as the Chinese trade negotiator joked following China's accession, 'a 15-year process is a blink of the eye in the 5,000-year history of China'. The Chinese were so eagerly waiting for this day that the media had convinced the population of its impending arrival years earlier, and also stressed its importance to China. There's no shortage of irony; a nation of 'communists' excited about free trade? The government was eager to get Most Favoured Nation status from the US. Finally they would end the annual humiliation of having their human rights abuses proclaimed and debated in the US congress. Plus, they would leave behind their former club members, the Least Favoured Nations: Afghanistan, Cuba, North Korea, Myanmar and other 'rogues'. My students had been telling me since I arrived that it was going to happen any day. Never cry wolf. I stopped listening to them and was actually a little surprised when the day finally came.

When we first arrived in China we read many naysayers in the West delighting in predicting the slowdown of China's 'unsustainable' growth of about 8 % annually. It was 1998, in the midst of the Asian slowdown, and we were surrounded by empty and half completed buildings. It is hard for Westerners to not agree with the pessimists, the Chinese economic model doesn't seem to make any sense. With WTO membership, China's economy grew at even higher rates and continues to do so. Go figure, they've proved us all wrong so far.

That settled it for me; China was officially non-communist in my books. But they are stubborn buggers, these party members, and in 2003 they launched a space-craft called the Shenzhou on a rocket called the Long March. I don't get it. Who doesn't have a rocket? The Chinese launched a manned space craft into outer space and made a national hero out of the pilot, Yang Li Wei, for doing something that was first done 40 years earlier. That's like me getting an Olympic medal for running a 4-minute mile. Or being able to eat with chopsticks. Somebody has already been there, done that.

'Let me get this straight,' I ask my students, 'by your own admission you are a developing country with hundreds of millions of people living in poverty, farmers and migrants without rights or steady jobs and homes, and you are spending billions, no trillions, on sending a man up in a rocket?'

'Yes, and soon we will go to the moon!'

Wow! Neil and Buzz and the other remaining seven moon-walkers should head over to China where their bouncing on green cheese routine is appreciated.

'Why is China doing this unilaterally?' I ask. 'Other countries are now cooperating with one another, even America and Russia'.

'To show how strong we are'.

I can almost hear the opening ceremony: 'Cold War II *xianzai kaishi!'* The problem is, for China, there may only be one guy competing in this new space race. Unless, and this may be the case, this is a bronze medal heat fought between a couple of slowpokes, China and India. In this case, we may be wise to recall the tale of the tortoise and the hare. At the very least, China now has some legitimacy to the notion of it becoming a superpower. No rocket, no super-power status. Every 10 year old boy knows that.

The real excitement in China in 2003 though, was not up in the sky, but down on earth, and it all started way down in Southern China. In January 2003, as we were getting ready for a trip to the South of China, I bumped into a friend in Kaifaqu who told me he was going down to Guangzhou for the holiday. I mention this because upon our return I happened to bump into him again, standing in the cold with a cup of coffee outside of McDonald's at Kaifaqu's busiest intersection.

'How was your trip?' I asked.

'I didn't go'.

'What happened?'

'You haven't heard? Apparently there is a terrible disease that has broken out down there and people are getting really sick, even dying'.

I thought this was rubbish, and frankly my friend is an odd fellow, so I laughed it off as the usual nonsense he comes up with. Later on, I was to realize that this was the first reference I heard to SARS, or Severe Acute Respiratory Syndrome, the flu that shocked the world and had China under a lock-down in the spring of 2003.

Like many strains of influenza, this one likely started in China, where animal-to-human transmission of viruses occurs regularly due to the close quarters that people and animals keep. Apparently civet cats, little racoon-like beasts were the culprits. While the civets were busy infecting humans, we were busy looking at civets, in Guangzhou's famed Qing Ping market.

When you hear stories about the Chinese eating everything with four legs except the table, they are especially talking about the Cantonese of Guangdong province. Qing Ping market has all the evidence: Buckets of scorpions, giant turtles, skinned dogs, civet cats. It's a wonder we didn't get sick. In fact I did get terrible sick, with a chest infection of some kind, for a whole month, the entirety of our holiday. Sara thinks it was SARS. Who knows, I was smart enough not to go to a Chinese hospital.

Had I gone to a Chinese hospital when I was sick, I likely would have been misdiagnosed and sent off with a crap-load of antibiotics, perhaps getting an intravenous injection, the method of choice in China. Those were the final days of Jiang Zemin's regime, when China was pretending that SARS didn't exist. To admit to SARS would have been a loss of face for China I guess. That logic turned out to be a tad short-sighted. Word of the disease spread and soon the Chinese officials were made out to be secretive fools by the Western media.

Shoppers pick through buckets of scorpions, Qing Ping Market.

By hiding the truth, they inadvertently promoted paranoia in the people. Foreigners were not immune, to the paranoia, that is. At least two female Canadian members of our staff truly thought they were going to die. One of them appeared at our door one night, in tears. Sara managed to talk her down, with the aid of numerous bottles of super-sweet Great Wall Cabernet. The paranoia got out of hand and eventually I sat down and wrote a mock newspaper article titled 'SARS Attacks Brain' and circulated it anonymously at work.

Once the Chinese decided this nasty flu was real and wasn't going away they had to look like they were in control and doing something about it. The 'pretend it isn't real approach' was replaced by another perennial Chinese favourite, the crackdown. Crackdowns occur periodically, usually to show, via media coverage, that the authorities are solving a problem. You can buy fake DVDs and Gucci purses 360 days a year, out in the open, but for five days a year you cannot. The SARS crackdown targeted anyone with sniffles, a cough, and a fever. It was accompanied by a lockdown. Every school and university campus either closed, or was sealed off. A veritable siege, with—and I'm not kidding here—barbed wire to cordon off the students on the inside from the outside world. It looked like a scene from Schindler's List, students sitting on either side of the fence, holding hands through barbed wire, and looking longingly at a loved one, wondering if they would ever live through this manic time. Stories circulated of neighbours ratting each other out.

'Old Wang has a cough, you know. Yes, he looked feverish'.

We Canadians couldn't be locked in the campus; we would have simply quit our jobs and returned to Canada. Instead we were prodded each morning with a little gun pointed at our neck that read our temperature. I was scared to exercise in case I appeared red faced and warm. The saddest, strangest, funniest thing I saw was the treatment of one of our students. Onion (and no, that's not the strangest name I encountered in China) was a top student, the class valedictorian. Unfortunately for her she came down with some kind of illness and was home from school for a few weeks right in the middle of the SARS madness, in the last semester of her graduating year. When she returned to school, she desperately needed to get caught up in order to prepare for her graduation exams, but instead she was placed under quarantine. Her quarters were a 2x3 metre guardhouse. Three times a day she was brought a meal on a metal tray that was placed on the steps outside her door. She opened the door, grabbed her meal, and retreated to her confinement, a modern Chinese Rapunzel. I will never be able to think of SARS without thinking of poor Onion.

A banner warns citizens about the dangers of SARS, Hailar, 2003.

On the bright side, we joked, we could actually smell chlorine bleach, which meant that things were being cleaned and disinfected for the first time in a long time, perhaps ever. The government started an anti-spitting campaign—more good news!—but it didn't really work. You were still just as likely then to hear the most Chinese of all noises, the clearing of the deepest, darkest, region of the throat, followed by the most dreaded of all sounds, the follow-up hork.

Poor Brownie. He and Alice got married that May and his parents didn't make it out from Canada due to the scare. Smirls gave them his-and-hers SARS masks as a wedding present.

The crisis came and went. Pity we never did make the 'I survived SARS' t-shirts.

In 2004, a surprising thing happened. A Chinese leader gave up his power. Yes, can you believe it? No revolution required. Jiang Zemin gave up his position as president of China and chairman of the Communist party. Hu Jintao took his place. Hu seemed a kinder, gentler Chinese leader, ready to move China towards more democracy, as Jiang Zemin had suggested was necessary in his final days in office. Cynics remind us that Hu was no stranger to toughness, having imposed martial law in Tibet in 1989, when he was governor there. Jiang Zemin was also seen lurking in the shadows, giving himself command of the People's Liberation Army. He was still pulling the strings, the Chinese said.

2006 saw the Three Gorges Dam finally finish and its massive reservoir began filling up. Building the largest dam in the world was an awesome feat, albeit a very Chinese thing to do. Mao once said that 'to attain freedom in the world of nature, people must use natural science to understand, conquer, and change nature and attain freedom from nature'. Indeed, they finally conquered the Chang Jiang (Yangtze River).

But the project was not without its costs and critics. Millions of people were forcibly relocated and their way of life irreparably changed. Known and unknown cultural treasures were forever buried under water. I showed my students an American-made documentary film on the project in which a geologist suggests the reservoir sits on a fault line and questions whether or not the weight of the water could instigate an earthquake. Such an event, if it damaged the dam, would kill millions in subsequent flooding. While the dam held up during the 2008 Sichuan earthquake, more than one student asked me if I thought the quake was caused by the reservoir.

When the 2010 Winter Olympics were announced in my hometown, Vancouver, you know what people were saying. To be read with your best sarcastic voice:

'Oh great, another colossal waste of taxpayers' money'.

'Wonderful, our city will be clogged with tourists and athletes. I'd better leave town'.

'Terrific, a chance to protest!'

From the few remaining non-cynics, there may even have been a celebration.

In China, by contrast, there was unanimous excitement and celebration. I remember the night the Beijing Olympics were announced. Toronto was also in the running. The Office Bar in Kaifaqu was packed with more Chinese than usual. We were cheering for Toronto, but only jokingly. We were mostly from BC and to cheer for Toronto, well, that would be wrong. The locals were glaring at us, taking our cheers as anti-Chinese. The whole bar was watching the announcement on the TV screen. When the IOC official said 'Beijing,' thereby defeating not only Toronto, but also Istanbul, Osaka, and Paris, the whole place erupted. The patriotic fervour the Olympic announcement brought out was incredible and barely fathomable for a Canadian. We simply don't feel this passionate about our country.

Prior to this, I was one of the naïve folks who thought the Olympics were about athletics. I guess I hadn't been paying attention. I couldn't help but think it absurd that Beijing, an incredibly polluted city, with terrible traffic, and little sports infrastructure, could host the Olympics.

Apparently the IOC members did hear and consider human rights abuse allegations and concerns about athletes' health and performance in the smog and dust laden mega-city, but decided to give the Chinese a chance anyway. There was never any doubt in my mind that the Chinese would put on a great show. They are masters at pulling off a gala performance, even on short notice. This gala they had years to prepare for. Anyone concerned about whether they could build facilities fast enough hasn't stepped foot in China. They can throw up a monster building in just months, whereas Canadians would take years and years to complete the same project.

As the Olympics got closer, the political dimension began to surface. In the spring of 2008, riots broke out in Lhasa, Tibet. The Chinese, as usual, blamed the riots not on Tibetans themselves, but on the 'Dalai Clique' and foreigners who hate China. When the Olympic torch passed through Paris, France, it was put out four times by pro-Tibet, AKA anti-China, protesters. The right to protest is considered sacred by Westerners and I agree with that sentiment. But I cannot condone the politicization of an Olympic torch relay that got so out of hand that someone attempted to rip the torch from the hands of Jin Jing, a wheel-chair bound Para-Olympian. Consider how Canadians would react if Rick Hanson was knocked out of his wheel-chair while carrying the torch, a symbol of peace among nations. Or Terry Fox.

Shame on them.

Naturally the Chinese were outraged, and calls for a boycott of French products, and especially French department store *Carrefour*, began immediately. Chauvinism reared its ugly head at our school, where the boys went crazy in their dorms, disregarding their usual Confucian respect for authority. The students chanted 'we love China' and 'f— you Canada' and made disparaging remarks about certain key figures of authority at our school. Bottles were launched out windows, one narrowly missing a Canadian teacher and the school's headmaster.

The day after the riot was one of the most difficult teaching days I have had in my career. The students were solemn, as if they had experienced something grave, some looked guilty and ashamed, others unrepentant. Teachers were shaken; one claimed this experience was the main reason for quitting.

What the protests and Chinese reaction did to me personally was to clear up in my mind how I felt about protesting in general. Public protest can be valid, but only in the right venue, with the right audience, otherwise it is pointless and can backfire. In this case, I believe the protests backfired. Rather than help the cause of Tibetan independence, they strengthened Chinese resolve. 'You see, they hate us,' was the message the Chinese got from it all, and all the more reason to ensure the integrity of a unified China, to accept hard-nosed approaches to dissent and separatism.

The protesters showed an ethnocentrism, a sad misunderstanding of China and the Chinese. Anyone who has lived in China for any length of time, regardless of how they feel about such issues as human rights or self-determination for nations, would never consider protesting in this way in China. It is simply not appropriate. Not only because it is disrespectful, but because it is not an effective way to influence the Chinese.

How, then, can we influence the Chinese, assuming that is a goal? I remember when I thought it was a cop-out for politicians and business leaders to say that the best way to influence change in China was to engage in trade. I'm not convinced that the main proponents of that argument cared for change, rather they wanted profit from trade, but ultimately I believe they are right. One result of engaging China with trade is a domestic demand for Western-style education, hence the flourishing market for Canadian curriculum schools like the one I work at. For the past twelve years, I have presented students with opportunities to consider democratic and human rights issues. Rather than dictate to them how it should be, I, and the other teachers—there are thousands of us now across the country—challenge the Chinese students to critically consider similarities and differences between such issues around the world and those in their own backyard. While the Vancouver Sun prints headlines like 'BC Teachers Muzzled in China,' we are busy in our classrooms comparing the struggle of the *Quebecois*, the Mohawks, and the Tibetans. And yes, we have been free to do this. Easy does it. Change is happening, social and political, and in some ways it is happening fast.

The Chinese know that their access to information is censored, and although they are somewhat understanding of the reasons for it, they don't like it. They reconcile their displeasure with their patriotism, like we all do when we consider the ugly truths about our country. It is inevitable that increased economic interdependence with the West will bring about change in China. Those of us who are here, on the inside, can see it happening. The ignoramuses attacking Para-Olympians unfortunately can't.

While the pre-Olympic tension rose in China, tragedy struck in May 2008. Mimicking geo-political events, India continued to rub China the wrong way, tectonically speaking. The result of the collision of plates was a massive earthquake, whose epicentre was in Wenchuan, Sichuan province. It was a tragedy of monumental proportions, making the top-twenty most disastrous earthquakes in human history. It is wrong and disrespectful to the victims to suggest this, but in some way, the earthquake created a diversion, and the whole of China rallied. They saw it as another obstacle to China's success and development, the Olympics being the best expression of this success to the outside world. The Tibet issue was largely forgotten.

One of the most interesting aspects of state-controlled media is the ability to redirect and refocus the population, literally overnight. The mood swings in China are radical, and leading up to the Olympics the mood cycle was excitement-pride-outrage-anger-grief-determination-celebration-pride.

Thankfully for China and everyone else, the Olympics were a great success. With fifty-one gold medals, fifteen more than second-place USA, what was not to be proud of?

The Western media couldn't accept the success though, and I watched with horror and disgust as journalists focussed not on the spectacular opening ceremony, but on evidence that a child lip-synched—as if it were a crime—and that firework displays seen on TV may not have been the real show from the smoky skies over Beijing. What bothered me even more, was how willing Canadians were to buy into those crappy stories, as if those revelations somehow reduced the magnificence of China's coming out gala performance. 'I can't wait for Vancouver's 2010 Olympics show, it will be an embarrassment in comparison,' I warned anyone who would listen.

The post-Olympic buzz was still on when another ethnic hotspot bubbled over, this time in China's far west, Xinjiang. Xinjiang, which means 'new frontier' in Chinese is an 'autonomous' region, AKA province, in China that borders diverse countries such as Russia, Mongolia, Kazakhstan, Kyrgyzstan, Tajikistan, Afghanistan, and Pakistan. Many of the major ethnic groups of these neighbouring countries also reside in Xinjiang, sometimes in pockets large enough to be designated autonomous counties. The major ethnic group in Xinjiang, however, is the Uyghur nation.

I have been enamoured with the Uyghurs since 1995, when I crossed over the Karakorum pass, from Pakistan into Xinjiang. Although the first Chinese citizens I saw, other than Han border patrol and soldiers, were Tajiks, the Uyghurs soon impressed me with their food and their proud and unique identity. I am convinced that Marco Polo got spaghetti from *laghman,* their superb hand-pulled noodles served with tomato, green pepper, onion, and lamb. They are a stunning looking race, the men resembling Mediterranean Europeans, dressed invariably in black leather shoes, dark slacks, white shirts, and caps, either traditional embroidered skull caps or Greek fisherman-style. The women wear bright coloured blouses and long skirts and cover their heads with scarves, although rarely in a full chador. But when they do wear them, the Uyghur chadors look hideous, like burlap sacks have been tossed over their heads.

The Uyghurs settled in the oases along the Silk Road and although they have a distinct culture, their ancestry, to my untrained eye, clearly shows a mixing of seeds over the centuries. In a single family of Uyghurs one may recognize faces of both Turks and Mongolians. Nearly all Uyghurs are dark haired, but a considerable number have blue or green eyes. One young woman I encountered from Khotan, had skin lighter than my red-haired sister, and bright blue eyes, shining from under her head scarf.

In a meagrely visited museum in Xinjiang's capital, Urumqi, several mummies found buried in the sand are on display in a poorly lit room. My dad had read a magazine article about the mummies prior to a family trip along the Silk Road in 2001. He insisted we have a look, and to this day, the exhibit remains the most powerful memory I have from any museum display I have seen. The bodies retain their hair—some of it red—and long noses. The kicker is that the carcasses are clothed in tartan. Celts in China, three thousand years ago!? Perhaps not Celts, these people have been proven, genetically, to be Caucasian, and furthermore, there is no evidence for another thousand years of any East Asian, or Mongoloid, peoples in Xinjiang. It's wrong to suggest that the present day

Uyghurs are the descendants of these folks, because we know the Uyghurs moved out from further west much later, perhaps 1200 years ago. Nevertheless, many Uyghurs have clasped onto the Beauty of Loulan and the other mummies as proof of their sovereign right to East Turkestan, as they sometimes call their homeland. In fact, DNA shows what we can clearly see about the Uyghurs, that they are, like Kazakhs and Uzbeks, mixed Caucasian and Mongoloid people. Their association with the mummies does tell us that they identify themselves as Caucasians, at least partially. It would be nice to pretend that race doesn't matter, but in this case, it seems to be very much a defining aspect of the Han-Uyghur split.

That the two groups are divided is not in dispute, except in official circles. In Xinjiang I witnessed a fascinating socio-cultural division. In an open-air, tarp-covered square in Kashgar—former center of Yakub Beg's independent Kashgaria state some 140 years ago—I watched dozens of Uyghur men playing chess. Turning 180 degrees, I surveyed dozens of Han Chinese men similarly playing chess. The difference was the game of chess itself; the Uyghurs played the familiar Western chess, with carved wooden pieces resembling kings, knights, *etc.;* the Chinese played Chinese chess, each piece a flat disc only distinguishable by the Chinese characters printed on them. There was no mixing. I snapped two photos.

I have always sought out Uyghurs wherever I have gone in China and they are always found. In Kaifaqu a Uyghur restaurant owned by a Zorba the Greek look-a-like built a tandoor-style brick oven on the sidewalk and the staff and Uyghur patrons—they blended together and we never knew who worked there and who was simply a guest—entertained us with singing accompanied by music played on guitar, *dutar*, a long-necked two-string instrument, and a *dap*, the common Uyghur hand tambourine-drum. Zorba and his troupe smoked hashish openly on the street. One day, without warning, they were gone and the restaurant never re-opened. Methinks it was the public hash smoking that did them in.

Once, on the streets of Guangzhou, a Uyghur man said to me, ironically in Mandarin, '*Ni shi waiguoren, wo ye shi waiguoren*'—You and I are both foreigners.

Coincidentally, it was in Guangzhou, the heart of Cantonese culture, that a Uyghur man was severely beaten in 2009 and left for dead by a gang of factory workers who believed the Uyghur had sexually assaulted a Chinese woman. The beating was captured on somebody's cell phone and uploaded onto the Internet, where Uyghurs saw it as a blatant example of the discrimination they have suffered for decades. Riots broke out in Urumqi, with Han Chinese shops and restaurants smashed and looted, and Chinese people were attacked physically. In the days following the initial riot, Han Chinese vigilante groups countered the violence with riots of their own. Martial law was declared. Nearly 200 were killed and over a thousand injured on both sides. It wasn't the first time things had got ugly in Xinjiang, but coming as it did, a year after the Tibetan riots, and just after the Olympics, it served as a reminder to any Chinese who had forgotten or who didn't care to notice in the first place, that the 56 nations of the People's Republic are not one big happy family. Never has it been easier to teach the concepts of regional identity and separatism in my social studies classes. Finally, they get it.

The government got it, too. They have, just months later, already tried, sentenced, heard appeals from, and executed perpetrators of the violence.

'I was expecting more of a parade, like at Discoveryland,' Hanna declared.

'This is dumb,' added Cosmo.

It was October 1ˢᵗ, 2009 and we were watching the sixtieth anniversary celebration of the founding of the People's Republic of China following the Communist Revolution in 1949. Every channel of CCTV, China Central Television, was showing the parade.

Tiananmen Square was filled with people dressed in colours, so that the square looked like the Chinese flag, with a rainbow at the front, directly across from Mao's portrait on the Forbidden City. When the people moved, colours changed, rendering Chinese characters that read 'People's Republic of China'

The Politburo leaders stood on the grandstand in front of the Forbidden City, in dark business suits with red ties, except for the military leaders who wore their medals and uniforms. The message was clear to me: the suits implied that the Chinese leadership saw itself as modern and business oriented, only the red ties symbolized their nearly forgotten ideology.

If you were feeling light-hearted with a sense of humour, it might have resembled a cross between a Shriner's parade, a Monty Python skit, and a 1930s European military parade— take your pick: communist or fascist. From under Mao's portrait shot out a black *Hong Qi* limousine with President Hu Jintao standing up, sticking out through the skylight. Unlike the other leaders on the grandstand, he wore a *zhong shan* suit, like Deng Xiaoping, Mao Zedong, and Sun Zhong Shan—Sun Yatsen—before him.

'*Tongzhimen Hao!*—Hello Comrades,' he calls to the crowd. Although I am familiar with the term *tongzhi*, or comrade, I had to ask my kids what he was saying, partly because of the echo effect from the amplification, but also partly because it is an archaic expression. Nobody calls anyone comrade anymore. In fact, in modern China a '*tongzhi*' or 'comrade' is more likely said to mean a homosexual than a stalwart communist. I chuckled to myself, like a thirteen year-old boy might, thinking it funny that the president of China was calling out 'hello homos!' It was rather like the prime minister of Canada celebrating Canada Day in 19th century fashion by hollering out, 'a gay day indeed!'

Turning onto *Chang An Jie*, Hu drove past thousands of soldiers, sailors, pilots, tanks, missiles, and fighter jets, repeating his 'tongzhimen hao!' routine.

'What are they saying?' I asked the kids when the TV commentary started. It's a sad state of affairs, having to ask your eight and ten-year old children to translate what was going on.

'Deng Xiaoping opened China. Nobody should ever forget that,' Cosmo said, and then added some commentary of his own. 'And I believe them, but I don't believe what they said about Mao Zedong'.

I wanted to quiz him on his eight-year old cynicism but we got distracted by scenes of nuclear warheads, fighter jets, and hundreds of sexy female militia, dressed in white, reminiscent of a 1980s Robert Palmer video; they were faceless, yet stunning.

'What are they saying now?'

'They are saying the same thing over and over again,'

Hanna said, with more than a hint of displeasure at having to sit through this, when the TV set could be put to much better use playing wii or at least a favourite DVD.

'Long live socialism!' Hu continues and then babbled on about the virtues of socialism, the minorities, democracy in China.

'Vive le People's Republic of China!' he calls out, using the preferred '*wan sui*,' or 10,000 years, to mean 'long live'.

Marching in the style we associate with fascist and communist totalitarian regimes, or Monty Python's John Cleese, legs kicking way out in front, the soldiers marched past the government leaders and the Forbidden City, every soldier the exact same height. I have to admit, that despite it being an out-dated expression of nationalistic fervour, it was impressive to see.

If only they could have done something about the cloud of blue smoke that rose over the tanks.

The changes that have taken place in the decade in between the fiftieth and sixtieth anniversaries of Communist China are immense and impressive, but I am left wondering about the next ten, twenty, fifty years. At one point in my early days in China I was convinced that another revolution was on the horizon, in perhaps ten to fifteen years, when the underclass would rise up against corruption, unemployment, classism, and broken dreams. I'm not ruling that possibility out completely but it seems less likely to me now since I have seen how well and seemingly easily the masses can be redirected, as evidenced by the many of the aforementioned events.

It looks as though my days in China are numbered, so I will likely view the *da wenti* from afar. I'll be the guy muttering to the TV set during the six o'clock news about Western bias, followed by 'when I lived in China...' I apologize in advance to all those who will have to suffer through this.

It will be sad.

18

A box of fireworks in front of grave, Manjiatan

Goodbye, Zaijian

Massoud lived a hell of a life, and I mean that in two senses. He lived a *hell* of a life at times, such as when he was persecuted—imprisoned for years and tortured—in his homeland, Iran, for his political views (he was a communist who idolized China!). After being smuggled to Turkey and then making his way to Europe, he undoubtedly had some tough times which certainly continued as he entered

Canada with refugee status in 1988. But he lived a *helluva* life too. He fell in love and married, had a child, travelled the world, and while doing so found a profession he was passionate about —teaching.

At the beginning of this book I described the experience of giving birth in China—the beginning of life. Unfortunately, I am now able to bring this book full circle and present a look at how life ends in China. I say 'unfortunately' because many of my observations happened only after Massoud passed away suddenly in March of 2009.

He collapsed from heart failure early one day at work, and so began a traumatic experience for our whole community. As described earlier, the community of Canadian teachers is much more a community than a staff. We work, live, eat, sleep (many of the teachers are married couples, and many more shack up while working in China), and play together. So it wasn't two colleagues that found Massoud collapsed on the stairs, it was two friends. And when a crowd gathered to help, it wasn't strangers and acquaintances, it was friends, who gave CPR, who held his hand, who pleaded with him to hang on, and who watched the life leave his eyes.

Sara came into my office and told me Massoud had been taken to the hospital up the road. We drove up a few minutes later. I had sounded optimistic with Sara in my office but in the car I had an ominous feeling. At the hospital, Sara comforted Massoud's wife, Anne. Bobbi, a former RCMP officer, stood looking very solemn while Tina Ho, relatively fluent in Mandarin, shifted anxiously outside the emergency room door. Bobbi whispered that it didn't look good and provided some details of Massoud's condition upon arrival. The door opened and a doctor rushed out, brushing past us, ignoring Tina's request for an update. Before the door swung shut I caught a glimpse of Massoud, lying face up, dressed in black corduroy pants, bare-chested, with a lifeless, ashen face in sharp contrast to his dark and grey-speckled goatee. His bare feet, almost a greenish-white, faced me. A moment or so later a male doctor came out and I listened in on Tina's question.

'*Ta yijing si le*,' said the doctor. He's already dead.

In retrospect, he may have said '*Ta yijing zou le*'. He's already *gone*. Regardless, he *was* dead, gone. Disbelief naturally followed this announcement. Anne began wailing, Sara cried 'No, no, no!' Anne demanded to see her husband and for some reason I can't explain, I was drawn into the room too.

We in the West are privileged for many reasons, one of which is that we are not faced with death all around us. In my twelve years in China I have seen many dead bodies. All but one were traffic accident fatalities, usually seen from a passing car. On my first backpacking trip to China in 1994, I thought I saw a corpse floating down the Pearl River, but now that memory is hazy and I wonder if it wasn't a coconut and a piece of wood. I haven't been to an open-casket funeral and other than Mao and Lenin—both surreal looking in their mausoleums—seeing Massoud's body lying there was a first for me, and a powerful experience. It definitely made me feel that this was now only a body and that his soul had most certainly left. In some ways that is a reassuring thought. I stayed only a minute, leaving Anne and Sara with Massoud. Bobbi, still standing strong in the hallway, asked me if I was okay and I replied that I was.

By chance, my mother had come to visit for a week from Canada and I went outside to call her. The minute I heard her voice, I cracked. I couldn't speak and my silence left her wondering what horrible thing might have happened to her family. When I regained my composure, I asked her to accompany me to our children's school. Anne was naturally worried about her son Jordan, just 9 years old. What was I going to tell him when I picked him up? I'm thankful that my mum was there to help at this difficult time.

We arrived at the school just as the students were lining up for their morning exercises. I looked out at a sea of black haired children in green uniforms. I soon spotted a Canadian girl in grade 1 and asked her where Jordan's class lined up. I found him and—just as I think Massoud knew he was going to die, so too did his son—he looked at me with a worried expression.

'Is it my dad?'

'Yes'.

'Is it his heart again?'

'Yes'.

'Is he going to be okay?'

'I don't know. He's in the hospital. Go jump in the car and I'll tell your teacher I'm taking you'.

I found his teacher, a Chinese man in his late twenties, and told him what had happened. Bewildered, his eyes glazed as he asked how it had happened. This is when I learned the Chinese term for heart attack: *Xin zang*. His face told me how much he cared for Jordan. He was deeply upset. I gathered my own children for the support that Jordan would surely need in the coming hours and days and we drove the 25 km home. On the way, Jordan revealed through several things he said that he, deep inside, knew his dad was dead. Mum and I did our best to entertain the kids with small talk.

I took the kids home to our place, knowing that Sara and Anne were by this time waiting there. What a horrible thing it is to witness a mother telling her child his father is dead.

Jordan ran to his mum and began wailing, grief pouring out of them both. Hanna stopped in disbelief and turned to me for confirmation, then aimlessly and slowly walked around. Cosmo, who had just days before ridden with Massoud in his sidecar, bolted to his bedroom, plopped himself on his bed, and cried his eyes out. Not knowing what to do, I tried my best to comfort him. It's hard to explain to an eight year-old child that there was a reason—heart disease—without scaring the child into thinking that you too, might die any day.

Our apartment soon turned into a grief and support centre for Anne and Jordan and our community of friends. Friends arrived to comfort Anne and within a couple of days her fridge was full of food baked by folks she hadn't even met. In times like this the expat community really pulls together.

Massoud happened to have a cousin living in Beijing, and he flew in for the weekend. His sister arrived from Canada too. We raised the issue of a memorial service but Anne wasn't ready to deal with it. Realizing that Massoud's cousin and sister would only be here for a few days, and that Anne was clearly not capable in her state of grieving to organize it, I took on the job of preparing a memorial service.

I had really no idea what to do but gathered some feedback from my mum and Sara. I had only been to three funerals in my whole life, two of which had taken place in churches— only my grandmother's had been a service at home. I got a little bit stressed out trying to balance perceived needs of the varied interest groups involved. First of all, I thought there had better be a strong Persian element, but I knew little of Persian culture. Thank goodness for the Internet!

When one thinks of Iranian culture invariable we think of Islam, but Anne was adamant that there should not be any religious overtones; Massoud had made a clear stance on that issue. Our friends Ladon and Foad, who are also Persian, hosted the memorial service at their house. They are Bahá'ís and requested that nobody bring or consume alcohol in their home; it wasn't to be an Irish wake. That was my challenge; to create a program that incorporated Persian elements, but was neither Muslim nor Bahá'í, was alcohol free, and most importantly, encapsulated the spirit of Massoud.

I felt it was a wonderful and moving evening. We began crowded together and seated on the floor in Ladon and Foad's living room. The house was packed and some people lined the stairwell that led upstairs. Persian traditional music played from the stereo for a minute or so before a voice was added to the instrumental music. The singing came out of the speakers like machine-gun fire, slaying us with its haunting, high-pitched vibrato. I instantly choked up. It was the saddest thing I have ever heard and seemed to sum up all of our thoughts at that moment.

Paddy O'Neil, our colleague and master of ceremonies, then introduced Massoud's cousin Younes. Younes was perfect; a natural speaker at ease in front of his cousin's mourning friends. He explained that the heart wrenching singing we had just heard was, in fact, light hearted and happy in the Farsi language and that was how we should be remembering Massoud. He went on to give a sketch of Massoud's early life in Iran, when they were boys. He hinted at, but did not give details of, the difficult days of Massoud's political imprisonment in Iran. He had us laughing at moments, especially when talking of the irony that Massoud was a teacher, given his unorthodox views of teaching and education. He then read from the thousand year old *Rubaiyat of Omar Khayyám*, Massoud's favourite poem, translating and explaining it as he read to us. It was almost as if Massoud himself were there teaching us about this ancient Persian cultural treasure.

Bijan, another Persian fellow in our community, read us the Farsi original version of the poem by the Persian poet Saadi, which adorns the entrance to the Hall of Nations at the UN building in New York. I felt this poem captured Massoud's outlook:

> Human beings are members of a whole,
> In creation of one essence and soul.
> If one member is afflicted with pain,
> Other members uneasy will remain.
> If you have no sympathy for human pain,
> The name of human you cannot retain.

Next, a few friends stood and said a few words about Massoud. I hadn't planned to say anything but I got up and told a few stories. I can't remember now what I said, only that I found it very difficult and got choked up, and that I did manage to make Jordan laugh for a moment, thinking about how he always told the crowd of kids around his dad how Massoud did his magic tricks.

We finished the service with Massoud's favourite song, Louis Armstrong's 'What a Wonderful World' and then his rendition of 'Somewhere over the Rainbow'. It was beautiful, and I have had those tunes in my head ever since.

I was talking with a friend about Massoud's memorial a few days later and he mentioned how his Chinese wife was quite bewildered by the service. She couldn't understand how we could tell jokes and laugh at such a sad event. Just what then, does a Chinese funeral look like? Strangely enough, we witness about one a week, right in front of our apartment.

That is not an exaggeration. Literally every week in the apartments just beside ours — inhabited by farmers and fishers who have just been relocated from their appropriated land—someone dies. I believe these old folks simply lose the will to live once they are pushed off their land and stuffed into concrete box apartments. But that's neither here nor there. In any event, they are dying in great numbers and their funerals are fascinating public displays of mourning.

They start early in the morning, sometimes by six am, with great eruptions of fireworks. Not the fancy colourful kind, but the simple bottle-rocket variety that shoot straight up about forty metres or so before exploding with a bright flash of white light. The sound is deafening. Amidst the noise of explosions, a loudspeaker, strapped to a bicycle or perhaps perched on a truck, blasts funeral music.

To the Western ear, much Chinese music sounds, well, God-awful. It is screechy, clanging, and all Chinese singers seem to be out of tune. Clearly, the scales they learned in music class are not the same as ours. Beijing Opera sounds like my mum's old Slumber Queen camper doing 60 km/h on a logging road with a child screaming in the back and pots and pans falling all over the place. It's pretty much like experiencing a massive earthquake while in the kitchen. So take that imagery and amplify it, literally and figuratively, and you have got Chinese funeral music. I have no idea what the message of the lyrics is, but as Sara said the other day, it definitely sounds like grieving. Not sobbing and weeping, mind you, but screaming and wailing grieving.

While the fireworks guy sets up a hundred metres farther down the road, the megaphone guy cycles along, slowly blasting the screeching music at full volume. Behind him comes a procession that appears at first to be a hybrid of a Latino religious festival, complete with giant piñatas, and a Ku Klux Klan parade. The convoys are made up of differing numbers of people; I can only assume more people means a better funeral, which in Chinese society likely translates to a better deal for the deceased in their afterlife.

Some mourners carry large, colourful pink and yellow placards covered with craft paper, resembling piñatas. Others walk silently along, with a white cloth belt fastened around their torsos; some are cloaked in white hoods, hence the KKK vibe. Some processions I have seen around our neighbourhood have only 15 or so people, others over 30 people. They move along slowly, catching up to the fireworks detonating overhead, only to find that the guy in charge of pyrotechnics has rushed ahead to set up the next set of explosions. They do a loop of several kilometres. Pallbearers carry a sedan on sticks that holds what look to me like offerings to the deceased that may come in handy in the after world: food, money, religious statues. They seem to repeat the process a couple of times a day and sometimes for several days.

In Canada, a funeral is a rather private affair, tucked away in a church, funeral parlour, or home. In China, it is an in-your-face public spectacle. Like many other things happening in China, it seems, from our perspective, to be an inconsiderate act, imposing this commotion on the whole neighbourhood. It is literally so loud that you can't think or have a conversation within a 500 metre radius of the procession. I rode by one on my motorbike earlier this year and nearly crashed as I passed. The fireworks scared the crap out of me. It honestly made me wonder how on earth anyone could keep their cool during wartime while under attack. That's how stressful it is to pass a Chinese funeral procession.

When the procession returns home the music continues and the loved ones wail, hanging around the body which is sometimes kept outside under a tent. Traditionally, the Chinese bury their dead in locations considering *feng shui*— literally wind and water, but referring to geomancy, the art of finding places with good *qi*—that are typically located on hillsides. All the hills in the area around where we live are dotted with graves and the colourful offerings that are left there by family. Given the population of China and the amount of land required to bury everyone, it's not surprising that the government declared that everyone should be cremated, not buried. Enforcement is difficult though, especially since the afterlife and treatment of the dead is taken so seriously in China. We still see fresh graves here.

Shortly after Massoud's passing, I was asked at work if I could accompany our school's secretary to the morgue. She was, like so many Chinese women I know, very superstitious —they are scared of the dark and believe in ghosts—and believed that Massoud's ashes would bring her bad luck, and so she refused to touch them. Could I come along to carry his ashes home?

We drove half an hour to Jinzhou and pulled into a complex that resembled a temple or cultural centre of some kind. It was nestled up against a mountain—good *feng shui*! Beside the morgue was a giant bathhouse hung with banners advertising cheap foot massages. The building was cold but clean.

'Do you want to see him one last time?' they asked us at the office.

'No,' I said.

'He doesn't want to see,' our secretary repeated.

Then the second man behind the counter asked me again.

'No!'

We signed some paperwork and paid cash, equalling a little over one hundred dollars, for the storage of the body and the cremation.

As the men walked out of their office to the morgue cooler rooms they couldn't resist and said to me one more time '*guo lai kan yi kan*'—Come and have a look. I didn't understand why they couldn't let it go, but it must be standard for people to watch the cremation take place in China. It has been suggested to me that the Chinese would wonder if the ashes were really his if they didn't see the cremation themselves.

What happened next I found very bizarre. Just as we might hear the manager at a grocery store yell to the bag boy 'Joe, can you give me a hand with a box of apples?' one of these guys yelled across the room—empty except for us, there was no need to yell—'we need a cremation over here!' It was as if there was little sensitivity and awareness that grieving people don't want to hear that. Everything here is matter of fact.

'*Deng yi hui er*'—wait a moment—, we were told.

Deng yi hui er turned out to be an hour. I sat in a waiting lounge with long wooden benches, like those found in old bus stations or churches. I was told to pick out an urn.

There were perhaps fifty different urns to choose from, ranging from simple brown boxes for eighty *renminbi* to elaborate jade and gold treasure chests that went for over

10,000 RMB. I chose a simple one near the cheaper end of the spectrum. I didn't think Anne would want a gaudy Chinese box. When our turn was up, we were summoned to a room to collect the ashes, placed in a red cloth bag that I held open. The bag was then folded and placed in the urn. Being a Chinese box, the lid didn't quite fit and it required a little bit of banging and pounding getting it on.

Back in the bus station waiting room we were to fill out some more paper work. Damn foreigners! Our names are too long. Just as Cosmo's name was too long for his birth certificate, so was Massoud's for his death certificate. After a few 'mei shirs' we managed to get out of there. Our poor secretary was not having a good time.

Once home, I knocked on Anne's door, and not knowing what to say I muttered 'special delivery' and handed over Massoud's remains.

19

Hanna in a calligraphy competition. Will she keep her Chinese in Canada?

Going Home

I don't want to go home and I've never been homesick for Canada. I am preparing mentally for it, because Sara's calls to return are growing in frequency and intensity.

She said 'You've lived your dream for a decade, what about my turn?'

She's got a valid point and I owe that to her. Perhaps this book will help me get ready.

Why don't I want to return? I guess the biggest reason is fear. What's to be afraid of, I'm returning to my home right?

I'm afraid of life, boredom, marriage, the kids' Chinese, jobs, friends...the list goes on.

We left Canada as young adults, just kids really, with no idea about what it meant to commit to a real job, to be parents, to struggle to maintain a loving relationship while overseas in a stressful environment. Leaving for China was risky and uncertain, to understate the situation somewhat. Twelve years on, we are seasoned professionals, confident at work, educated with master's degrees, with a happy home life and wonderful children. Ironically, returning to Canada brings unfathomable uncertainty.

Will we have jobs? We are teachers. One of the fantastic things about teaching is that there are opportunities all over the world for us, but there may not be in the old neighbour-hoods where we grew up. We hear stories of teachers return-ing to Canada only to find themselves on teacher-on-call lists, subbing sporadically for a year or more. If you are lucky, you land a part-time temporary contract in your first year. That's fine and dandy if you are a 25 year-old recent graduate from the education program at the local university, but we are experienced professionals, well into our careers, and perhaps more importantly, we have bills to pay! Can we afford to live in Vancouver without jobs, or underemployed as substitute teachers? I cringe at the thought that I might not be able to afford hockey fees for my kids, if they should want to play. If we can't even afford to put our kids in hockey, what is the point of living in Canada?

I predict some difficult days ahead.

Readers may wonder where our stash of gold is, after all, don't people go overseas to teach so they can come home with a whack of cash in savings? Believe it or not, after 12 years overseas, we still live pay cheque to pay cheque. We chose to live life to the fullest, which meant making 11 tropical holidays, 12 trips to Canada, and gallivanting with our kids all over China's hinterlands: Tibet, Xinjiang, Inner Mongolia, Manchuria, Hainan, and Yunnan. We did this while paying off exorbitant student loans and, after Sara went back to work, paying off a small piece of land and cabin in BC's Cariboo region.

So no, we won't be coming home with a whack of cash in hand, ready to buy a house in Vancouver. Even if we had saved a hundred thousand dollars, that still wouldn't buy us anything in Vancouver. I try to be positive about the move home, but I can't help wondering if we will be happy living in a dump, knowing that that's what we will be living in, if and when we find something we can afford.

Sure, we could choose not to live in Vancouver, but that is the only place our kids have any chance of keeping their Chinese language. What a travesty it would be to lose that after all the tribulation they have faced and overcome growing up in China and attending Chinese school.

To be hired as a teacher in a public school in British Columbia, you pretty much have to move to the district you want to work in, apply to be a teacher-on-call, and then wait by the phone hoping that your subbing job turns into something long term. There is virtually no chance of landing a job before we arrive. Without the two of us having regular, full time work, there is no chance to get a mortgage, so buying a home is not an option for us when we return.

Luckily, we have a soft landing; my mother has a house, in a wonderful neighbourhood and she will be retiring just as we return to Canada. We are blessed to have this option, but I can't help but feel like we are downgrading. We have been independent of our families for ages, providing for ourselves and our children and now, after all this time, there is the danger that I won't be able to fulfill my responsibility to myself and my wife and children to take care of us financially. That uncertainty is hard to live with.

What is certain is that the transition will be tough for all of us. The kids will start school in a new environment, a new society, one that is familiar yet foreign. They will be exposed to, for the first time, the ugly elements of Canadian schools and youth culture that they are sheltered from in China: Sex, drugs, gangs, and violence.

Assuming Sara and I do find teaching jobs there will be a major transition for us too, reconnecting with Canadian youth, whose independence and lack of respect for authority will likely be shocking to us after the amazing, smiling, and respectful faces we have been looking upon for years in our classrooms in China. We have heard from numerous friends who have returned home after teaching in Asia that the first year back is one of the hardest years of their lives.

How will Sara and I manage our own relationship with financial worries, adjusting children, a potentially less rewarding work life, and reverse culture shock? That remains to be seen.

In the preface to this book I wrote that my reasons for writing it were twofold: to tell our tales for all those who have expressed interest in our lives, and to provide a glimpse of the 'real' China, however biased my views may be, to counter the ignorant and superficial coverage that China gets in the Western media. I see now, as this book comes to a close, that perhaps its greatest value is not for you, dear reader, but for me, a therapeutic preparation to say goodbye to this marvellous land and people who have both challenged and nurtured us, as we learned to be a simple Canadian family overseas.

20

A Glossary of Life in China

This final chapter is a blatant rip off...er...I mean this chapter honours two pieces of writing on China that I greatly admire. The first is Bill Holm's *Coming Home Crazy*, a brilliant and hilarious collection of essays on China, each one named after the letters of the alphabet, and the second is an article that Jan Wong wrote detailing ten things the Chinese do better than us. I'll do more than Jan Wong's ten, but write much less than Bill Holm's essays. It will serve as a final snapshot of the China I've come to know and love.

A—Ayi

Ayi, or Auntie, is what you call an older woman in China. Your *Ayi* is the nanny who helps make life in China bearable, and sometimes even awesome. She does your laundry, washes your floors, picks up groceries, pays your bills, teaches you about China and Chinese culture, and is, best of all, a Chinese Grandma for your children. Ayi will drive you nuts at times. She never cleans as well as you'd like, but when she cooks up a batch of *jiaozi* you brag to all your friends that your Ayi makes the best.

β—Baijiu for Bai Qiu En

Just hearing the word *baijiu*—white liquor—can bring back the horrible sensation of the *baijiu* belching that inevitably takes place following its consumption. Beware of Chinese weddings and other formal events where foreigners will be targeted by *ganbei*-ing heavy drinkers with a penchant for *baijiu*. After drinking *baijiu*, tequila tastes like lemonade. The Chinese are proud of this stuff. It's their Scotch, and they will spend hundreds of *renminbi* for a good bottle of *Moutai*, the celebrated national brand. On the other hand, the low-end stuff sells for just a couple of bucks for a gallon, sold in a plastic Jerry can, or for just pennies for a plastic bag.

Bai Qu En is the Chinese name for Canadian doctor Norman Bethune, who died while operating mobile blood transfusion units during the second Sino-Japanese war in 1939. In his essay *In Memory of Norman Bethune* Mao Zedong wrote: 'We must all learn the spirit of absolute selflessness from him'. When we tell the Chinese we are Canadians we get a thumbs up and a reference to Bai Qui En.

Raise your *baijiu beizi* and *ganbei* for Bai Qiu En!

C—Chinglish

The Chinese are crazy about English right now but they are not exactly crazy about getting it right. Chinglish is the form of English that appears when you translate Chinese literally. Things that make sense in Chinese very often sound ridiculous in English. Add to this mess a penchant for mis-spelling words, compounded by sign makers who don't actually know what Roman letters look like. Some classics that appeared at the school I work at include 'Wok hard, broad leaning' (which was meant to say 'work hard, broad learning') and 'EXCELLEИCE IИ EDUCATIOИ' (with a Cyrillic backwards И instead of an English N). I see countless examples of Chinglish every single day but I will never forget in my first year in China passing a restaurant called 'Fat Pevson Bone Vestevant'

D—Donkey Dumplings

Wednesday was *baozi*—steamed bun—day at our school cafeteria. But just what was in those buns? When I asked, I thought I heard *niu rou*—beef—but the taste didn't seem quite right. It turns out it was *lu rou*—donkey. It sounds disgusting but really isn't that bad. The best part is nearly none of the foreigners I work with have any idea that's what they are eating.

E—Er

It takes a while to get used to the spoken sounds of Mandarin Chinese. One of the conventions of Beijing dialect is to add the sound *er* to the end of nouns. You know you are catching on when you find yourself adding the character 儿 to your words too. Do it once and your cab driver will think you are fluent.

F—Feng le

It is funny how nearly all foreigners in China learn to say *feng le* early on in their stay. It means crazy. China certainly seems crazy to us, and perhaps we seem crazy to the Chinese.

G—Gou rou

People back in Canada often joke about neighbourhood cats that go missing ending up in Chinese restaurants. They don't, at least not in Northern Chinese restaurants. Dogs, on the other hand, are a different story. *Gou rou* is a delicacy, especially in Korean restaurants. One night in 2002, while standing amidst a crowd of several hundred Koreans, all wearing red and screaming during a World Cup of Soccer game between Korea and Italy, I jokingly declared out loud that if Korea won the game then dog meat was my treat. The game went into extra time and the Koreans did the impossible, beating the favourites Italy. I bucked up and treated my friends to a dog meat stew.

Interestingly, the Manchu refuse to eat dog meat ever since, as legend has it, a dog saved the life of their first emperor, Nurhachi. Most foreigners share the feeling that eating dog is taboo and cringe at the sight of a skinned dog hanging in a market or at a restaurant door. I think they taste pretty good.

H—Heller

When we arrived in China, next to nobody could speak English, but it seems that everyone was fond of calling out 'hello' to any foreigner they saw, regardless of whether or not that foreigner might speak a language that uses the word hello. Mostly it comes out sounding like 'heller,' with a guttural, throat-cleaning sound at the end. It sounds friendly at first, but soon becomes annoying and it seems that yelling out 'heller' may not always actually mean hello. At times it seems to be more about showing off to friends. 'Heller' is often followed by a bout of laughter. Sometimes it even resembles 'f— off,' when delivered with a bite. The Chinese tell us they just want us to feel welcome. I'm guilty of it too. I once screamed 'Tashi Delek' to a group of Tibetans I saw walking in the streets in downtown Dalian. Sara scolded me for it...I was just trying to make them feel welcome!

|— I is for...

Interestingly, when Chinese is transliterated into the Roman script (i.e. Pinyin) there is not a single word that starts with i, but those Chinese who can speak English are particularly fond of saying the word 'interesting'. In Chinese 'interesting' is *you yisi*—have meaning. Now isn't that interesting?

J—Jiang Si Kele

On a typical winter day in Dalian you can easily be fooled by the glorious sunshine into thinking that it might be warm outside. Luckily, the creaking windows and howling sounds that kept you up all night indicate there is a nasty northerly wind blowing Siberia's dry continental polar air down your way. So you know to wear a down jacket and you take your toque and gloves with you, but it's not enough. You are absolutely frozen by the time you walk up the road at lunch, reaching the nearest Dong Bei restaurant. Anywhere else in the world and you would be ordering up a coffee or a hot chocolate, but not here. Nope, here in Manchuria it's time for a teapot, or perhaps bowl, full of *jiang si kele*—piping hot Coca-Cola steeped with slices of ginger. To the uninitiated it sounds disgusting; to those in the know, it's a magic winter tonic.

K—KTV is Ku, OK 了!

The Chinese are exceptionally proud of their unique language that has developed over 5000 years, and so they should be.

With the advent and influx of modern technology there has been an increase in loan words from English and other languages. KTV is a Chinese word that is seen everywhere and means *karaoke*. K for karaoke and TV for, well, you know. There are a few other loan words that pop up daily. The most common is probably 'OK' which usually gets the character 了 attached to the back to make it past tense. It is then pronounced 'OK le!' Anyone who uses such hip loan words must also be *ku,* or cool, minus the l.

L—Lao wai

Lao wai is a colloquial form of the word *wai guo ren*—foreigner. While *wai guo ren* literally means 'outside country person,' *lao wai* translates as 'old outsider'. It creates some uneasiness because it appears to some foreigners to be a derogatory term, much like *gwailow*—old ghost—in Cantonese. Many Chinese insist, rather, that is a term of respect. I guess it's better than what they called the Russians up in the northern border regions. They were known as *lao maozi*—old hairy.

M—Mao Zedong

If he sat up from his embalmed horizontal position in his mausoleum in Tiananmen Square, the Great Helmsman would crap his pants. He would find himself in a staring contest with another great man, albeit a capitalist, Colonel Saunders. Never mind that his dream of a Communist paradise is dead, the Chinese still, for the most part, revere Mao Zedong, the architect of the Chinese Revolution and it's nasty echoes, the Great Leap Forward and the Great Cultural Revolution. Taxi drivers often still hang his portrait from their rear-view mirrors, Communist cling-ons dangling like fuzzy dice, unaware of the irony as they race dangerously for their next fare, no less desperate than the rickshaw pullers of pre-Communist China.

N—Negativity

Negativity is the evil trap that many foreigners fall into during the various stages of culture shock. Negativity is contagious...beware of foreigners complaining about life in China! On the contrary, the Chinese seem to live in a stupor of positivity when they speak of, and think about their country. Perhaps a balanced appraisal in between the two extremes is needed.

O—Ou tu

Ou tu means to vomit, to barf. It is not a pleasant thing but for some reason regurgitation seems to be a way of life in China. People are simply puking everywhere. Lunch chunks can be found on nearly every sidewalk, pathetic heads hang out of car and bus windows. Much of this can be attributed to the drinking habits of the locals but certainly the flu and food poisoning play a role. I myself once puked right on the floor in the middle of the hallway at my school one day. Sorry about that.

P—Pi jiu

It's cheap, it's plentiful, it's beer. The national brand Tsingtao (Qingdao, in pinyin), is celebrated but I prefer Harbin Beer, abbreviated so nicely as Hapi (Ha for Harbin, pi for pijiu). German *braumeisters* set up the breweries, the former in 1903 and the latter in 1900. The Chinese have continued the tradition, and thank goodness too. Beer in China is exceptionally cheap, ranging in price from 30 to 60 cents for a bottle of regular brew. My only complaint is the lack of variety. With few exceptions, Chinese beer is light lager.

Q—Qian

Qian means money and the first sentence a foreigner needs to know is '*duo shao qian*'—how much money? Chinese money takes getting used to. First of all, the currency is called *renminbi*, or people's money. The unit equivalent to a dollar is called a *yuan*. To complicate things it is commonly referred to as *kuai*, which means a lump of something, roughly equivalent to saying 'bucks' in English. One yuan is divided not into cents, but rather into dimes, which are called *jiao*, although on the street they may be called *mao*. Each jiao is further divided into *fen* but these days you can't find anything that costs so little to use your fen. The *fen* are so worthless now that the Chinese make paper sculptures out of the notes.

When you make a decent salary and everyday things are cheap, money loses it's meaning and value. We throw hundred *yuan* notes around like they are napkins. In the end it adds up. The Chinese, too, seem to throw it around a lot. There is always money changing hands in China, and cash is the means of choice for transactions.

The Chinese scrutinize every bill to make sure it is not counterfeit. You usually get passed fake bills when getting change from taxi drivers. Just tuck it away until you take another cab at night when it's too dark for them to see. It's the counterfeit game.

R—Re Nao

Re nao means hot and noisy, which China definitely is, except in winter, when it's decidedly cold and noisy. *Re nao* refers to the atmosphere the Chinese like to create. Whereas 'hot and noisy' doesn't sound comfortable to most Westerners, for the Chinese it means to be surrounded by friends and family, yelling and screaming excitedly about something over a plate of steaming *jiaozi* and other dishes.

∫—Sh*t

There's no way to avoid it, there's a lot of it in China. Young children are dressed in split-bottom pants, rather than in diapers, so when they have to go, they go wherever they happen to be. I'll never forget my first trip backpacking around China when I went to the bank to cash a traveller's cheque. A woman was holding her child while he crapped right on the top step at the front door of the Bank of China. It's not just the kids though. With millions of migrant workers roaming the country with no decent facilities to use, they find anywhere quiet and hidden. Quiet and hidden are relative concepts in China. When you step in poop in China (and yes, you will) unfortunately it is human excrement, not doggy doo. And nowhere is sacred. The staircase in an apartment block, a children's playground; all are fair game for the desperate dumpers.

T—Tiananmen

You knew of Tiananmen Square from the events of 1989 long before you came to China, but you are still drawn there time and time again. Mao Ze Dong, lying embalmed in an orange hue, pulls you into his mausoleum and his portrait welcomes visitors to the Forbidden City. You'll never forget the day your kids came home from school singing the patriotic classic kids' tune *'Wo ai Beijing Tiananmen'*—I love Beijing's Tiananmen.

U—Ugly

I blame Stalin for this, but the Chinese sure took to ugly, rectangular, concrete buildings. So many of China's cities are simply ugly although the beauty in China is there, found in little things that get dwarfed by the big uglies; the faces on the street, a blossoming tree, a lonely garden, a door poster that says 'luck'.

V—Vacancy

One of the great mysteries of the planned economy that is China, is the astronomical number of half-built, abandoned, and completed but empty buildings. They are everywhere. It makes one wonder about the sense of the planning. This whole pace of development is a sham! But wait a few years and sooner or later things do fill up. Or they don't, and the buildings are torn down, only to be replaced by more vacant buildings, which in turn, will also be pulled down. It's a great place to be a squatter!

W—Wei shenme?

When you arrive in China you have so many questions. Most of them start with 'wei shenme'—why? Why can't I buy train tickets? Why is this office closed now? Why can't we get rice at lunch? Why is it pronounced this way? There is no short-age of opportunities to ask why. The problem is, even after years and years, I rarely understand the answer I'm given. The seasoned Old China Hands say 'don't ask why, this is China' but I keep asking.

Ӿ—Xie xie

Thank you, or *xie xie*, is perhaps the most important word you can learn in China. You'll say it hundreds of times a day. The Chinese are helpful, and you will be grateful. I've yet to hear a foreigner newly arrived in China who can pronounce it properly. I probably still can't either.

Ϋ—Yin-yang

After living in China the harmonious balance of opposites that is represented by the symbol ☯ seems so appropriate. China is a paradox, backwards yet modern, planned yet chaotic, and so too are the people. Reflecting on the yin-yang helps deal with this place.

Ƶ—Zaijian Zhong guo

Zhong guo, the Middle Kingdom, China; the place I've spent the past 12 years; the place I became a man, father and husband; the place I will always miss; the land of dragons, donkeys, and dust.

Index

BLB

BING LONG BOOKS

Bing Long Books is an independent Canadian publisher of important literary and other work by, and of interest to, the Canadian expatriate community. China and Asia are of particular interest to many of our authors.

Visit us at **www.binglongbooks.com**

For comments, suggestions, questions, or orders email:

info@binglongbooks.com

If you find an error in this book please inform us. If it is new to us and we feel the need to correct it we may send you a complimentary book or ebook.

About the author

Rudy Kong is an intrepid traveler, teacher, geographer, and hockey ambassador. He moved to China in his twenties with his very pregnant girlfriend, eventually proposing marriage on the shores of Dalai Lake in Inner Mongolia and was married on the sand at Mui Ne, Vietnam. When not riding his vintage People's Liberation Army motorcycle with his kids in the sidecar around the Chinese countryside he is playing hockey with the team he put together from local Chinese and expats, somewhere on a frozen pond in Manchuria.

LaVergne, TN USA
24 August 2010
194420LV00001B/141/P